ASEAN–India Development and Cooperation Report 2015

India's engagement with the Association of Southeast Asian Nations (ASEAN) is at the heart of its Look East Policy. As a regional bloc, ASEAN has developed much faster than any of the other blocs in the Asia-Pacific. With ASEAN and India working towards establishing a Comprehensive Free Trade Area through the Regional Comprehensive Economic Partnership Agreement (RCEP), their cooperation will be key to promoting economic stability, competitiveness, growth and integration in the region.

This Report:

- provides a comparative analysis of the global and regional economies;
- examines the impact and implications of India–ASEAN integration;
- assesses policy priorities, effectiveness, implementation imperatives and challenges; and
- discusses themes central to the economic sustainability of the region, including public and foreign policy, trade facilitation, financial and scientific cooperation, food security, energy cooperation and productivity and opportunities in the manufacturing and service sectors.

It will be invaluable to scholars and researchers of economics, international relations, development studies, area studies, as well as policy-makers, administrators, private sector professionals and non-governmental organisations in the field.

ASEAN–India Centre (AIC) was established at the Research and Information System for Developing Countries (RIS) and has been working to strengthen India's strategic partnership with ASEAN. AIC undertakes research, policy advocacy and networking activities with organizations and think tanks in India and ASEAN countries for strengthening ASEAN–India strategic partnerships.

Research and Information System for Developing Countries (RIS) is an autonomous policy research institute that specializes in issues related to international economic development, trade, investment and technology. It is envisioned as a forum for fostering effective policy dialogue and capacity building among developing countries on global and regional economic issues.

ASEAN–India Development and Cooperation Report 2015

ASEAN–India Centre
Research and Information System for Developing Countries

NEW DELHI LONDON NEW YORK

First published 2015
by Routledge
2 Park Square, Milton Park, Abingdon, Oxon OX14 4RN

and by Routledge
711 Third Avenue, New York, NY 10017

Routledge is an imprint of the Taylor & Francis Group, an informa business

© 2015 ASEAN–India Centre, Research and Information System for Developing Countries

The right of ASEAN–India Centre, Research and Information System for Developing Countries to be identified as author of this work has been asserted in accordance with sections 77 and 78 of the Copyright, Designs and Patents Act 1988.

All rights reserved. No part of this book may be reprinted or reproduced or utilised in any form or by any electronic, mechanical, or other means, now known or hereafter invented, including photocopying and recording, or in any information storage or retrieval system, without permission in writing from the publishers.

Trademark notice: Product or corporate names may be trademarks or registered trademarks, and are used only for identification and explanation without intent to infringe.

British Library Cataloguing-in-Publication Data
A catalogue record for this book is available from the British Library

Library of Congress Cataloging-in-Publication Data
A catalog record has been requested for this book

ISBN: 978-1-138-92603-5 (pbk)

Typeset in Sabon 10.5/12.5pt by Glyph Graphics Private Limited Delhi 110 096

Contents

List of illustrations	vii
Foreword by Ambassador Shyam Saran	xi
Preface by Professor Sachin Chaturvedi	xiii
Acknowledgements	xv
List of abbreviations	xvii
Executive Summary	xxiii
Introduction	xxxi
1 Economic Outlook and Prospects	1
2 Trends and Patterns of Merchandise Trade	16
3 Services Trade Patterns and Key Policies	32
4 Investments, Prospects and Challenges	47
5 Emerging Production Networks	59
6 Corridors, Connectivity Challenges and New Direction	68
7 Removing Non-Tariff Measures	87
8 Energy Market Integration and Cooperation	98
9 Strengthening Monetary and Financial Cooperation	106
10 Science and Technology Cooperation Blueprint	114
11 Expanding Food Security and Food Reserves	122
12 Towards a Stronger Cultural Link	132
References	140

Illustrations

FIGURES

0.1	ASEAN Integration over Time	xxxii
0.2	Trends in ASEAN–India Trade	xxxiii
1.1	Trends in Growth Rates of the World Economy	2
1.2	GDP Growth Rate of Some ASEAN Countries	3
1.3	Trend in World Fiscal Deficit	4
1.4	Trends in Road Density	6
1.5	Trends in World Exports	7
1.6	Trends in Trade for India and ASEAN Countries	8
1.7	Foreign Reserves of Three Types of Economies	10
1.8	Trend in World GDP per Capita	11
1.9	GDP per Capita for ASEAN Economies	12
1.10	Trends in India's GDP per Capita	13
3.1	Trends in World Services	33
3.2	Trends in Total Services Exports of Selected ASEAN Countries and India	33
3.3	Intra-ASEAN Exports in Services	45
4.1	Top Foreign Direct Investing Countries in ASEAN	47
6.1	Stages of Development of Economic Corridor	68
6.2	Gateways, the Border and Beyond	70
6.3	Moving Towards Economic Corridor	75
6.4a	Trends in Cost to Export and Import	78
6.4b	Trends in Time to Export and Import	79
6.5	One-Stop Border Post	82
7.1	AIFTA Total TBT and SPS Measures January 1995–April 2014	89
7.2	SPS Measures under the AIFTA	90
7.3	TBT Measures under the AIFTA	91
7.4	Market Access under the Tariffs at Aggregated Heading level	94
7.5	TBT Measures under the AIFTA: 2000–2013	94
7.6	SPS Measures under the AIFTA: 2000–2013	95

TABLES

0.1	India's Trade with ASEAN: Number of Products Traded	xxxiii
1.1	Forecast of GDP Growth Rates	3
1.2	Rankings of ASEAN Countries by Logistics Performance Index	6
1.3	India's Trade with EAS Countries in 2013	9
1.4	Tariff Rate, Most Favoured Nation, Simple Mean, All Products	9
1.5	Current Account Balance for ASEAN+6 Countries	10
1.6	Foreign Exchange Reserves, 2013–14	10
1.7	ASEAN Countries' HDI Rankings of 2012 and 2013	13
2.1	India's Trade Intensity with ASEAN Countries	18
2.2	RTI Index	19
2.3a	AIFTA Tariff Elimination Schedule	21
2.3b	AIFTA Tariff Elimination Schedule for Special Products	21
2.4a	Welfare Effect of the FTA with Reduced Trade Costs on Partners	23
2.4b	Welfare Effect of the FTA with Reduced Trade Costs on Other East and South Asian Countries	24

A2.1	Sectors among Top 20 Exports Sectors with >10% CAGR since 2009–10	28
A2.2	New Export Commodities in 2013–14 Relative to 2009–10	28
A2.3	Commodity Exports in 2013–14 with >10% CAGR since 2009–10	29
A2.4	New Import Commodities in 2013–14 since 2009–10	30
A2.5	Import Commodities with >10% CAGR since 2010	30
3.1	Services Trade Volume and Share	32
3.2	CAGR for Exports in Services, 2000–13	34
3.3	Revealed Comparative Advantage for Selected Countries and Sectors	35
3.4	Services Trade Restrictiveness Index	36
3.5	Market Access Commitments (under GATS) in Mode 3 and Mode 4	38
3.6	Targets on Foreign (AMS) Equity Participation in Mode 3 as per AEC Blueprint	43
3.7	Commitments under GATS and AFAS: A Comparison	44
3.8	Intra-ASEAN Exports in Services, 2005–13	45
4.1	Major Indian Investments in ASEAN	48
4.2	Select ASEAN Countries' Equity, Inflows in India	50
4.3	Potential Sectors for FDI in India	57
5.1	Participation in GVC by Asian Countries: Year-wise Participation Index	61
5.2a	'Distance to Final Demand Index' Reflecting Country's Position in Industry-Wise Value Chain	62
5.2b	'Distance to Final Demand Index' Reflecting Country's Position in Industry-Wise Value Chain	63
5.3a	Index of Number of Production Stages in Selected Countries: Electrical and Optical Equipment Sector	64
5.3b	Index of Number of Production Stages in Selected Countries: Transport Equipment Sector	64
5.4	Share of Value Added from Selected Trade Partners Embodied in India's Gross Exports	65
5.5	Share of Foreign Value Added Embodied in ASEAN's Exports in Selected Sectors in 2009	66
5.6	Frequency of Sector-wise Tariff Rates under India–ASEAN FTA	66
6.1	Corridor Development Policy	76
6.2	Trade Cost Elements Holding Back ASEAN–India Integration	78
6.3	Key Trade Facilitation Priorities	83
6.4	UNCTAD's Liner Shipping Connectivity Index	84
6.5	ASEAN–India Maritime Connectivity Projects	85
7.1	SPS and TBT Measures by AIFTA Parties: 1995 to 2013	89
7.2	NTMs and Its Significance for Preferential Market Access under AIFTA	93
7.3	Compositions of National and International TBT Measures under AIFTA	96
7.4	Compositions of National and International SPS Measures under AIFTA	96
8.1	Energy Indicators in India and ASEAN Countries, 2011	98
8.2	Energy Balances in India and ASEAN Countries, 2011	99
8.3	Indian Imports of Oil (Crude) from ASEAN Countries	100
8.4	Indian Imports of Coal from ASEAN Countries	101
8.5	Indian Oil (Refined) Trade with ASEAN Countries (2710)	101
8.6	Indian Trade in Electric Motors and Generators (8501) with ASEAN Countries	102
A8.1	Energy Reserves and Resources in India and ASEAN Countries	105
9.1	Size of Bond Market, 2012	110
9.2	Insurance Indicators in ASEAN Countries, 2012	111
10.1	R&D Inputs	114
10.2	R&D Outputs	115
11.1	Prevalence of Undernourishment in Asia	123
11.2	Inadequate Access to Food	124
A11.1	Incidence of Poverty in India and ASEAN	131

Boxes

0.1	ASEAN Economic Community's Post-2015 Vision	xxxvi
6.1	Benefits of Economic Corridors	69
7.1	NTM in AIFTA	88
9.1	Major Banking Sector Reforms in India Since 1991	107
10.1	India's S&T Cooperation with ASEAN	117
11.1	SEWA's Model of Institution Building: Empowering Small-scale Women Farmers	126
11.2	National Food Security Bill of India	128
12.1	Nalanda University	138

Maps

6.1	Trilateral Highway Alignment	71
6.2	Kaladan Multimodal Transit Transport Project	73
6.3	New Shipping Routes between ASEAN and India	85

Foreword

Relations between India and ASEAN are poised to reach new heights and cross new frontiers. We have moved into a proactive 'Act East' policy, which envisages accelerated and broad-ranging engagement between ASEAN and India. The two sides are stepping up their collaboration across a range of economic and strategic issues, including trade and connectivity, culture, people-to-people contacts, transnational crime and international terrorism, and maritime security. With ASEAN and India working towards establishing a comprehensive free trade area through the proposed Regional Comprehensive Economic Partnership (RCEP), their cooperation will be key to promoting economic stability, competitiveness, growth and integration in the region.

The leaders of ASEAN and India, who attended the ASEAN–India Commemorative Summit in 2012, accorded several recommendations made by the *ASEAN–India Eminent Persons' Report*. The Report emphasized the need for further enhancing and upgrading the strategic and economic cooperation on a mutually beneficial basis. A better understanding of the issues relevant to such cooperation will help policymakers to formulate appropriate policy responses and direct the necessary technical and financial resources to where they are needed. It will also contribute to more balanced ASEAN–India relations and improved dialogue on trade policy issues.

Research and Information System for Developing Countries (RIS) has been playing a catalytic role to strengthen ASEAN–India economic integration. ASEAN–India Centre (AIC) has been setup at RIS to work exclusively on ASEAN–India relations. The *ASEAN–India Development and Cooperation Report 2015* prepared by the ASEAN–India Centre at RIS under the guidance and editorship of Dr Prabir De, Coordinator of AIC, highlights a number of key issues that are relevant from the point of view of deepening the relations between India and ASEAN. This Report explores themes central to the economic prosperity of the ASEAN–India region, including in the areas of foreign policy, trade and trade facilitation, financial and scientific cooperation, food security, energy cooperation and productivity, and for opportunities in the economic front. The Report addresses the prospects and challenges concerning ASEAN–India economic relations and provides a framework for strengthening the regional integration.

This publication by the ASEAN–India Centre at RIS is an effort to improve existing knowledge on relevant issues related to Asian integration, with particular attention to those more relevant for India and ASEAN. I am confident that this Report will assist ASEAN countries and India to strengthen economic integration in the shared region.

ASEAN–India Development and Cooperation Report 2015 is an outcome of a series of studies undertaken at the ASEAN–India Centre at RIS with the support of the Ministry of External Affairs, Government of India. I am thankful to Ambassador Anil Wadhwa, Secretary (East) and Ms Pooja Kapur, the present Joint Secretary (ASEAN ML) in the Ministry of External Affairs, Government of India and Ms Renu Pall and Ms Vani Rao, who both served earlier as Joint Secretary (ASEAN ML), for their continuous cooperation to the ASEAN–India Centre.

I thank Ambassador V. S. Seshadri, Vice-Chairman, RIS and AIC, and Prof. Sachin Chaturvedi, Director General, RIS and AIC, for their wholehearted support to this Report.

I am certain that this Report will be a valuable reference for policymakers, academics and practitioners.

Ambassador Shyam Saran
Chairman, ASEAN–India Centre (AIC) and Research and Information System for Developing Countries (RIS)

Preface

India and ASEAN countries share long history and civilizational linkages. India's relation with the ASEAN is one of the cornerstones of India's foreign policy and the foundation of our 'Act East' policy. ASEAN and India are natural partners in defining their perspectives and addressing their common requirements of economic growth and prosperity. They are together in the East Asia Summit, ASEAN Regional Forum, ADMM+ and the Expanded ASEAN Maritime Forum, which are important initiatives for evolving an open and inclusive regional architecture. The economic underpinnings of the ASEAN–India Strategic Partnership have been strengthened by the signing of the India–ASEAN Free Trade Agreement in Goods in 2010. India–ASEAN Free Trade Agreement (FTA) in services and investments is likely to come into force very soon. The services and investment agreements complete the India–ASEAN FTA and are expected to deepen our economic partnership. The volumes of trade and investment flows between ASEAN and India have been increasing, but remain below the potential. The negotiations for arriving on a common ground on the Regional Comprehensive Economic Partnership (RCEP) are also underway. We are working with ASEAN in enhancing physical and institutional connectivity.

Research and Information System for Developing Countries (RIS) has been focusing on regional cooperation in its work programme. *The ASEAN–India Development and Cooperation Report 2015* (AIDCR) is an outcome of the project undertaken at the ASEAN–India Centre (AIC) at RIS. The project brought together experts and researchers from a wide range of subjects in an effort to offer insights and better understanding of the ASEAN–India Strategic Partnership, particularly with regard to economic relations. It presents, among others, a list of recommendations for deepening our partnership with ASEAN and beyond. My colleague Professor Prabir De led and co-ordinated the project with incredible professionalism.

I hope this Report will be a valuable reference for policymakers, academics and practitioners.

Sachin Chaturvedi
Director-General, Research and Information System for
Developing Countries and ASEAN-India Centre (AIC)

Acknowledgements

The *ASEAN–India Development and Cooperation Report* (AIDCR) 2015 has been prepared under the guidance of Dr Prabir De, Professor, Research and Information System for Developing Countries (RIS) and Coordinator, ASEAN–India Centre (AIC). He is also the editor of this Report. The AIDCR 2015 collects select papers written exclusively in connection with the preparation of this Report. This publication places together key messages emerging out of the ASEAN–India Summit 2014, held at Nay Pyi Taw on 12 November 2014, along with background research papers prepared for further dissemination in view of their relevance to policy. It also carries important messages for the forthcoming 13th ASEAN-India Summit and 10th East Asia Summit, to be held at Kuala Lumpur in November 2015.

We are grateful to Ambassador Shyam Saran, Chairman, RIS; Ambassador V. S. Seshadri, Vice-Chairman, RIS; and Prof. Sachin Chaturvedi, Director-General, RIS, for their continuous guidance and encouragement. We are especially thankful to Ambassador Anil Wadhwa, Secretary (East), Ministry of External Affairs (MEA), Government of India and Ms Pooja Kapur, Joint Secretary (ASEAN-ML), Ministry of External Affairs (MEA), Government of India for their support. We also wish to extend our thanks to all the Heads of Indian Missions in ASEAN; Ambassador Suresh K. Reddy, Indian Ambassador to ASEAN; and all the ASEAN Ambassadors in India for sharing their views on ASEAN–India relations, further enriching the Report.

Principal authors of the chapters of this Report are as follows — Dr Prabir De (Overview chapter); Dr Ranajoy Bhattacharya, Indian Institute of Foreign Trade (IIFT) Kolkata (Chapter 1); Dr Amita Batra, Jawaharlal Nehru University, New Delhi (Chapter 2); Dr Prabir De and Dr Sabyasachi Saha, RIS (Chapter 3); Dr Geethanjali Nataraj, Observer Research Foundation (ORF) and IPE Global, New Delhi and Dr Ashwani (Chapter 4); Dr Biswajit Nag, Indian Institute of Foreign Trade (IIFT) New Delhi (Chapter 5); Dr Prabir De (Chapter 6); Dr Murali Kallummal, Centre for WTO Studies, Indian Institute of Foreign Trade (IIFT) New Delhi (Chapter 7); Mr Nitya Nanda, The Energy and Resources Institute (TERI), New Delhi (Chapter 8); Dr Soumya Kanti Ghosh, State Bank of India (SBI), Mumbai (Chapter 9); Dr Sabyasachi Saha, RIS (Chapter 10); Dr Beena Pandey, RIS (Chapter 11); and Dr Baladas Ghosal (Chapter 12). Additionally, substantial research inputs were received from Dr Chandrima Sikdar, Narsee Monjee Institute of Management Studies (NMIMS), Mumbai; Mr Pranav Kumar, Confederation of Indian Industry (CII), New Delhi; and Ms Sreya Pan, RIS.

Many research assistants contributed to the Report through compilation, tabulation and analysis of statistical data; the preparation of country and subregional trade briefs; and undertaking background research and referencing. These were: Mr Manmeet Singh Ajmani, Mr Sunando Basu, Mr Supratik Guha and Ms Sreya Pan.

This Report has benefitted from the discussion and feedback received during the preparatory workshop organized under this project at AIC/RIS. We appreciatively acknowledge the efforts of the following peer reviewers for ensuring the quality and relevance of the *ASEAN–India Development and Cooperation Report 2015*. These were Dr Mia Mikic (UNESCAP, Bangkok); Dr Rajan Ratna (UNESCAP, Bangkok); and Dr Ajitava Raychaudhuri (Jadavpur University, Kolkata).

Occasionally discussions were held with many researchers and policymakers on several chapters of the Report such as Prof. Manoj Pant (Jawaharlal Nehru University, New Delhi); Prof. Suthiphand Chirathivat (Chulalongkorn University, Bangkok); Dr Amitendu Palit (ISEAS, Singapore); Dr Sankaran Nambiar (MIER, Kuala Lumpur); Dr Gilberto M. LLanto (PIDS, Manila); Dr Yose Rizal Damuri (CSIS, Jakarta); Dr Florian A. Alburo (CATIF, Manila); Dr Tin Htoo Naing (CEES-Myanmar, Yangon); Dr Nguyen Huy Hoang (VASS, Hanoi); Dr Selim Raihan (SANEM, Dhaka); to mention a few.

We would like, in particular, to acknowledge the support of the Ministry of External Affairs (MEA), Government of India. This Report benefitted greatly from the assistance and support by the RIS Administration. Ms Kiran Wagh provided administrative assistance. Copy editing of the Report was carried out by Mr. Vivek Gopal, and Routledge India, New Delhi, helped in the production of the Report. We hope the recommendations in this Report will help India and ASEAN in strengthening their economic relations. The ASEAN–India Centre (AIC) and RIS stand ready to contribute to the fulfillment of the ASEAN–India Strategic Partnership.

Views expressed in this publication are those of the authors of the Report and not the views of the Governments of India, ASEAN countries, Research and Information System for Developing Countries (RIS), ASEAN–India Centre (AIC) or the ASEAN Secretariat. Usual disclaimers apply.

Abbreviations

AANZFTA	ASEAN-Australia-New Zealand Free Trade Agreement
ABAPAST	ASEAN Advisory Board for Plan of Action on S&T
ABMI	Asian Bond Markets Initiative
ACARE	Advanced Centre for Agricultural Research and Education
ACCC	ASEAN Connectivity Coordinating Committee
ACFTA	ASEAN-China Free Trade Agreement
ACI	Air Connectivity Index
ACU	Asian Clearing Union
ADB	Asian Development Bank
ADBI	Asian Development Bank Institute
ADD	Anti-Dumping Duty
ADF	ASEAN Development Fund
AEC	ASEAN Economic Community
AECA	ASEAN Energy Co-operation Agreement
AEGC	ASEAN Experts Group on Competition
AEO	Authorized Economic Operator
AEP	Act East Policy
AEPSS	ASEAN Emergency Petroleum Sharing Scheme
AERPD	ASEAN+3 Economic Review and Policy Dialogue
AFAS	ASEAN Framework Agreement on Services
AFCC	ASEAN Multi-Sectoral Framework on Climate Change and Food Security
AFSIS	ASEAN Food Security Information System
AFTA	ASEAN Free Trade Agreement
AIC	ASEAN–India Centre
AIDCR	ASEAN–India Development and Cooperation Report
AIF	ASEAN Infrastructure Fund
AIFS	ASEAN Integrated Food Security
AIFTA	ASEAN India Free Trade Agreement
AIRM	ASEAN Insurance Regulators Meeting
AISTDF	ASEAN–India S&T Fund
AITRI	ASEAN Insurance Training and Research Institute
AITTA	ASEAN–India Transit Transport Agreement
AKFTA	ASEAN-Korea Free Trade Agreement
AMRO	ASEAN+3 Macroeconomic Research Office
AMS	ASEAN Member States
APAST	Action Plan of Action on Science and Technology
APG	Asia Pacific Group
APSA	ASEAN Petroleum Security Agreement
APTDPC	Andhra Pradesh Technology Development & Promotion Centre
APTERR	ASEAN Plus Three Emergency Rice Reserve
ARC-ICT	Advanced Resource Centre in Information and Communications Technology
ARF	ASEAN Regional Forum
ASCC	ASEAN Socio-cultural Community
ASCOPE	ASEAN Council for Petroleum
ASEAN	Association of Southeast Asian Nations
ASEAN+3	ASEAN, China, Japan, and South Korea
ASW	ASEAN Single Window

ATSN	Air Transport Sectoral Negotiation
ATSP	ASEAN Tourism Strategic Plan
ATWG	Air Transport Working Group
BG	Broad Gauge
BHEL	Bharat Heavy Electricals Limited
BIMSTEC	Bay of Bengal Initiative for Multi-Sectoral Technical and Economic Cooperation
BOPS	Balance of Payments Statistics
BRICS	Brazil, Russia, India, China and South Africa
BRO	Border Roads Organisation
BTDIxE	Bilateral Trade Database by Industry and End-Use Category
CAGR	Compound Annual Growth Rate
CAREC	Central Asia Regional Economic Cooperation Programme
CBTA	Cross-Border Transport Agreement
CCI	Coordinating Committee on Investment
CCS	Coordinating Committee on Services
CDAC	Centre for Development of Advanced Computing
CEAC	Comprehensive Economic Agreement
CELT	Centres for the English Language Training
CENVAT	Central Value Added Tax
CEP	Cultural Exchange Programme
CEPT	Common Effective Preferential Tariff
CGE	Computable General Equilibrium
CIDB	Construction Industry Development Board
CII	Confederation of Indian Industry
CLMV	Cambodia, Lao PDR, Myanmar and Vietnam
CMI	Chiang Mai Initiative
CMIM	Chiang Mai Initiative Multilateralization
COMA	Control of Manufacture Act
COST	Committee on Science and Technology
CPC	Central Product Classification
CPI	Consumer Price Index
CSSTEAP	Centre for Space Science and Technology Education in Asia and the Pacific
CTD	Custom Transit Document
CTSH	Change in Tariff Sub-heading
DDA	Doha Development Agenda
DFC	Dedicated Freight Corridor
DHRL	Delhi–Hanoi Railway Link
DMIC	Delhi-Mumbai Industrial Corridor
DSC	Decision Support Centre
EAERR	East Asia Emergency Rice Reserve
EAS	East Asia Summit
EC	Election Commission
EDC	Entrepreneurship Development Centre
EDI	Entrepreneurship Development Institute
EEP	Educational Exchange Programme
ESCAP	Economic and Social Commission for Asia and the Pacific
ETP	Economic Transformation Programme
EU	European Union
EXIM Bank	Export–Import Bank of India
FAO	Food and Agriculture Organization
FDI	Foreign Direct Investment
FICCI	Federation of Indian Chamber of Commerce and Industry
FIPB	Foreign Investment Regulator

FTA	Free Trade Agreement
GAP	Good Agricultural Practices
GATS	General Agreement on Trade in Services
GATT	General Agreement on Tariff and Trade
GCC	Gulf Cooperation Council
GCSS	General Cultural Scholarship Scheme
GDP	Gross Domestic Product
GERD	Gross Expenditure on Research and Development
GHI	Global Hunger Index
GITA	Global Innovation & Technology Alliance
GMS	Greater Mekong Sub-region
GPRS	General Packet Radio Service
GQ	Golden Quadrilateral
GRiSP	Global Rice Science Partnership
GTAP	Global Trade Analysis Project
GVCs	Global Value Chains
HDI	Human Development Index
HS	Harmonized System
IAI	Initiative for ASEAN Integration
IAMMST	Informal ASEAN Ministerial Meeting on Science and Technology
ICCR	Indian Council for Cultural Relations
ICIO	Inter-Country Input-Output
ICP	Integrated Check-Post
ICT	Information and Communication Technology
IDFC	Infrastructure Development Finance Company
IFC	International Finance Cooperation
IIFT	Indian Institute of Foreign Trade
IIIT	Indian Institute for Information Technology
IIM	Indian Institute of Management
IIT	Indian Institute of Technology
IMCEITS	India–Myanmar Centre for Enhancement of IT Skills
IMF	International Monetary Fund
IMTTH	India–Myanmar–Thailand Trilateral Highway
IPNs	International Production Networks
IPR	Intellectual property Right
IRRI	International Rice Research Institute
ISRO	Indian Space Research Organization
IT	Information Technology
ITEC	Indian Technical and Economic Co-operation
IWT	Inland Water Transport
JIT	Just-in-Time
JWG	Joint Working Group
KMTTP	Kaladan Multimodal Transit Transport Project
LEP	Look East Policy
LNG	Liquefied Natural Gas
LSCI	Liner Shipping Connectivity Index
M&As	Mergers and Acquisitions
MA	Market Access
MEA	Ministry of External Affairs
MGCSS	Mekong Ganga Co-operation Scholarship Scheme
MIE	Minimally Invasive Education
MIEC	Mekong–India Economic Corridor
MIEDC	Myanmar India Entrepreneurship Development Centre

MIFCRSDP	Myanmar-India Friendship Centre for Remote Sensing and Data Processing
MIIT	Myanmar Institute of Information Technology
MMIF	Actuarial Review of Money Market and Investment Funds
MNC	Multi-national Cooperation
MPAC	Master Plan of ASEAN Connectivity
MRA	Mutual Recognition Agreements
MRL	Maximum Residual Limit
MTSF	Medium-Term Strategic Framework
NAFTA	North American Free Trade Agreement
NER	North Eastern Region
NFA	National Food Authority
NFMAP	National Farm Mechanization and Automation Plan
NFSP	National Food Security Policy
NMIMS	Narsee Monjee Institute of Management Studies
NTBs	Non-Tariff Barriers
NTMs	Non-Tariff Measures
OECD	Organisation for Economic Co-operation and Development
ONGC	Oil and Natural Gas Corporation
OP	Operating Procedures
ORF	Observer Research Foundation
OSBP	One Stop Border Post
OVL	ONGC Videsh Limited
PAECE	Programme of Action for Enhancement of Co-operation in Energy
PDC	Project Development Company
PDF	Project Development Facility
POA	Plan of Action
POC	Programme of Co-operation
PPD	Public–Private Dialogue
PPP	Public–Private Partnership
PSE	Public Sector Enterprises
R&D	Research and Development
RBI	Reserve Bank of India
RCA	Revealed Comparative Advantage
RCEP	Regional Comprehensive Economic Partnership
RFID	Radio Frequency Identity
RGC	Royal Government of Cambodia
RIS	Research and Information System for Developing Countries
RITES	Rail India Technical and Economic Service
RMU	Regional Monetary Unit
RTC	Rural Tele Centres
RTI	Regional Trade Introversion
S&T	Science and Technology
SAARC	South Asian Association for Regional Cooperation
SATIS	South Asia Agreement on Trade in Services
SBI	State Bank of India
SCOSA	Sub-Committee on Space Technology Applications
SEZ	Special Economic Zone
SFFSN	Strategic Framework for Food Security and Nutrition
SKRL	Singapore-Kunming Rail Link
SMEs	Small and Medium Enterprises
SPS	Sanitary and Phytosanitary
SPVs	Special Purpose Vehicles
STATEVAT	State Value Added Tax

STI	Science, Technology and Innovation
STRI	Services Trade Restrictiveness Index
TBT	Technical Barriers to Trade
TERI	The Energy and Resources Institute
TEU	Twenty-Foot Equivalent Unit
TF	Trade Facilitation
TFA	Trade Facilitation Agreement
TH	Trilateral Highway
TI	Trade Intensity
TICP	Technology Information & Commercialization Portal
TIFAC	Technology Information, Forecasting and Assessment Council
TIVA	Trade In Value Added
TNTDPC	Tamil Nadu Technology & Development Promotion Centre
TOE	Ton Oil Equivalent
TPES	Total Primary Energy Supplies
TPP	Trans-Pacific Partnership
TTIP	Trans-Atlantic Trade and Investment Partnership
UBI	United Bank of India
UK	United Kingdom
UNCOMTRADE	United Nations Commodity Trade Statistics Database
UNCTAD	United Nations Conference on Trade and Development
UNESCAP	United Nations Economic and Social Commission for Asia and the Pacific
UNESCO	United Nations Educational, Scientific, and Cultural Organization
USA	United States of America
VIIP	Virtual Institute for Intellectual Property
VOA	Visa on Arrival
WCO	World Custom Organization
WDI	World Development Indicators
WTO	World Trade Organization

Executive Summary

The Association of Southeast Asian Nations (ASEAN) has been the most successful regional organization in Asia and the Pacific. As the geographically adjacent, western neighbour of ASEAN, India's relations with ASEAN have grown from strength to strength. India's partnership with ASEAN has successfully moved from a sectoral dialogue partnership in 1992 to a summit partnership in 2002 to the strategic partnership in 2012. On the economic front, India and ASEAN signed a free trade agreement in 2009 and have been working together to establish a free trade area. Besides, India is also part of Regional Comprehensive Economic Partnership (RCEP) Agreement, which is currently being negotiated among the ASEAN+6 countries. Today, ASEAN not only lies at the core of India's 'Act East' Policy but also one of the cornerstones of India's foreign policy. The wave of ASEAN–India strategic partnership is sweeping across the region.

The growth pole of Asia may be shifting. The International Monetary Fund (IMF) has recently predicted India's economic growth will overtake China's in 2016. India aims to play a proactive role in Asia. India has moved into a proactive Act East Policy, which envisages accelerated engagement between ASEAN and India. The relationship is set to deepen in days to come as the two sides step up their collaboration across a range of economic and strategic issues, including trade, investment and connectivity, energy, culture, people-to-people contacts, and maritime security. Regional cooperation will be key to promoting economic stability, competitiveness, growth and integration in the region. A stronger ASEAN–India partnership would also enhance our participation in global economic governance and work towards building a common position, voice, and visibility in addressing the global governance.

Significant achievements in ASEAN–India relations have been witnessed. During the last two decades and a half, India's efforts in improving relations with Southeast and East Asian countries have resulted in increased trade and investment, better provision of trade facilitation measures, more engagements in non-traditional areas of cooperation, and have reduced the connectivity gaps. However, there are still untapped potentials for further enhancing ASEAN–India integration. Moving from cooperation to integration, there is a need to jointly address challenges to strengthening the partnership between ASEAN and India in various areas. Understanding the core challenges that result in deeper integration requires better understanding the underlying dimensions: enhancing macroeconomic and financial stability; trade integration and investment promotion; higher competitiveness and innovation; connectivity improvement; sharing resources and knowledge; supporting equitable growth; strengthening regional institutions; among others.

The ASEAN–India Development and Cooperation Report 2015 (AIDCR) is built upon the independent study commissioned by the ASEAN–India Centre (AIC) at RIS to explore further scopes and opportunities in deepening the ASEAN–India Strategic Partnership. One of the objectives of the Report is to bring together ideas, perspectives and experiences as part of our efforts to promote ASEAN–India integration in the context of ASEAN Economic Community (AEC). This Report provides a comparative analysis of the global and regional economies; examines the impact and implications of India–ASEAN integration; assesses policy priorities, effectiveness, implementation imperatives and challenges; and discusses themes central to the economic sustainability of the region, including public and foreign policy, trade facilitation, financial and scientific cooperation, food security, energy cooperation, and productivity and opportunities in the manufacturing and service sectors. Most specifically, it aims to provide insight into the work of regional cooperation and integration and suggest implications for both policy and programme interventions to strengthen the relations and introduce more academic substance into the policy making process. This Report presents comprehensive regional cooperation and integration issues, not only on partnership between ASEAN and India but also on East Asia Summit (EAS) Group relations. Findings of this Report would help making an Action Plan in order to translate the ASEAN–India Strategic Partnership Vision into concrete action. In addition, recommendations of this Report also offer inputs to the proposed ASEAN–India Plan of Action for the period 2016–2021. Taking account of the multidimensional nature of ASEAN–India cooperation, the Report is divided into 12 chapters, discussed briefly in the subsequent sections.

Economic Outlook and Prospects

The latest edition of IMF's *World Economic Outlook*, predicts that the developed countries have left their worst behind them and are on a path to recovery. It also comments that this is good news to the emerging market economies as the demand for their exports will increase. However, it remarks that full recovery of these countries will take more time. As far as Asia, especially Southeast Asia is concerned, the OECD reports that Southeast Asia is expected to fully recover from the effects of the global financial crisis in the medium term (the next five years). The same cannot be said about India and China. Both these countries are showing signs of a more gradual recovery. The economies of the ASEAN region plus India and China are on a road to recovery as well. At the same time, both China and India are facing delectation in exports in recent months.

The main factor in this prolonged recovery and the lagged response of emerging market economies is the contagion associated with globalization. Though the major source of growth in Asia remains domestic demand, outside factors, especially those in Europe and North America are increasingly exerting their influence on the performance of this region. It appears that these effects have become stronger during this financial crisis compared to the earlier two crises and will become even stronger as globalization progresses.

The main macro-economic challenge for these economies is therefore to combat this contagion. If the advanced economies recover strongly, there is every chance that investment flowing into Asian economies from these countries during their recessionary period will reverse. The twin options open to these economies then would be to increase returns on assets and simultaneously reduce risk associated with investments. Both monetary and fiscal tightening appears to be a good option under the circumstances. However, it should not be forgotten that these economies still depend substantially on domestic investments to fuel their growth and domestic investments may be crowded out in a bid to attract foreign investment. To ensure that this does not happen, extra sops need to be given to domestic investments.

Another important method of combating the contagion will be to define an economic subregion within the larger context of globalization by systematically facilitating trade and investments among the countries in the region — to an extent that goes much beyond what is true for the rest of the world. South and Southeast Asia can be such an economic subregion. The only problem in this respect is the pulls of gravity. Being in the low to middle income category, these countries have an inherent vulnerability to engage more with nations that have greater size as well as levels of economic development. For instance, most major trading partners of all these countries are either in North America or Europe. The doors of contagion from these countries are therefore wide open.

Lowering transport and transaction cost among these economies to a much larger extent than what has been achieved with the rest of the world can clearly help. And this is the crux of India–ASEAN economic cooperation. While the Free Trade Agreement (FTA) between the ASEAN countries themselves and between India and the ASEAN countries are a step in the right direction much more remains to be done. The investments agreements and the infrastructure agreements that are planned between India and ASEAN will without any doubt take this much further.

But the main issue remains implementation and ensuring effectiveness. The signing of an agreement does not automatically ensure that it is effective. Is trade taking place through the FTA route? Is the reduction in tariff too small compared to the loads of extra paperwork that needs to be dealt with to take advantage of the reduced tariff? Is connectivity between countries acting as a hindrance? Another issue that needs to be clarified is: are the right goods being targeted for tariff reduction? Are the goods for which tariff is relaxed tariff elastic? Recent evidence shows that most of the goods for which tariff was relaxed in the India ASEAN FTA have insignificant tariff elasticity, meaning that their imports are not expected to respond significantly to tariff reductions. Tariff negotiations before the signing of an FTA have its own logic. That logic may not coincide with the economic logic of the agreement: the incremental impact of the negotiation on the volume of trade. Subsequent policy must ensure this. Current policy priorities need to be focused in these directions.

Trends and Patterns of Merchandise Trade

The ASEAN–India bilateral trends in trade have been analyzed in this chapter at four reference time points, that is, 2009, the year immediately preceding the FTA, 2013 to observe the consequences of completion of first phase of FTA implementation and 2000 and 2005 for a relatively longer comparative perspective prior to the FTA. Our results show that the AIFTA does not appear to have resulted in any distinct break in the trade trends in the previous decade. Exports and imports have registered a consistent increase in volume over the last decade. Trade continues to be in favour of ASEAN. The share of ASEAN in India's total trade has been close to 10 per cent through the last decade. The implementation of the AIFTA in 2010 has not altered ASEAN's ranking among the regions that India trades with. ASEAN member countries that show an increase in India's share in their exports relative to the pre-FTA shares include Lao PDR, Malaysia, Thailand and Vietnam. The AIFTA does not appear to have made a positive impact on trade intensity among member countries and in fact leads to a decline in intra-regional trade bias.

Trade patterns show a very small share of component trade and hence do not seem to reflect India's integration in regional supply chains in any significant manner, despite the AIFTA. While India could be emerging as the alternative market for ASEAN, particularly in the post global financial crisis scenario, it would also need to upgrade its manufacturing abilities and participate in regional production networks as these constitute an integral component of intra-Southeast Asian trade.

Given the reality of mega-regional agreements in Asia, both ASEAN and India will have to accelerate the pace of their economic reform processes in order to participate in and benefit from their trade creation possibilities. For ASEAN, this would entail consolidation of the ASEAN Economic Community (AEC) and ensure thereby a stable centre for the RCEP. India will also have to undertake major reforms so as to overcome competitive pressures from China, a country with which India has resisted a formal trade agreement so far, as also from members common to the RCEP and the more advanced Trans-Pacific Partnership (TPP).

SERVICES TRADE PATTERNS AND KEY POLICIES

Trade in services has gained more importance in recent years as advances in technology have resulted in new means of providing services across borders. While there is little doubt that services trade is an essential ingredient to economic growth and sustainable development, it is widely accepted that it can only make such positive contribution if appropriately liberalized and implemented across countries. Services have become an important component of the global economy. ASEAN and India are no exception. The services sector has already become an important source of both output and employment in ASEAN and India. While India and some of the ASEAN member countries are services-driven, a large part of ASEAN has an equally fast growing manufacturing sector. The structural asymmetries in production and trade may tend to suggest that the opportunities for two-way services exports among ASEAN countries and with India in particular are substantial. Nevertheless, an efficient services sector is not only crucial for the performance of the ASEAN economies but also critical to its competitiveness.

Total intra-ASEAN exports in services have more than doubled between 2005 and 2012. In the services trade, the AEC Blueprint had set out targets to substantially remove all restrictions on trade in services for air transport, ICT and e-commerce, health care and tourism, and logistics services. Most ASEAN countries have allowed foreign entry in services, but limits vary in a significant manner. Moreover, the limits of foreign equity shareholding in various sectors are often different for GATS and AFAS. Under the GATS, countries usually indicate a threshold value in terms of commitments. However, improvements under AFAS suggest willingness towards deeper integration among ASEAN economies. India has already signed Services Trade and Investment Agreement with ASEAN, which is likely to be implemented very soon.

Under the WTO, India's requests profile gives a glimpse into India's core interests. At the same time requests received by India tell us about barriers to service trade faced by other countries in India. This is true for ASEAN countries as well. India has been asked to take commitments with regard to transparency in domestic regulations, simplify procedures, eliminate differential treatment of foreign suppliers of services and facilitate the movement of natural persons under Mode 4. However, India, at present, also has a growing interest in Mode 3 in areas related to computer, education, health and tourism. These are the sectors where barriers on the ASEAN side exist in terms of domestic regulations. The prospect that India could gain in roads into ASEAN markets (market access) depends on streamlined and favourable domestic regulations in ASEAN member countries. India has often faced barriers in terms of different levels of openness (market access) offered by countries on Mode 3 and Mode 4. This has implications for commercial operations that involve presence of personnel from abroad for execution of projects.

India has made a request under GATS to take full commitments with respect to the category of independent professionals, de-linked from the commercial presence. India has also requested others to follow a liberalized visa system by ensuring the fulfillment of horizontal and sectoral commitments that were undertaken, such as multiple entry visas for professionals and allowing inter-firm mobility to professionals. India has longstanding interests in Mode 4 (cross-border mobility of its large number of highly skilled individuals). We stress that one crucial bottleneck for ASEAN–India trade in services concerns skilled labour mobility. Negotiating for recognition of academic and professional qualifications is a complex and time-consuming process given the wide divergence in the levels of development among ASEAN countries and absence of comprehensive or single MRAs for a broad range of professional categories among ASEAN members. However, both India and ASEAN should make attempts at sealing MRAs mutually in such sectors, where ASEAN has successfully completed MRAs. This could significantly improve prospects of cross-border movements of professionals from either side.

INVESTMENTS PROSPECTS AND CHALLENGES

ASEAN region has been very resilient in terms of receiving foreign investment, while posting an 18 per cent growth in the capital inflows particularly when world economies are striving to manage their economic fundamentals. The growing trade and investment relations between ASEAN and India justify further areas for economic collaboration. Singapore being the largest investment contributor to India and having core competence in areas such as air and sea transport, innovation, technology etc. sets a clear roadmap for collaboration. Malaysia and Thailand are sound in logistics performance and automatically enhance the scope for further tie-up. The growing middle income class in the region amid more active policy measures in all countries of the region is adding a significant scope for bilateral investment.

Major hurdles for investors in both India and ASEAN continue in terms of legal environment, poor infrastructure, lack of transparency and regulatory issues, among others. The issues for restrictions in ownerships in sectors such as banking, construction, hotel and restaurant, mining and quarrying etc. need to be considered at par for further investment and economic cooperation. The attraction of investment from ASEAN into India largely depends on the policy responses to macroeconomic problems. Country needs to enhance its business environment by reducing corruption and strengthening the rule of law, faster clearances for projects, develop infrastructure, boost manufacturing, simplify the taxation system, ease FDI regulations and increase awareness about its emerging cities, flexibility in the Public–Private Partnership (PPP) contracts through renegotiations, among others.

The growth prospects of ASEAN region provide the best avenue for India to encash on the region's service sector potential in which India enjoys a comparative advantage. Besides, the Indian target of uplifting manufacturing sector has great potential for the ASEAN region to exploit. India has strong comparative advantage in export of computer and information services, other business services such as financial, medical tourism, insurance, etc., and movement of natural persons such as IT professionals and seafarers. Likewise, ASEAN countries have comparative advantage in logistics-related services that can be of great help to India. Complementarities among the two exist in terms of trade in energy, consumer durables and food items. Addressing the above mentioned competitive sectors coming into the ambit of services sector may enhance the scope of India-ASEAN FTA in services and investment.

EMERGING PRODUCTION NETWORKS

There is need for research and policy focus on ways and means for advancing India's participation and integration in regional production networks. Policy measures in the direction of developing manufacturing sector competitiveness supplemented with further liberalization of trade and investment climate and developing necessary infrastructure and trade logistics need to be formulated.

Developing IPNs depends on host of conditions ranging from infrastructure, conducive industrial policies, encouragement towards technological innovation, to absorptive capacity of SMEs and end market competitiveness. It has been observed that India is slowly but steadily getting integrated with the industries of Southeast Asia especially in machinery, electrical products and automobile sector. This also carries some ramifications for Indian SMEs because all the above mentioned industries are closely tied with domestic medium and small enterprise. Thus, if SMEs could overcome technological, financial and other barriers, the IPN in these sectors might act as a growth facilitator for them as well. It is observed that so far, in India's exports of the mentioned products (that is, electric, machinery and automobile), contribution of Europe and the United States has been higher than Southeast Asia and China but the scenario is changing fast. India is mostly importing components and engaging itself in downstream activities. China has moved towards upstream activities and thereby has better control of the value of chain activities. India is ahead of Indonesia, the Philippines and CLMV countries but behind Malaysia, Singapore and Thailand in terms of value addition capability in the production system. India's contribution in the global value chain is not only limited to downstream final assembly but also in various business services, which are required in the manufacturing process. India's engagement in trading, transport, storage and telecommunication are also important for the exports from ASEAN region. It is noted that in post-FTA period, India has surged ahead with exports of automobile components implying its strong presence in ASEAN IPN. On the other hand, in machinery, imports from Southeast Asia is used both in final goods production for domestic consumption as well as for international use. In case of electronic and optical equipment, India is still on the fringe with limited connectivity. India lacks attractiveness in terms of possible investment in these sectors especially in developing joint ventures with SMEs. Though India is ranked high in terms of adopting new technology, major skill gap in manufacturing sector is a stumbling block for converting this into a productivity gain. Coupled with this, as discussed earlier, most SMEs still face certain barriers in the form of lack of financing, exposure to new technology and ability to conduct small innovation. An effective handholding, proper policy support and awareness about global business strategy can help Indian SMEs to become more connected with emerging international production network.

REMOVING NON-TARIFF MEASURES

It is not the tariff liberalization but the disciplining of non-tariff measures (NTMs) which is important for achieving preferential market access. Only then any FTA would achieve its true goal of promoting trade and investment. Some interesting facts about the role of NTMs which have come to light from the analysis is that although AIFTA has come up with considerable tariff reduction, at the same time it is equally important for such agreements to come to an understanding on the issue of NTMs. This is critical because of its nature of impact on a product or group of products whereby these measures have possibility of totally denying market access. Therefore, there is a growing urgency for negotiations and immediate solution on this issue, by creating and strengthening the discipline around the mutual recognition agreements (MRAs) while dealing with the SPS and TBT measures.

Currently, there is discord in the tariff lines. There is a need to harmonize the tariff schedules of two parties to the agreement. This is important in the context of ASEAN moving towards a common tariff by 2015. A majority of ASEAN members have different Scheduling under the AIFTA. This in itself is very challenging and to add to this is how the measure is applied at the border, sometime it may lead to discrimination due to lack of transparency built-in-to the procedures of application of domestic regulation. Finally, there is a need to build sectoral MRAs. This is important especially when it is found that a lot of TBT measures are based on national standards. This would help countries to protect the industries within the FTA.

CONNECTIVITY CHALLENGES AND NEW DIRECTION

With India's FTA with the ASEAN in 2010 and the proposed RCEP, economic integration between India and Southeast and East Asia is set to gain new momentum. More production and services networks between ASEAN and India may emerge if the regional economy is adequately supported by cross-border infrastructure facilities, both hardware and software.

ASEAN and India have undertaken several connectivity projects, physical or otherwise. India, Myanmar and Thailand have been negotiating the Motor Vehicle Agreement (MVA) to facilitate movement of goods and passengers along the Trilateral Highway. Before moving to an economic corridor, ASEAN and India may have to pass through trade corridors. The transformation of the transport corridors into economic corridors will depend on the volume, types and pattern of corridor trade and how it encourages certain level of development in the areas surrounding the corridors. Spatial planning going beyond national policies is needed to support the development of the corridors between ASEAN and India at the same time, development of one area of the corridor is conditional upon the trading conditions along the entire area of the corridor across countries. Building corridor nodes and gateways and linking the nodes along the corridor would help the region in moving towards economic corridor.

Efforts to promote regional infrastructure such as economic corridor need to address policy reform in a number of areas. Institutions and investment have an important complementary role in enhancing infrastructure development between ASEAN and India. Regional cooperation also has an important catalytic role to play in this process. By sharing each other's experiences, regional cooperation can make countries efficient by integrating them to the regional market. Economic corridor integrates the markets by fostering trade. Finally, economic corridor can have huge payoffs at a time when the region is looking for higher investments in industrial sector, and planning to deepen regional trade through global and regional value chains. Making trade between ASEAN and India faster and seamless would require complementary policy initiatives by countries, regional organizations, and multilateral development institutions to strengthen the capacity of countries for development of economic corridors.

ENERGY MARKET INTEGRATION AND COOPERATION

India is already engaged in energy infrastructure development in the ASEAN region, particularly in the CLMV countries. India is building hydropower projects, power transmission lines and substations, and oil and gas pipelines in these countries. Indian companies have also invested in energy assets in ASEAN countries in sectors like coal, oil and gas. When it comes to trade in energy commodities, it is largely limited to Indian imports of coal from Indonesia and Indian exports of petroleum products. However, the resource positions of India and ASEAN indicate that India can import much more, particularly natural gas and electricity. Energy sector machineries, equipments and other goods can also open up possibilities for substantial trade.

ASEAN is in the process of developing region wide grid of natural gas pipelines and electricity transmission lines. India can get connected through these two ASEAN wide grids by developing transmission line and gas pipeline connections through Myanmar. Indian electricity grid is already connected with Bangladesh electricity grid and Bangladesh is planning to link its electricity grid with that of Myanmar. There has been a significant change in the attitude of Bangladesh with respect to Myanmar–Bangladesh–India natural gas pipeline. India and Myanmar have also revived the discussions on the gas pipeline connection between India and Myanmar through Bangladesh. The proposed pipeline would extend from Block A-1, through Bangladesh, to India and various design options are being considered, including a land route via the eastern Indian states of Tripura and Mizoram, an offshore route through the coastal areas of Bangladesh, and a deep sea route. In future, it will be possible for India not only to access electricity and gas from Myanmar but also gas from faraway fields in Indonesia and Brunei and electricity from Lao PDR.

The official discussion on energy cooperation between India and ASEAN has so far focused on renewable energy only. The electricity generation sources indicate that India has developed significant capability in wind energy whereas Indonesia and the Philippines have the same in geothermal energy and Singapore is generating significant electricity from waste. India and Thailand have some experience in solar power as well. India is also the only country to generate nuclear power and use bio-fuel to generate significant quantity of electricity. These countries can help others in developing energy production capabilities in the respective sub-sectors. While India–ASEAN energy cooperation focuses on renewable energy only, India, along with some of its South Asian neighbours and some members of ASEAN are part of BIMSTEC, where energy has been identified as one of the important sectors for comprehensive cooperation including all types of energy. The ASEAN–India energy cooperation would depend very much on BIMSTEC energy activities, work as a bridge between SAARC and ASEAN in promoting a comprehensive energy cooperation regime.

STRENGTHENING MONETARY AND FINANCIAL COOPERATION

The Chiang Mai Initiative (CMI) is a good starting point to build on the various existing initiatives. Although under the present dispensation the CMI is complementary to similar IMF initiatives, it has an important symbolic value in as much as it can signal the markets a regional commitment to supporting any member country's currency that is under speculative pressures. It also recognizes that establishing swap arrangements does not obviate the need to address structural and financial sector weaknesses. It may also be added that while CMI might have contributed to the exchange rate stability in the region, it has also contributed to closer regional economic and financial integration and cooperation. It is useful to explore ways of carrying this process forward.

Developing corporate bond market also needs a special focus. Some of the suggestions may include: (*a*) set up specific development banks to meet the financial needs of the member countries; (*b*) to allure individuals to invest, the Government should provide tax incentives like in Malaysia and other countries and (*c*) there is a need to promote guarantee in bond market and for that an organization on lines of deposits insurance be promoted. There is a need to build capacity and lay the long-term infrastructure for development of ASEAN capital markets, with a long-term goal of achieving cross-border collaboration between the various capital markets in ASEAN.

There is a need for integration between India and ASEAN to penetrate the underdeveloped insurance market in India. This will help the member countries to coordinate themselves, which may help in developing products and policies for a developed insurance markets. This is in line with the efforts by the ASEAN Insurance Regulators Meeting (AIRM) that include sharing of insurance statistics among countries with the end goal of achieving a unified form of statistics; exchange of views on regulatory issues and observance of core principles related to insurance markets.

Science and Technology Cooperation Blueprint

The enabling role of science and technology (S&T) for economic development has been fully recognized under the ASEAN Framework and a target for the year 2020 has been set to make the ASEAN region technologically competitive through competence in strategic and enabling technologies, with an adequate pool of technologically qualified and trained manpower, and strong networks of scientific and technological institution and centres of excellence. However, as a group of 10 developing countries with great variance in the level of S&T capability, ASEAN faces considerable difficulties in achieving these goals. The overwhelming concern for India, on the other hand, has been its inability to transform India's S&T potential into outcomes that could measure up in terms of industrial competitiveness and human development. ASEAN–India cooperation in S&T is based on complementarities, where India has generously shared its 'technical knowledge' and 'resources' with ASEAN member states at various levels.

The India–ASEAN partnership platform offers the most in terms of opportunities in this regard with maximum consensus on both sides. Over the recent years, India has taken a keen interest in furthering cooperation with the poorer ASEAN members, namely, the CLMV by implementing capacity building programmes in areas, in which India has proven expertise like information technology, agriculture and space. Deepening of such cooperation between CLMV–ASEAN and India is called for, particularly in the area of space science and technology where India can be a lead partner. However, practical bottlenecks like long drawn approvals arising out of multiple stakeholders have slowed the pace of such efforts. There is also a need for greater optimism on both sides about beneficial outcomes of development cooperation between India and ASEAN in the area of S&T.

Expanding Food Security and Food Reserves

ASEAN region along with India has been struggling hard in reducing food insecurity, as the fruits of efforts have not been distributed evenly across the region. The challenge of ensuring food security for the growing population cannot be tackled only with the increase in agricultural productivity or food-stocking mechanisms, but greater attention is needed for achieving nutritional security. Despite the numerous measures like food reserves system and price stabilization of rice for food emergency purposes by almost all the member countries of ASEAN to resolve the challenges of food security issues, there is need for long-term solutions rather than the short one. One suitable option to deal with this is the establishment of regional food bank in collaboration with India. SAARC Food Bank offers several lessons with respect to meeting food demands under disaster conditions and other climate-driven uncertainties. It would maintain food reserves and support national as well as regional food security through collective action among member countries.

An integrated food security approach may be initiated with ASEAN dialogue partners such as India. It may be emphasized here that the results achieved so far in terms of food availability and reduction in hunger, have been the outcome of the positive initiatives undertaken at the regional level. ASEAN governments with involvement of the NGOs and civil societies have to play very effective role in order to bring significant improvement in enhancing food security through regional cooperation. Both ASEAN and India gain from a deeper cooperation.

Towards a Stronger Cultural Link

Durable and abiding relationships are based not on inter-governmental contacts, but on people-to-people contacts. Culture is the best bond between people of India and ASEAN. Even though tourism is an important item in Indian dialogue with ASEAN, not much has been done to develop this area to promote people-to-people contacts. So far, tourism has been moving in only one direction — Indians going to Southeast Asia but not the reverse. Imaginative packages need to be evolved and sufficient incentives offered to attract tourists from countries in Southeast Asia, and from Myanmar, Malaysia, Indonesia, Thailand and Vietnam in particular, by promoting cultural and religious tourism. This will not only bring revenues to India but will also cement civil society interactions, an important component of mature and enduring state-to-state relations.

Cooperation in the field of education needs to be widened and deepened further by showcasing some of our premier educational institutions like the Indian Institute of Technology and the Indian Institute of Management. Educational and cultural agreements need to be concluded with a view to narrow the knowledge gap that exists between India and Southeast Asian countries. The future educational and cultural interactions should be carried out with a clear-cut view of training a core of experts in each country who would be able to provide better perspective of their country of specialization and give nuanced feedback to their respective policymakers. Finally, cultural and religious tourism need to be promoted to bring the people from India and Southeast closer to each other. It would be appropriate if both ASEAN and India initiate an innovative political, educational and cultural charm to give more substance to economic engagement process.

Introduction

The year 2015 will long be remembered for India's new foreign policy — 'Neighbourhood First' or 'Act East Policy' — that has influenced all countries, smaller or bigger, across the world, especially in the area of trade and investment. Regional economic integration agenda has become a priority as we turn our focus towards economic goals with ASEAN and beyond. A series of agreements over past two decades put regional integration at the centre of economic agenda of Association of Southeast Asian Nations (ASEAN) and India. Today, relations with ASEAN are the foundation of India's Act East Policy (AEP). There has been deepening of cooperation between India and ASEAN across the three pillars of relationship, namely, politico-security, economic and sociocultural. Down the line, the trade between ASEAN and India has grown 20 times in the last 20 years to reach over US\$ 77 billion in 2014–15. ASEAN is currently India's fourth largest trading partner. Adding China, Japan and Korea in it, countries falling under the coverage of AEP contribute to about 1/3rd of India's global trade. Quite naturally, relations with ASEAN are one of the cornerstones of India's foreign policy. The wave of the ASEAN–India Strategic Partnership is sweeping across the region. However, there are still untapped potentials for further enhancing ASEAN–India integration.

There has been steady progress in the ASEAN–India partnership since the Look East Policy (LEP) was initiated in 1991. India became the sectoral dialogue partner of ASEAN in 1992. In 1996, this was upgraded to full dialogue partnership. In 2002, India became summit-level partner of ASEAN. These political level interactions are further strengthened through the Senior Officials' Meetings, as also specialized working groups in the various functional areas. India has been increasingly engaged with ASEAN, and that is also growing rapidly. At present, there are 26 Dialogue mechanisms between India and ASEAN, cutting across all the sectors. In 2012, ASEAN and India commemorated 20 years of dialogue partnership and 10 years of summit level partnership. The Commemorative Summit, attended by the Leaders from all the 10 ASEAN countries, endorsed elevating the ASEAN–India partnership to the Strategic Partnership level.

The combined region of ASEAN and India represents a total population of 1.8 billion, which is about one-quarter of the global population, and with a total GDP of over US\$ 3.8 trillion, the region presents one of the largest economic spaces in the world, thereby offering immense opportunities not only for the region but also for the entire world. Acceding to open regionalism, political foundation of ASEAN at the same time has grown stronger since its establishment in 1967. In the last four decades and a half, ASEAN integration has crossed many milestones one after another (see Figure 0.1). Today, it's free trade area with six neighbouring countries, of which two are the world's top emerging markets, is the foundation of the Asian integration process. Deeper integration between India and ASEAN will provide a strong platform for the larger economic integration being negotiated under the Regional Comprehensive Economic Partnership (RCEP) Agreement framework. Any further efforts to deepen integration between India and ASEAN will therefore have renewed importance as the global economy enters new phase of integration.

POLICY CHANGES POSTED BY ECONOMIC INTEGRATION PROCESS

Significant achievements in ASEAN–India relations have been witnessed. During the last two decades and a half, India's efforts in improving relations with Southeast and East Asian countries have resulted in increased trade and investment, better provision of trade facilitation measures, more engagements in non-traditional areas of cooperation, and have reduced the connectivity gaps. The implementation of the ASEAN–India Free Trade Agreement (FTA) in goods, which was signed in 2009, has translated into a significant increase in bilateral trade, which has increased from under US\$ 44 billion in 2009–10 to over US\$ 77 billion in 2014–15. However, it remains relatively low compared with the other dialogue partners of ASEAN. But, more and more Indian products are getting market access in ASEAN. As seen in Table 0.1, a number of export products at 8-digit HS level from India to ASEAN increased, particularly after the ASEAN–India FTA, while the number of import products from ASEAN to India had fallen. India's rising trade deficit with ASEAN has been debated widely in recent months. Figure 0.2 clearly shows India's trade deficit has widened in the post-FTA period. However, the

Figure 0.1 ASEAN Integration over Time

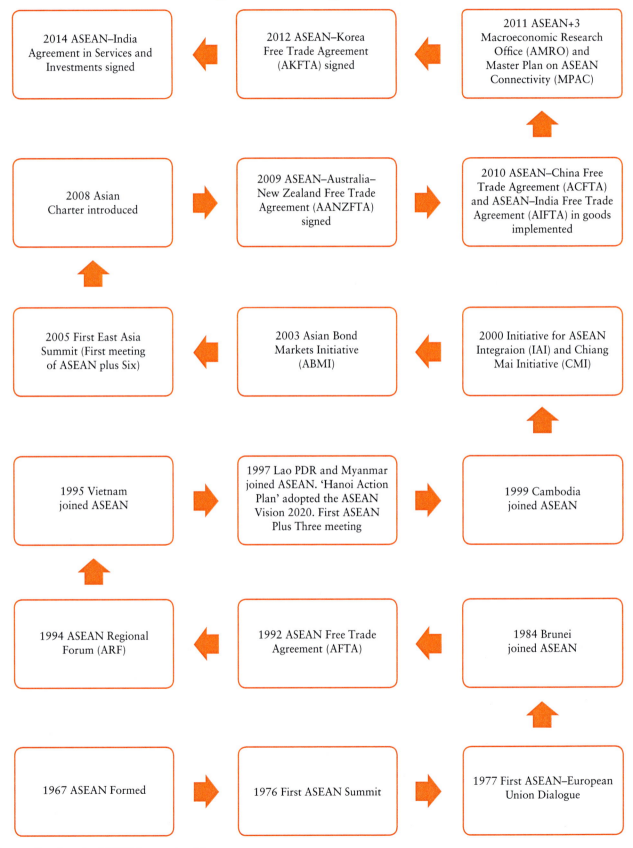

Source: Based on the ASEAN Secretariat, Jakarta.
Note: Illustrated by Sreya Pan

TABLE 0.1
India's Trade with ASEAN: Number of Products Traded

Year	HS Code	Total No. of Products Exported by India ASEAN	World	Share in Total Exports to World (%)	Total No. of Products Imported by India ASEAN	World	Share in Total Imports from World (%)
2000–01	8 digit	5878	9800	59.98	4729	8295	57.01
2005–06	8 digit	6912	10639	64.97	5769	9810	58.81
2009–10	8 digit	6905	10297	67.06	5626	9494	59.26
2013–14	8 digit	7067	10367	68.17	5522	9541	57.88

Source: Figures have been calculated based on Comtrade.

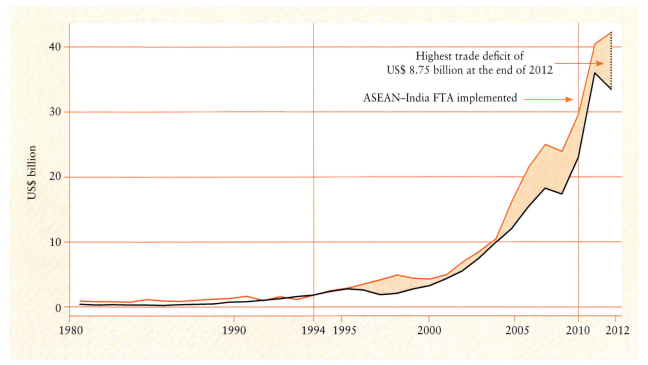

FIGURE 0.2
Trends in ASEAN–India Trade

Source: Based on the Direction of Trade Statistics, International Monetary Fund (IMF).

Services and Investment Agreements, which were signed in 2014 between India and ASEAN, are expected to raise the trade flow between the two partners. Nevertheless, a large part of bilateral trade between them is yet to be unlocked.

In terms of FDI inflows, India–ASEAN region has significantly outpaced many other regions in the world. ASEAN drew more FDI than China for the second straight year in 2014. Overall FDI into Singapore, Indonesia, Malaysia, the Philippines, Thailand and Vietnam rose to a record US$ 128 billion in 2014. That surpassed the US$ 119.56 billion which flowed into China. FDI into the Philippines grew the fastest, at 66 per cent, while in Thailand inflows fell. FDI into Indonesia, the region's biggest economy, rose around 10 per cent.

In the recent past, investment flows have also expanded with US$ 25 billion FDI equity flowing into India from ASEAN countries and US$ 31 billion in outflows from India to ASEAN over the last seven years between the period of April 2007 to March 2014. It is expected that the increased economic relevance and dynamism of the ASEAN–India partnership will boost the bilateral FDI flows. As intra-regional FDI flows are fast replacing those from the developed countries, India has the potential to become a major investor in the region and so also ASEAN in India.

As China's troubled manufacturing sector loses momentum, Chinese businesses will be venturing abroad to cut operating costs and to search for new markets. Rising wages in China are leading low-end manufacturers to look for other low-cost locations for their factories, with countries like Myanmar, Vietnam and the Philippines looking like attractive alternatives. ASEAN and India are also large markets in their own rights, with good long-term growth prospects. Investment reform is therefore the biggest challenge for both India and ASEAN.

ASEAN–India Partnership for Peace, Progress and Shared Prosperity sets out the roadmap for long-term ASEAN–India engagement, which was signed at the 3rd ASEAN–India Summit, on 30 November 2004 at Vientiane. A Plan of Action (2004–10) was also developed to implement the Partnership. Encouraged by the efficacy and usefulness of the Plan of Action in steering concrete sectoral cooperation between ASEAN and India, a second Plan of Action for the period 2010–15 was adopted at the 8th ASEAN–India Summit in Hanoi on 30 October 2010. The Plan of Action (PoA) 2010–15 envisages cooperation in a range of sectors in the political, economic and socio-cultural spheres for deepening and intensification of ASEAN–India cooperation. The PoA for 2016–21 is currently under preparation.

ASEAN Multilateral Division of MEA offers project-based financial assistance to ASEAN countries. Financial assistance has been provided to ASEAN countries through (a) ASEAN–India Cooperation Fund, (b) ASEAN–India S&T Development Fund, and (c) ASEAN–India Green Fund. At the 7th ASEAN–India Summit in 2009, India announced a contribution of US$ 50 million to the ASEAN–India Cooperation Fund to support the implementation of the ASEAN–India PoA 2010–15. Till October 2014, projects worth US$ 6 million have been completed, whereas projects worth US$ 14.15 million are at implementation stage. At the 6th ASEAN–India Summit in 2007, India announced the setting up of an ASEAN–India Science & Technology Development Fund with a US$ 1 million contribution from India to promote joint collaborative R&D research projects in Science & Technology sectors. This Fund became operational in 2009–10 and expenditure began in 2010–11. Till 2014, projects worth US$ 0.36 million are the implementation stage. ASEAN–India Green Fund was set up in 2007 with an initial contribution of US$ 5 million to support the collaboration activities relating to environment and climate change. Project proposals worth US$ 1.27 million are the implementation stage and US$ 0.86 million are at the planning stage.

In order to facilitate investments from the Indian private sector in CLMV countries (Cambodia, Laos, Myanmar and Vietnam), a Project Development Company (PDC) has been announced by India. It will, through separate Special Purpose Vehicles (SPVs), set up manufacturing hubs in CLMV countries. Underlining the importance of connectivity, Prime Minister of India during the 12th ASEAN–India Summit, announced establishment of a special facility to facilitate project financing and quick implementation of ASEAN–India connectivity projects with provision of US$ 1 billion over a 10-year period to catalyze investment from the Indian private sector to the tune of US$ 10 billion over the same period. This will also include identification of economic nodes and development of backend linkages to achieve a symbiotic model of development and integrate northeastern part of India with regional value chains in the ASEAN region.

ASEAN and India are now a driving force for the global economy. But, if the region is to grow further, it is essential to press ahead with the infrastructure development that underpins industrial activity such as 'Make-in-India', improves people's livelihoods and facilitates the distribution of goods. The biggest challenge is to bring in private-sector funds. To attract private capital in infrastructure, public–private partnership (PPP) shall be promoted. Globally, the private sector has accumulated large amounts of capital, in part because of monetary easing measures. This private capital, used wisely, will pave the way for not just infrastructure development, but also sustainable economic growth, worldwide.

As a regional bloc, ASEAN has developed much faster than any of the other blocs in the Asia-Pacific. With ASEAN and India working towards establishing a Comprehensive Free Trade Area through the RCEP Agreement, their cooperation will be the key to promoting economic stability, competitiveness, growth and integration in the region. As long-term patterns of economic integration shift, new international relationships are being built. ASEAN and India are increasingly important to each other in trade, finance, investment, connectivity, and in regional and global policy. Will India's growth strengthen the partnership with ASEAN or what would be the policies that will provide a new tool for building dynamism between ASEAN and India?

The chapters that follow examine the dimension of ASEAN–India economic integration challenges they bring, and the regional cooperative mechanisms that could provide solutions to them. The major issues are divided into three broad areas: (a) economic performance, trade, investment, (b) trade barriers and connectivity, and (c) sectoral cooperation.

Moving from cooperation to integration, there is a need to jointly address challenges to strengthening the partnership between ASEAN and India in various areas. Understanding the core challenges that result in deeper integration requires better understanding of the underlying dimensions: enhancing macroeconomic and financial stability; trade integration and investment promotion; higher competitiveness and innovation; connectivity improvement; sharing resources and knowledge; supporting equitable growth; strengthening regional institutions; among others.

ASEAN–India Development and Cooperation Report 2015 (AIDCR) is built upon the independent study commissioned by the ASEAN–India Centre (AIC)at RIS to explore further scope and opportunities in deepening the ASEAN–India Strategic Partnership. One of the objectives of the report is to bring together ideas, perspectives and experiences as part of our efforts to promote ASEAN–India integration in the context of ASEAN Economic Community (AEC).

The chapters provide a comparative analysis of the global and regional economies; examine the impact and implications of India–ASEAN integration; assess policy priorities, effectiveness, implementation imperatives and challenges; and discuss themes central to the economic sustainability of the region, including public and foreign policy, trade facilitation, financial and scientific cooperation, food security, energy cooperation and productivity and opportunities in the manufacturing and service sectors. Most specifically, the chapters aim to provide insight into the work of regional cooperation and integration and suggest implications for both policy and programme interventions to strengthen the relations and introduce more academic substance into the policy making process. This Report presents comprehensive regional cooperation and integration issues, not only on the partnership between ASEAN and India but also on East Asia Summit (EAS) Group relations. Findings of this Report would help making an Action Plan in order to translate the ASEAN–India Strategic Partnership Vision into concrete action. In addition, recommendations of this Report also offer inputs to the proposed ASEAN–India Plan of Action for the period 2016–2021.

ASEAN Economic Community and India: Major Challenges beyond 2015

An Asian Development Bank Institute (ADBI) study suggests that ASEAN economies can enter a high-growth trajectory by tripling their per capita incomes by 2030 and raising the quality of life to current levels of OECD countries. Another scenario, however, leads to a major GDP growth slowdown to no more than 3 per cent per year, as countries fall into the middle income trap and are unable to manage natural disasters and climate change, or resolve political tensions.

According to the same ADBI Study, an ASEAN Economic Community (AEC) for 2016–25 may include an integrated and highly cohesive economy, a competitive, innovative and dynamic ASEAN, a resilient, inclusive and people-oriented, people-centred ASEAN, enhanced sectoral integration and cooperation and a global ASEAN. Box 1 presents some stylized facts about AEC's post-2015 vision. AEC will generate tremendous growth potential and new opportunities for promoting bilateral trade between ASEAN and India and building business partnerships in the private sector. However, the few major challenges facing AEC are: (*a*) enhancing macroeconomic and financial stability; (*b*) supporting equitable growth; (*c*) promoting competitiveness and innovation and (*d*) protecting the environment. Overcoming these challenges by building a truly borderless economic region implies sound macroeconomic management, promoting inclusive development and 'green' growth, eliminating barriers to the flow of goods, services and production factors, branding ASEAN through standardization and harmonization and strengthening regional institutions. While these are some macro challenges faced by the AEC, major micro challenges for ASEAN beyond 2015 were identified as follows.

a) An elimination of non-tariff barriers (NTBs) is much more difficult than tariff reductions. Virtually tariff reduces closer to zero for the ASEAN-6 countries; it is now non-tariff measures (NTMs) that have become particularly salient as a potential barrier to smoother trade linkages among member states.

b) National Single Windows are not yet fully operational in most ASEAN member states. The ASEAN Single Window (ASW) is not yet operative. ASW would greatly facilitate regional trade volume by using a standardized process with less documentation.

c) Reducing development gaps (income inequality) among ASEAN member states

d) Need to improve competitiveness of ASEAN countries

e) ASEAN member states (AMS) have mixed record on services and investment liberalization, given the different political economy challenges facing each of the member states. It is likely that negotiations for the ASEAN Framework Agreement on Services (AFAS) beyond AFAS-8 would be increasingly much more

Box 0.1
ASEAN Economic Community's Post-2015 Vision

- Create a deeply integrated and highly cohesive ASEAN economy that would support sustained high economic growth and resilience even in the face of global economic shocks and volatilities.
- Incorporate a sustainable growth agenda with green technology and green energy.
- More equitable and inclusive growth in ASEAN to narrow the development gaps among the ASEAN countries.
- Promote good governance, transparency and responsive regulations and regulatory regimes through active engagement with the private sector, community based organizations and other stakeholders of ASEAN.
- Enhanced Dispute Settlement Mechanism and developing other approaches to speed it up.
- Foster robust productivity growth through innovation and technology development, which entails human resource development and intensified regional research and development with commercial application to increase ASEAN's competitive edge to move up the global value chain into higher technology-intensive manufacturing industries and knowledge intensive market services.
- Promote connectivity with infrastructure connectivity, people-to-people connectivity and movement of skilled people and talents.
- Address issues related to food security, energy security, natural disasters and other economic shocks, emerging trade-related issues and global mega trends with more dynamic ASEAN (national and regional) mechanism.
- Maintain ASEAN's role as the centre and facilitator of economic integration in the East Asian region to reinforce ASEAN centrality in the emerging regional economic architecture.
- Enhance ASEAN's participation in global economic governance and work towards building a common position, voice and visibility in addressing.

Source: ASEAN Secretariat, Jakarta.

difficult since the deepening and widening of services liberalization efforts would almost certainly touch the more sensitive sectors in each of the AMSs. AMSs may have to determine the degree of liberalization of the services sector that would be consistent with a highly contestable services sector in the region needed for greater competitiveness vis-a-vis other major economies in the region.

Post-2015 Plans

The ASEAN Experts Group on Competition (AEGC) gathered at the ASEAN Secretariat from 9–10 September 2014 to set new targets and a regional plan of action on competition for the period 2015–25. It was proposed to develop the ASEAN High-Level Task Force on Economic Integration (HLTF-EI) for a strategic framework towards 2025. The post-2015 Competition Action Plan is set to be finalized soon. However, some decisions have been taken on sectoral Action Plan such as tourism. For example, in Kuala Lumpur, on 13 January 2015, ASEAN member states have agreed to build new ASEAN Tourism Strategic Plan (ATSP) 2015–25. ATSP aims to explore the quality tourism destination with a unique and diverse ASEAN experience. It, among others, will enhance ASEAN's competitiveness as a single tourist destination through the development and adoption of tourism standards. Certified tourism professionals, security and safety and other promotional activities are taken by the Community to enhance further tourism.

A Public–Private Dialogue (PPD) focusing on the ASEAN Strategic Action Plan for Small and Medium Enterprises (SME) Development 2015–25 (Post-2015 SME Vision) was held on 25 November 2014 in Siem Reap, Cambodia. The five key strategic goals of the post-2015 SME Action Plan, namely; (*a*) promote productivity, technology and innovation; (*b*) increase access to finance; (*c*) enhance market access and internationalization (*d*) enhance policy and regulatory environment and (*e*) promote entrepreneurship and human capital development. The private sector provided a number of inputs highlighting the need for information and facilitative measures as well as the need for monitoring through Key Performance Indicators to ensure success of the implementation of the post-2015 Plan.

The growth pole of Asia may be shifting. The International Monetary Fund (IMF) has recently predicted India's economic growth will overtake China's in 2016. India aims to play a proactive role in Asia. India has moved into a proactive Act East Policy, which envisages accelerated engagement between ASEAN and India. The relationship is set to deepen in days to come as the two sides step up their collaboration across a range of economic and strategic issues, including trade, investment and connectivity, energy, culture, people-to-people contacts and maritime security. Regional cooperation will be key to promoting economic stability, competitiveness, growth and integration in the region. A stronger ASEAN–India partnership would also enhance our

Introduction xxxvii

participation in global economic governance and work towards building a common position, voice and visibility in addressing the global governance.

ECONOMIC OUTLOOK AND PROSPECTS

The latest edition of IMF's *World Economic Outlook* predicts that the developed countries have left their worst behind them and are on a path to recovery. It also comments that this is good news to the emerging market economies as the demand for their exports will increase. However, it remarks that full recovery of these countries will take more time. As far as Asia, especially Southeast Asia, is concerned, the OECD reports that Southeast Asia is expected to fully recover from the effects of the global financial crisis in the medium term (next five years). The same cannot be said about India and China. Both these countries are showing signs of a more gradual recovery. The economies of the ASEAN region as well as India and China are on a road to recovery as well.

The main factor in this prolonged recovery and the lagged response of emerging market economies is the contagion associated with globalization. Though the major source of growth in Asia remains domestic demand, outside factors, especially those in Europe and North America are increasingly exerting their influence on the performance of this region. It appears that these effects have become stronger during this financial crisis compared to the earlier two crises and will become even stronger as globalization progresses.

The main macro-economic challenge for these economies is therefore to combat this contagion. If the advanced economies recover strongly, there is every chance that investment flowing into Asian economies from these countries during their recessionary period will reverse. The twin options open to these economies then would be to increase returns on assets and simultaneously reduce risk associated with investments. Both monetary and fiscal tightening appears to be a good option under the circumstances. However, it should not be forgotten that these economies still depend substantially on domestic investments to fuel their growth and domestic investments may be crowded out in a bid to attract foreign investment. To ensure that this does not happen, extra sops need to be given to domestic investments.

Another important method of combating the contagion will be to define an economic subregion within the larger context of globalization by systematically facilitating trade and investments among the countries in the region — to an extent that goes much beyond what is true for the rest of the world. South and Southeast Asia can be such an economic subregion. The only problem in this respect is the pull of gravity. Being in the low to middle income category, these countries have an inherent vulnerability to engage more with nations that have greater size as well as levels of economic development. For instance, most major trading partners of all these countries are either in North America or Europe. The doors of contagion from these countries are therefore wide open.

Lowering transport and transaction cost among these economies to a much larger extent than what has been achieved with the rest of the world can clearly help. And this is the crux of India-ASEAN economic cooperation. While the FTA between the ASEAN countries themselves and between India and the ASEAN countries are a step in the right direction, much more remains to be done. The investments agreements and the infrastructure agreements that are planned between India and ASEAN will without any doubt take this much further.

But the main issue remains implementation and ensuring effectiveness. The signing of an agreement does not automatically ensure that it is effective. Is trade taking place through the FTA route? Is the reduction in tariff too small compared to the loads of extra paperwork that needs to be dealt with to take advantage the reduced tariff? Is connectivity between countries acting as a hindrance? Another issue that needs to be clarified is: are the right goods being targeted for tariff reduction? Are the goods for which tariff is relaxed tariff elastic? Recent evidence shows that most of the goods for which tariff was relaxed in the India ASEAN FTA have insignificant tariff elasticity, meaning that their imports are not expected to respond significantly to tariff reductions. Tariff negotiations before the signing of an FTA have its own logic. That logic may not coincide with the economic logic of the agreement: the incremental impact of the negotiation on the volume of trade. Subsequent policy must ensure this. Current policy priorities need to be focused in these directions.

TRENDS AND PATTERNS OF MERCHANDISE TRADE

The ASEAN–India bilateral trends in trade have been analyzed in this chapter at four reference time points — that is, 2009, the year immediately preceding the FTA; 2013, to observe the consequences of completion of first phase of FTA implementation; and 2000 and 2005, for a relatively longer comparative perspective prior to the FTA. Our results show that the AIFTA does not appear to have resulted in any distinct break in the trade trends in the previous decade. Exports and imports have registered a consistent increase in volume over the last decade. Trade continues to be in favour of ASEAN. The share of ASEAN in India's total trade has been close to 10 per cent through the last decade. The implementation of the AIFTA in 2010 has not altered ASEAN's ranking among the regions that India trades with. ASEAN member countries that show an increase in India's share in their exports relative to the pre-FTA shares include Lao PDR, Malaysia, Thailand and Vietnam. The AIFTA does not appear to have made a positive impact on trade intensity among member countries and in fact leads to a decline in intra-regional trade bias.

Trade patterns show a very small share of component trade, and, hence, do not seem to reflect India's integration in regional supply chains in any significant manner, despite the AIFTA. While India could be emerging as the alternative market for ASEAN, particularly in the post global financial crisis scenario, it would also need to upgrade its manufacturing abilities and participate in regional production networks as these constitute an integral component of intra-Southeast Asian trade.

Given the reality of mega-regional agreements in Asia, both ASEAN and India will have to accelerate the pace of their economic reform processes in order to participate in and benefit from their trade creation possibilities. For ASEAN, this would entail consolidation of the AEC by 2015 and ensure thereby a stable centre for the RCEP. India will also have to undertake major reforms so as to overcome competitive pressures from China, a country with which India has resisted a formal trade agreement so far, as also from members common to the RCEP and the more advanced TPP.

SERVICES TRADE PATTERNS AND KEY POLICIES

Trade in services has gained more importance in recent years as advances in technology have resulted in new means of providing services across-borders. While there is little doubt that services trade is an essential ingredient to economic growth and sustainable development, it is widely accepted that it can only make such positive contribution if appropriately liberalized and implemented across countries. Services have become an important component of the global economy. ASEAN and India are no exception. The services sector has already become an important source of both output and employment in ASEAN and India. While India and some of the ASEAN member countries are services-driven, a large part of ASEAN has an equally fast growing manufacturing sector. The structural asymmetries in production and trade may tend to suggest that the opportunities for two-way services exports among ASEAN countries and with India in particular are substantial. Nevertheless, an efficient services sector is not only crucial for the performance of the ASEAN economies but also critical to its competitiveness.

Total intra-ASEAN exports in services have more than doubled between 2005 and 2012. In the services trade, the AEC Blueprint had set out targets to substantially remove all restrictions on trade in services for air transport, ICT and e-commerce, healthcare and tourism, and logistics services. Most ASEAN countries have allowed foreign entry in services, but limits vary in a significant manner. Moreover, the limits of foreign equity shareholding in various sectors are often different for GATS and AFAS. Under the GATS, countries usually indicate a threshold value in terms of commitments. However, improvements under AFAS suggest willingness towards deeper integration among ASEAN economies. India has already signed Services Trade and Investment Agreement with ASEAN, which is likely to be implemented very soon.

Under the WTO, India's requests profile gives a glimpse into India's core interests. At the same time, requests received by India tell us about barriers to service trade faced by other countries in India. This is true for ASEAN countries as well. India has been asked to take commitments with regard to transparency in domestic regulations, simplify procedures, eliminate differential treatment of foreign suppliers of services and facilitate the movement of natural persons under the Mode 4. However, India, at present, also has a growing interest in Mode 3 in areas related to computer, education, health and tourism. These are the sectors where barriers on the ASEAN side exist in terms of domestic regulations. The prospect that India could gain in roads into ASEAN markets (market access) depends on streamlined and favourable domestic regulations in ASEAN member countries. India has often faced barriers in terms of different levels of openness (market access) offered by countries on Mode 3 and Mode 4. This has implications for commercial operations that involve the presence of personnel from abroad for the executing projects.

India has made a request under GATS to take full commitments with respect to the category of independent professionals, de-linked from the commercial presence. India has also requested others to follow a liberalized visa system by ensuring the fulfilment of horizontal and sectoral commitments that were undertaken, such as multiple entry visas for professionals and allowing inter-firm mobility to professionals. India has longstanding interests in Mode 4 (cross-border mobility of its large number of highly skilled individuals). We stress that one crucial bottleneck for ASEAN–India trade in services concerns skilled labour mobility. Negotiating for recognition of academic and professional qualifications is a complex and time-consuming process, given the wide divergence in the levels of development among ASEAN countries and absence of comprehensive or single MRAs for a broad range of professional categories among ASEAN members. However, both India and ASEAN should make attempts at sealing MRAs mutually in such sectors, where ASEAN has successfully completed MRAs. This could significantly improve prospects of cross-border movements of professionals from either side.

INVESTMENTS PROSPECTS AND CHALLENGES

ASEAN region has been very resilient in terms of receiving foreign investment, while posting an 18 per cent growth in the capital inflows, particularly when world economies are striving to manage their economic fundamentals. The growing trade and investment relations between ASEAN and India justify further areas for economic collaboration. Singapore is the largest investment contributor to India, with core competence in areas such as air and sea transport, innovation and technology, and sets a clear roadmap for collaboration. Malaysia and Thailand are sound in logistic performance and automatically enhance the scope for further tie-ups. The growing middle income class in the region amid more active policy measures in all countries of the region is adding a significant scope for bilateral investment.

Major hurdles for investors in both India and ASEAN continue in terms of legal environment, poor infrastructure, lack of transparency, and regulatory issues, among others. The issues for restrictions in ownerships in sectors such as banking, construction, hotel and restaurant, mining and quarrying, etc. need to be considered at par for further investment and economic cooperation. The attraction of investment from ASEAN into India largely depends on the policy responses to macroeconomic problems. Country needs to enhance its business environment by reducing corruption and strengthening the rule of law, faster clearances for projects, develop infrastructure, boost manufacturing, simplify the taxation system, ease FDI regulations and increase awareness about its emerging cities, flexibility in the public–private partnership (PPP) contracts through renegotiations, among others.

The growth prospects of ASEAN region provide the best avenue for India to encash on the region's service sector potential in which India enjoys a comparative advantage. Besides, the Indian target of uplifting manufacturing sector has great potential for the ASEAN region to exploit. India has strong comparative advantage in export of computer and information services, other business services, such as financial, medical tourism and insurance, and movement of individuals, such as IT professionals and seafarers. Likewise, ASEAN countries have comparative advantage in logistic-related services that can be of great help to India. Complementarities among the two exist in terms of trade in energy, consumer durables and food items. Addressing the given competitive sectors coming into the ambit of services sector may enhance the scope of India–ASEAN FTA in services and investment.

EMERGING PRODUCTION NETWORKS

There is need for research and policy focus on the ways and means of advancing India's participation and integration in regional production networks. Policy measures in the direction of developing manufacturing sector competitiveness supplemented with further liberalization of trade and investment climate and developing necessary infrastructure and trade logistics need to be formulated.

Developing International Production Networks (IPNs) depends on host of conditions ranging from infrastructure, conducive industrial policies and encouragement towards technological innovation to the absorptive capacity of SMEs and end-market competitiveness. It has been observed that India is slowly but steadily getting integrated with the industries of Southeast Asia especially in machinery, electrical products and automobile sector. This also carries some ramifications for Indian SMEs because all these industries are closely tied with domestic small and medium enterprises. And thus, if SMEs could overcome technological, financial and other barriers, the IPN in these sectors might act as a growth facilitator for them as well. It is observed that so far, in India's exports of products (such as, electric, machinery and automobile), contribution of Europe and the United States has been higher than Southeast Asia and China but the scenario is changing rapidly. India is mostly importing components and engaging itself in downstream activities. China has moved towards upstream activities and thereby has better control of the value chain activities. India is ahead of Indonesia, the Philippines and CLMV countries but behind Malaysia, Singapore and of Thailand in terms of value addition capability in the production system. India's contribution in the global value chain is not only limited to downstream final assembly but also in various business services, which are required in the manufacturing process. India's engagement in trading, transport, storage and telecommunication are also important for the exports from ASEAN region. It is noted that in the post-FTA period, India has surged ahead with exports of automobile components, implying its strong presence in ASEAN IPN. On the other hand, in machinery, imports from Southeast Asia is used both in final goods production for domestic consumption as well as for international use. In case of electronic and optical equipment, India is still on the fringe with limited connectivity. India lacks attractiveness in terms of possible investment in these sectors especially in developing joint ventures with SMEs. Though India is ranked high in terms of adopting new technology, major skill gap in manufacturing sector is a stumbling block for converting this into a productivity gain. Coupled with this, as discussed earlier, most SMEs still face certain barriers in the form of lack of financing, exposure to new technology and ability to conduct small innovation. An effective handholding, proper policy support and awareness about global business strategy can help Indian SMEs to become more connected with emerging international production network.

REMOVING NON-TARIFF MEASURES

It is not the tariff liberalization but the disciplining of non-tariff measures (NTMs) which is important for achieving preferential market access. Only then any FTA would achieve its true goal of promoting trade and investment. Some interesting facts about the role of NTMs which have come to light from the analysis is that although AIFTA has come up with considerable tariff reduction, at the same time it is equally important for such agreements to come to an understanding on the issue of NTMs. This is critical because of its nature of impact on a product or group of products whereby these measures have possibility of totally denying market access. Therefore, there is a growing urgency for negotiations and immediate solution on this issue, by creating and strengthening the discipline around the mutual recognition agreements (MRAs) while dealing with the Sanitary and Phytosanitary (SPS) and Technical Barriers to Trade (TBT) measures.

Presently, there is discord in the tariff lines. There is a need to harmonize the tariff schedules of two parties to the agreement. This is important in the context of ASEAN moving towards a common tariff by 2015. A majority of ASEAN members have different Scheduling under the AIFTA. This in itself is very challenging and to add to this is how the measure is applied at the border — sometimes it may lead to discrimination due to lack of transparency built into the procedures of application of domestic regulation. Finally, there is a need to build sectoral MRAs. This is important especially when it is found that a lot of TBT measures are based on national standards. This would help countries to protect the industries within the FTA.

CONNECTIVITY CHALLENGES AND NEW DIRECTION

With India's FTA with the ASEAN in 2010 and the proposed RCEP, economic integration between India and Southeast and East Asia is set to gain momentum. More production and services networks between ASEAN and India may emerge if the regional economy is adequately supported by an improved connectivity.

ASEAN and India have undertaken several connectivity projects, physical or otherwise. India, Myanmar and Thailand have been negotiating the Motor Vehicle Agreement (MVA) to facilitate movement of goods and passengers along the Trilateral Highway. Before moving to an economic corridor, ASEAN and India may have to pass through trade corridors. The transformation of the transport corridors into economic corridors will depend on the volume, types and pattern of corridor trade and how it encourages certain level of development in the areas surrounding the corridors. Spatial planning, going beyond national policies, is needed to support the development of the corridors between ASEAN and India; at the same time, development of one area of the corridor is conditional upon the trading conditions along the entire area of the corridor across countries. Building corridor nodes and gateways and linking the nodes along the corridor would help the region moving towards economic corridor.

Efforts to promote regional infrastructure, such as the economic corridor, need to address policy reform in a number of areas. Institutions and investments have an important complementary role in enhancing infrastructure development between ASEAN and India. Regional cooperation also has an important catalytic role to play in this process. By sharing each other's experiences, regional cooperation can make countries efficient by integrating them to the regional market. Economic corridor integrates the markets by fostering trade. Finally, economic corridor can have huge pay-offs at a time when the region is looking for higher investments in the industrial sector, and is planning to deepen regional trade through global and regional value chains. Making trade between ASEAN and India faster and seamless would require complementary policy initiatives by countries, regional organizations and multilateral development institutions to strengthen the capacity of countries for development of economic corridors.

ENERGY MARKET INTEGRATION AND COOPERATION

India is already engaged in energy infrastructure development in the ASEAN region, particularly in the CLMV countries. India is building hydro-power projects, power transmission lines, sub-stations, and oil and gas pipelines in these countries. On the other hand, Malaysia is engaged in similar infrastructure development in India. While Malaysia has invested in energy assets in India, Indian companies have also invested in energy assets in the ASEAN countries in sectors like coal, oil and gas. When it comes to trade in energy commodities, it is largely limited to Indian imports of coal from Indonesia and Indian exports of petroleum products. However, the resource positions of India and ASEAN indicate that India can import much more, particularly natural gas and electricity. Energy sector machineries, equipments and other goods can also open up possibilities for substantial trade.

ASEAN is in the process of developing region-wide grid of natural gas pipelines and electricity transmission lines. India can get connected through these two ASEAN-wide grids just by developing transmission lines and gas pipeline connections through Myanmar. Indian electricity grid is already connected with Bangladesh electricity grid and Bangladesh is planning to link its electricity grid with that of Myanmar. There has been a significant change in the attitude of Bangladesh with respect to the Myanmar–Bangladesh–India natural gas pipeline. India and Myanmar have also revived the discussions on the gas pipeline connection between India and Myanmar through Bangladesh. The proposed pipeline would extend from Block A-1, through Bangladesh to India, and various design options are being considered, including a land route via the eastern Indian states of Tripura and Mizoram, an offshore route through the coastal areas of Bangladesh and a deep-sea route. In future, it will be possible for India to not only to access electricity and gas from Myanmar, but also gas from faraway fields in Indonesia and Brunei Darussalamand electricity from Lao PDR.

The official discussion on energy cooperation between India and ASEAN has so far focused only on renewable energy. The electricity generation sources indicate that India has developed significant capability in wind energy, Indonesia and the Philippines have the same in geothermal energy and Singapore is generating significant electricity from waste. India and Thailand have some experience in solar power as well. India is also the only country to generate nuclear power and use bio-fuel to generate significant quantity of electricity. These countries can help others in developing energy production capabilities in the respective sub-sectors. While India–ASEAN energy cooperation focuses only on renewable energy, India along with some of its South Asian neighbours and some members of ASEAN are part of Bay of Bengal Initiative for Multi-Sectoral Technical and Economic Cooperation (BIMSTEC), where energy has been identified as one of the important sectors for comprehensive cooperation including all types of energy. ASEAN–India energy cooperation would greatly depend on BIMSTEC energy activities, work as a bridge between SAARC and ASEAN in promoting a comprehensive energy cooperation regime.

STRENGTHENING MONETARY AND FINANCIAL COOPERATION

The Chiang Mai Initiative (CMI) is a good starting point to build on the various existing initiatives. Although under the present dispensation the CMI is complementary to similar IMF initiatives, it has an important symbolic value as it can signal to the markets a regional commitment to supporting any member country's currency that is under speculative pressures. It also recognizes that establishing swap arrangements does not obviate the need to address structural and financial sector weaknesses. It may also be added that while CMI might have contributed to the exchange rate stability in the region, it has also contributed to closer regional economic and financial integration and cooperation. It is useful to explore ways of carrying this process forward.

Developing corporate bond market also needs a special focus. Some of the suggestions may include: (*a*) setting up specific development banks to meet the financial needs of the member countries; (*b*) to allure individuals to invest, the government should provide tax incentives like in Malaysia and other countries and (*c*) there is a need to promote guarantee in bond market, and for that an organization on lines of deposits insurance be promoted. There is a need to build capacity and build the long-term infrastructure for development of ASEAN capital markets, with a long-term goal of achieving cross-border collaboration between the various capital markets in ASEAN.

There is a need for integration between India and ASEAN to penetrate the underdeveloped insurance market in India. This will help the member countries to co-ordinate themselves, which may help in developing products and policies for a developed insurance market. This is in line with the efforts by the ASEAN Insurance Regulators Meeting (AIRM) that include sharing of insurance statistics among countries with the end goal of achieving a unified form of statistics; exchange of views on regulatory issues and observance of core principles related to insurance markets.

SCIENCE AND TECHNOLOGY COOPERATION

The enabling role of science and technology (S&T) for economic development has been fully recognized under the ASEAN Framework and a target for the year 2020 has been set to make the ASEAN region technologically competitive through competence in strategic and enabling technologies, with an adequate pool of technologically qualified and trained manpower, and strong networks of scientific and technological institutions and centres of excellence. However, as a group of 10 developing countries with great variance in the level of S&T capability, ASEAN faces considerable difficulties in achieving these goals. The overwhelming concern for India, on the other hand, has been its inability to transform its S&T potential into outcomes that could measure up in terms of industrial competitiveness and human development. ASEAN–India cooperation in S&T is based on complementarities, where India has generously shared its 'technical knowledge' and 'resources' with ASEAN member states at various levels.

The India–ASEAN partnership platform offers the most in terms of opportunities in this regard with maximum consensus on both sides. In recent years, India has taken a keen interest in furthering cooperation with the poorer ASEAN members, namely, the CLMV by implementing capacity building programmes in areas, in which India has proven expertise like information technology, agriculture and space science. Strengthening such cooperation between CLMV–ASEAN and India is called for, particularly in the area of space science and technology where India can be a lead partner. However, practical bottlenecks, such as long-drawn approvals arising out of multiple stakeholders have slowed the pace of such efforts. There is also a need for greater optimism on both sides about beneficial outcomes of development cooperation between India and ASEAN in the area of S&T.

EXPANDING FOOD SECURITY AND FOOD RESERVES

ASEAN region along with India has been struggling hard in reducing food insecurity, as the results of efforts have not been distributed evenly across the region. The challenge of ensuring food security for the growing population cannot be tackled only with the increase in agricultural productivity or food-stocking mechanisms, but greater attention is needed for achieving nutritional security. Despite numerous measures, such as food reserves system and price stabilization of rice for food emergency purposes, by almost all the member countries of ASEAN to resolve the challenges of food security issues, there is a need for long-term solutions rather than the short ones. One suitable option to deal with this is the establishment of a regional food bank in collaboration with India. SAARC Food Bank offers several lessons with respect to meeting food demands under disaster conditions and other climate-driven uncertainties. It would maintain food reserves and support national as well as regional food security through collective action among member countries.

An integrated food security approach may be initiated with ASEAN dialogue partners such as India. It may be emphasized here that the results achieved so far, in terms of food availability and reduction in hunger, have been the outcome of the positive initiatives undertaken at the regional level. ASEAN governments with involvement of the NGOs and civil societies have to play very effective roles in order to bring significant improvement in enhancing food security through regional cooperation.

TOWARDS A STRONGER CULTURAL LINK

Durable and abiding relationships are based not on inter-governmental contacts, but on people-to-people contacts. Culture is the best bond between the people of India and ASEAN. Even though tourism is an important agenda in Indian dialogue with ASEAN, not much has been done to develop this area to promote people-to-people contacts. So far, tourism has been moving in only one direction — Indians going to Southeast Asia but not the reverse. Imaginative packages need to be evolved and sufficient incentives offered to attract tourists from countries in Southeast Asia, and from Myanmar, Malaysia, Indonesia, Thailand and Vietnam, by promoting cultural and religious tourism. This will not only bring revenues to India but will also cement civil society interactions — an important component of mature and enduring state-to-state relations.

Cooperation in the field of education needs to be widened and deepened further by showcasing some of our premier educational institutions, such as the Indian Institute of Technology (IIT) and the Indian Institute of Management (IIM). Educational and cultural agreements need to be concluded with a view to narrow the knowledge gap that exists between India and Southeast Asian countries. The future educational and cultural interactions should be carried out with a clear-cut view of training a core of experts in each country, who would be able to provide a better perspective of their country of specialization and give nuanced feedback to their respective policymakers. Finally, cultural and religious tourism needs to be promoted to bring the people from India and Southeast closer to each other. It would be appropriate if both ASEAN and India initiate an innovative political, educational and cultural charm to give more substance to economic engagement process.

Overall, this Report presents compelling and wide-ranging evidence on India's deepening interdependence with ASEAN and vice-versa and on its implications for policymaking. This Report shows that many complex problems require increasing regional cooperation and explains why this cooperation is not difficult, in the light of the region's varied economic interests. Looking forward, ASEAN–India partnership will continue to be the cornerstone of India's foreign policy. While growth remains fragile around the world, trade, investment and connectivity can be a powerful policy tool to leverage economic growth and development.

1
Economic Outlook and Prospects

As a regional bloc, ASEAN has developed much faster than any of the other blocs in Asia-Pacific. It has an active Free Trade Agreement (FTA), almost free movement of factors of production and an ASEAN identity building process. ASEAN, in addition to China and India, is one of the three pillars of growth in Asia, with an average GDP growth at around 6 per cent per annum over the past 15 years. Today, ASEAN is an economic bloc having an aggregate economic size of US$ 2.3 trillion. The Indian economy, on the other hand, is the world's 10th largest by nominal GDP (US$ 1.8 trillion).[1] Economic cooperation between ASEAN and India would, therefore, be a huge step towards regional integration of the Asian economy. There has been a high possibility of success due to the economic integration of the two as well as a keen intent on both sides to achieve this. There is now a sense prevailing on both sides that any cooperation would be beneficial to both.

In the following sections, we, first, take a descriptive look at the global economy and then the ASEAN economy with the aim to discover what India–ASEAN integration implies in the perspective of current global developments. In a nutshell, the global economy entered this century with economic gloom, then bounced back and then relapsed again into a prolonged period of depression, while the ASEAN economy as well as the Indian economy also behaved likewise albeit with a lag.

1. Performance and Prospects of the Global Economy

The world economy entered this century under duress. A severe winter (2000–01) pushed up oil prices to US$ 54 per barrel, the Euro slumped and a strong US dollar depressed their exports. The Consumer Price Index (CPI) rose above 5 per cent in the United States and the Fed tightened monetary policy.[2] Bond yields rose, but the yield curve remained inverted through the mid-2001. During this period most of the countries witnessed very low GDP growth rates (with major exceptions like Myanmar and Andorra).[3] During the crisis, two alternative economic scenarios were predicted by economists: a low growth scenario with weak domestic demand and world growth, and a high growth scenario with stronger economic recovery.

Fortunately, the world economy took the second course and bounced back quickly (see Figure 1.1). According to the *Actuarial Review*, the US CPI was back under 2 per cent by the spring of 2002. By the summer of 2003, the US unemployment was back under 5per cent after peaking at 6.5 per cent in the spring of 2002. GDPs started growing once again.

The upward trend in GDP continued until 2004, when it grew at the rate of 4.19 per cent per annum, before falling to 3.62 per cent in 2005 and was revived by registering an annual growth rate of 4.10 per cent in 2006. At one stage, the consumption growth rate was much higher than the GDP growth rate, but as the years progressed, the GDP growth rate surpassed the consumption growth rate and savings (as a per cent of GDP) gradually increased.

As it turned out, the revival of the world economy was short lived. Recession returned by 2008–09 (see Figure 1.1). The recession spread from the United States and Europe to the rest of the world. The downward trend continued till 2009, when the global economy witnessed a negative growth rate and a consumption growth rate close to zero.

---

[1] This data has been sourced from the World Bank's World Development Indicators (WDI) Database. Available at http://databank.worldbank.org/data (accessed 16 February 2015).

[2] Refer to the Disaster Recovery Institute (DRI). 2000. *Actuarial Review of Money Market and Investment Funds* (MMIF). New York: McGraw-Hill Financial.

[3] All figures are from the World Bank's World Development Indicators (various issues) unless otherwise mentioned.

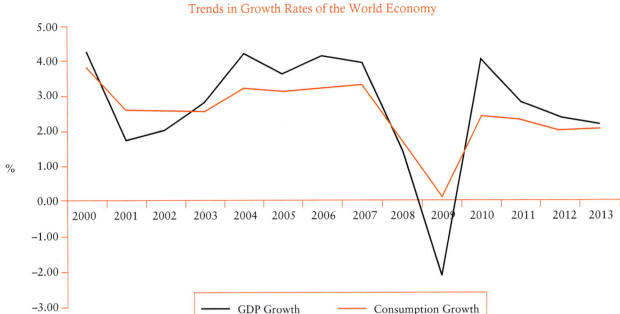

FIGURE 1.1
Trends in Growth Rates of the World Economy

Source: Data in figures and tables have been sourced from the World Bank's World Development Indicators (various issues) unless otherwise mentioned.

Around 2010, the global economy showed some positive signs with government bail outs of insolvent banks, provision of credit facilities to unclog financial markets, and expansionary monetary and fiscal policies. However, according to the United Nation's *World Economic Situation and Prospects (WESP) 2013*, four years after the crisis, the global economy was still struggling to recover. During 2012, the growth of the world economy further weakened. However, thereafter, it showed a positive trend. The global economy grew at 3 per cent in 2013 and 3.6 per cent in 2014 and is expected to grow at 3.9 per cent in 2015 (IMF, 2014).

The Asian financial crisis of 1997–98 affected Indonesia, the Philippines, Malaysia, and Thailand and their fiscal balances (measured as a proportion of GDP) further worsened. Fiscal deficits created huge public debts and high budget deficits. Excessive government borrowing crowded out domestic investment spending, limiting capital accumulation and economic growth through higher domestic interest rates. For Indonesia, the Philippines and Thailand, the consolidated central government revenue was under 20 per cent of respective GDPs. The combination of lower central government revenue and higher central government expenditure shares manifested in bigger budget deficits for these economies in the post-Asian financial crisis. From 2000 onwards, Malaysia and the Philippines have persistently posted deficits between four to six per cent of GDP. Even the public debt to GDP ratio was very high. Thus, the ASEAN nations were not prepared for another crisis when the global financial crisis hit in 2007–08.

Among the ASEAN members, Brunei Darussalam was the worst affected nation during the euro crisis in 2009 since its growth rate turned negative (see Figure 1.2). Countries like Lao PDR and Indonesia suffered the least as their real sector continued to perform fairly well even in the crisis period (World Bank, 2009). Singapore also weathered the crisis better than most Asian economies and used the exchange rate and wage instruments effectively during the crisis. Despite the crisis, Singapore has pressed ahead with financial reforms including liberalizing the Singaporean dollar to ensure the long-term competitiveness of its economy (for more details, see Siriwardana and Schulze, 2000). According to the *World Economic Outlook 2014*, the performance of the ASEAN economies will remain uneven in 2014–15 (IMF, 2014). Some of the ASEAN countries will perform much better during 2015–19 (see Table 1.1). Overall, however, the emerging and developing Asian economies and the ASEAN-5 are expected to grow at about 6.6 per cent and 6.54 per cent per annum during 2015–19, respectively. These projected growth rates are higher than the growth prior to the financial crisis.

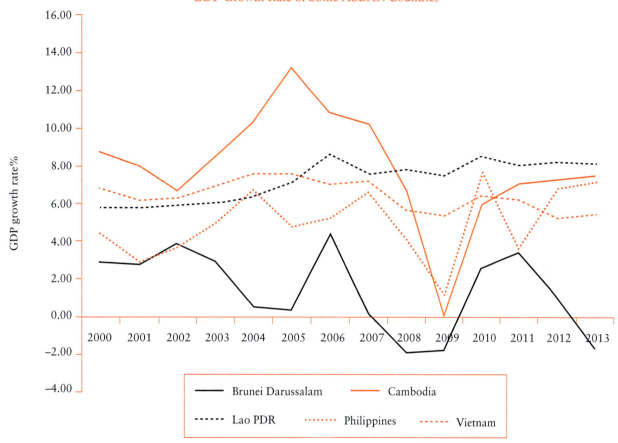

FIGURE 1.2
GDP Growth Rate of Some ASEAN Countries

TABLE 1.1
Forecast of GDP Growth Rates

Country	2015	2016	2017	2018	2019
Australia	2.703	2.949	2.970	2.979	3.041
Brunei Darussalam	3.014	3.743	5.516	5.641	3.492
Cambodia	7.318	7.289	7.538	7.459	7.484
China	7.283	6.970	6.761	6.629	6.520
India	6.353	6.479	6.650	6.734	6.765
Indonesia	5.800	6.000	6.000	6.000	6.000
Japan	0.965	0.670	0.992	1.006	1.125
Korea	3.796	3.776	3.820	3.752	3.763
Lao PDR	7.806	7.995	7.681	7.478	7.510
Malaysia	5.000	5.000	5.000	5.000	5.000
Myanmar	7.800	7.800	7.800	7.800	7.699
New Zealand	3.006	2.597	2.540	2.492	2.548
The Philippines	6.505	6.209	6.014	6.019	6.024
Singapore	3.629	3.635	3.607	3.712	3.778
Thailand	3.779	4.793	4.730	4.499	4.473
Vietnam	5.700	5.800	5.900	6.000	6.000

Source: International Monetary Fund (IMF), Washington DC.
Note: Shaded cells indicate IMF staff estimates. GDP growth represents annual percentages of constant price GDP are year-on-year changes; the base year is country-specific.

On the other hand, India's growth performance during the pre-euro crisis has been phenomenal. The growth rate, which traditionally hovered around 3 per cent, witnessed a steep increase from 1997. Just before the euro crisis, the Indian economy witnessed a very high growth rate of 9.8 per cent.[4] India's increase in growth rate over the last two decades was due to the structural changes in industrial, trade and financial sectors.

However, India could not isolate itself from the adverse impacts of the global crisis. Economic growth declined to 6.7 per cent in 2008–09, which was much below its average growth rate in last five years (8.8 per cent) (for more details, see World Bank, 2014). To counter this economic slowdown, the government responded by providing fiscal stimulus packages in the form of tax reliefs to boost demand, increased expenditure on public projects to create employment and public assets. India's central bank, the Reserve Bank of India (RBI) also adopted a number of monetary policies like liquidity enhancing measures to facilitate the flow of funds from the financial system to the productive sectors.

India made a promising start to this decade. According to the RBI, GDP growth in 2010–11 was 8.4 per cent, fiscal deficit was 4.7 per cent of GDP (from 6.4 of GDP in 2009–10). However, the GDP growth decelerated sharply to a nine-year low of 6.5 per cent during 2011–12. The slowdown was reflected in all sectors of the economy but the industrial sector suffered the sharpest deceleration (growth rate fell to 2.9 per cent during 2011–12 from 8.2 per cent in 2010–11).[5] India's growth rate has remained poor since 2011–12. In 2012, the growth rate was 3.7 per cent and the projected growth rate for the period 2015–19 is 6.60 per cent (see Table 1.1) (OECD, 2014).

2. FISCAL POSITION

There was a sharp increase in fiscal deficits of many countries just after the beginning of the financial crisis (see Figure 1.3) as the governments of countries across the world took steps to improve the economic situation through increased government expenditure. The fiscal deficits declined gradually after 2009. It was expected that due to high deficits, countries would witness very high interest rates, which in turn would crowd out private investment. But that prediction was proved wrong. In the United States (US), at least, there was a record deficit and simultaneously a record low interest rate (IMF, 2013).

From the early 1990s to 2006, most of the OECD countries had deficits. But in 2007, half of these became surpluses. In 2007, the total deficit for OECD countries was only 1.3 per cent of OECD GDP. But it changed with the crisis. During 2007–08, the deficits of these countries became at par with the rest of the world. However, the crisis in 2007–08 acted as the trigger that set the snowball of debt rolling across Europe and in the euro zone as

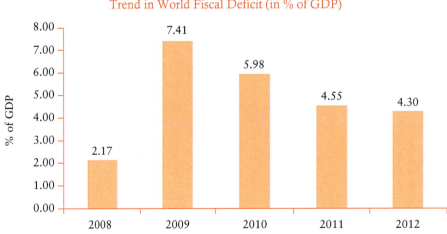

FIGURE 1. 3
Trend in World Fiscal Deficit (in % of GDP)

Source: Fiscal Affairs Department, IMF, Washington DC.

---

[4] This data has been sourced from the World Bank's World Development Indicators (WDI) Database. Available at http://databank.worldbank.org/data (accessed 16 February 2015).
[5] Taken from Reserve Bank of India's Annual Report, 2011–12.

growth declined sharply.[6] The IMF's *World Economic Outlook 2014* also points out that the fiscal balance of the world as a whole is expected to be –3.006 for 2014 with India leading the field, followed by the Middle East and North Africa. The European position is expected to improve substantially.

In 2009, East and North East Asia had fiscal deficits but China recorded a fiscal surplus of 1.1 per cent of GDP. But that surplus turned into a deficit of 2.2 per cent of GDP in 2009 due to fiscal expansion undertaken by the government to stimulate the domestic economy during the crisis. Korea also recorded a relatively high fiscal deficit of 1.7 per cent of GDP in 2009 after a long time. Hong Kong, however, witnessed six consecutive years of budget surpluses during this period due to cuts in public spending and high growth in revenue. In North and Central Asia, most of the countries had declining fiscal balance in 2009. Among them, Tajikistan recorded high deficit of 7.1 per cent of GDP. The Southeast Asian nations that witnessed a trend of fiscal surpluses since 2005, witnessed a significant deterioration of fiscal balances in 2009. This is due to the fall in revenue collection with public revenue falling to 17 per cent of GDP compared to 21 per cent in 2008. Excessive lending had left banks with bad debts and governments with large fiscal deficit and public debt in the peripheral economies.

According to the *Statistical Yearbook for Asia and the Pacific 2011* of the Asian Development Bank (ADB), Vietnam and Malaysia also recorded large fiscal deficits just after the crisis in 2009 (7.7 per cent and 7 per cent of GDP, respectively) (see, for example, UNESCAP, 2012). The deficit widened due to slow revenue growth which was a result of subdued economic activity. In Malaysia, too, public spending increased due to the implementation of fiscal stimulus packages. On the other hand, the revenue collection was also affected because of the fall in oil prices. Thailand and the Philippines too recorded significant fiscal deficits in 2009 (4.1 per cent of GDP and 3.9 per cent of GDP) respectively due to the same reason. In India, fiscal deficit increased from 2.7 per cent of GDP in 2007–08 to 6.2 per cent of GDP in 2008–09.

The fiscal balance in Asia is expected to improve substantially from –4.26 (as a per cent of GDP) in 2009 to –2.25 in 2015. For the emerging market economies, the improvement for the same period is from –4.55 to –2.25. For India, as we already pointed out, the deficits are significantly higher. It was –10.07 in 2007 and marginally improved to –8.44 in 2014 (IMF, 2014).

3. BUSINESS AND INFRASTRUCTURE

3.1 Ease of Doing Business

Singapore ranked 1st in the Ease of Doing Business Index, published by the World Bank in 2012 and 2013.[7] Among other ASEAN nations, Malaysia was ranked 6th in 2013. Thailand also figures among the top 20. But, the other seven ASEAN members as well as India are not even in the top 50. India ranked 134 out of 185 economies with almost no change in overall ranking from 2012 (131). According to the World Bank's *Doing Business Report 2014*, Singapore again topped the list. Among the other countries who are in the top 10 are Hong Kong, China, New Zealand, the United States, Denmark, Malaysia, Korea, Georgia, Norway and the United Kingdom. India ranks 134 in the index, which indicates no change in the rankings compared to the previous year. It has been reported that there is a strong correlation (0.84 in 2014) between *Doing Business* rankings and World Economic Forum rankings on 'Global Competitiveness', thereby indicating ease of business and competitiveness are correlated.

3.2 Logistics

The quality of logistics services — such as customs brokerage, freight forwarding and express delivery — also varies substantially from country to country. Logistics services are world-class in Singapore but poor in Lao PDR, Cambodia and Myanmar. Singapore was ranked 5th in the Logistics Performance Index (2014), while Myanmar ranked 145th among 155 countries (see Table 1.2).

---

[6] For more details, refer to the Organisation for Economic Cooperation and Development (OECD) Statistics, OECD Database.

[7] Refer, the World Bank's *Doing Business* Database. Available at http://www.doingbusiness.org. (accessed on 16 February 2015).

TABLE 1.2
Rankings of ASEAN Countries by Logistics Performance Index (LPI)

Country	2007	2010	2012	2014
Singapore	1	2	1	5
Malaysia	27	29	29	25
Thailand	31	35	38	35
Indonesia	43	75	59	53
Vietnam	53	53	53	48
The Philippines	65	44	52	57
Cambodia	81	129	101	83
Lao PDR	117	118	109	131
Myanmar	147	133	129	145

Source: World Bank, Washington, DC.

As far as trade logistics is concerned, procedures for trading in Singapore, Thailand and Malaysia are relatively easy to complete, but it is very difficult in Lao PDR and Cambodia. The ASEAN Single Window (ASW) is one of the most visible efforts to facilitate trade among its members. However, development of the ASW has proceeded slowly.

3.3 Transport Infrastructure

Among the ASEAN members, Indonesia has relatively higher road network with a total system length of 496,607 km in 2011. Indonesia's transport system has been shaped overtime and all transport modes play a role in the country's transport system. Among the other ASEAN members, Malaysia also has a good coverage of roads with 155,427 km of road length. Since Lao PDR has no proper railway system, it depends mainly on road transport and to some extent on river and air transport. According to the World Bank's *World Development Report 2004*, Lao PDR has a total road network of 31,210 km, which is comprised of national roads making up 23 per cent, 21 per cent of provincial roads and the remaining other types of roads including district, rural, urban and special roads. Lao PDR's road network increased to 41,029 km in 2011. Myanmar also has moderate road connectivity with 37,785 km of road length in 2011. Being a large country, India is just after the United States in terms of total area under road coverage. In terms of road density (km of road per sq km of land), with approximately 480 km of road per sq km of land, Singapore has the highest road density, compared to the other ASEAN members and India. India ranks next to Singapore in terms of road density, followed by Brunei Darussalam . Road density in both India and Singapore increased over the years (see Figure 1.4).

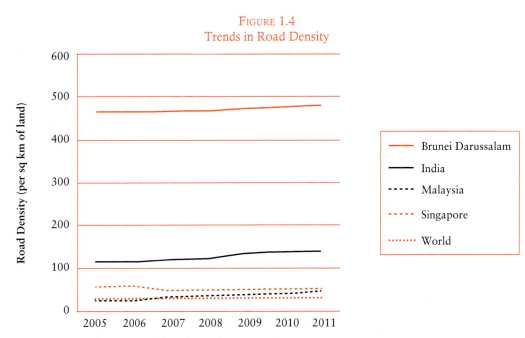

FIGURE 1.4
Trends in Road Density

Source: World Development Indicators, World Bank, Washington, DC.

India ranks 4th in terms of the rail network after the United States, China and Russia. In contrast, India's air transport facilities are not that impressive, compared to her road and rail connectivity. According to the Air Connectivity Index (ACI) of the World Bank, India ranks 88th among 195 nations in the world with a share of 3.82 per cent in world air cargo volume. Among the ASEAN members, Singapore has the best air connectivity with a rank of 74, followed by Thailand (rank 75) and Malaysia (rank 83). Brunei Darussalam, on the other hand, has a poor air network, since it ranked 129th among 195 countries in the world. Thus, among the ASEAN members, Singapore, Malaysia and Thailand have the best transport infrastructure (World Bank, 2012).

4. The External Sector

4.1 Trade

During the global crisis, international merchandise trade witnessed its greatest plunge since the Second World War. By the end of 2011, some of the developed countries and countries in Southeast Europe, where the trade collapse was the sharpest, still did not reclaim the pre-crisis level trade figures. In contrast, the developing countries had been more impressive since their trade volumes exceeded their pre-crisis level by 2011 (UNCTAD, 2012).

In 2010, the value of total merchandise exports from all countries of the world was US$ 15 trillion, of which the share of developed countries was 54 per cent, down from 60 per cent in 2005. As the world's leading merchandise exporter since 2009, China's share of world exports climbed to 10 per cent in 2010, ahead of the United States (8 per cent), Germany (8 per cent), and Japan (5 per cent). On the import side, the ranking still shows the United States in 1st place (13 per cent), followed by China (9 per cent), Germany (7 per cent) and Japan (4.5 per cent).[8]

World exports as a significant percentage of GDP also grew over the years except in 2009, when it witnessed a steep decline (see Figure 1.6). From the given figure, it can be observed that among the ASEAN members, Singapore is the most liberalized or open country, followed by Malaysia and Thailand. It can be also observed that Singapore's openness gradually increased when we compare it with other ASEAN members.

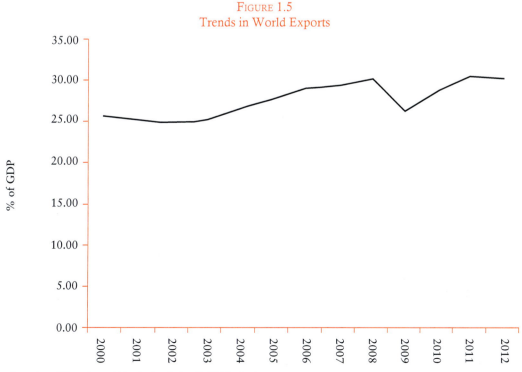

FIGURE 1.5
Trends in World Exports

Source: Drawn based on Direction of Trade Statistics (DOTS), IMF.

---

[8] Data up to 2012 in this section is sourced from the UNCTAD Report on *Development and Globalization, 2012*. Data since 2012 is taken from *World Economic Outlook, 2014*.

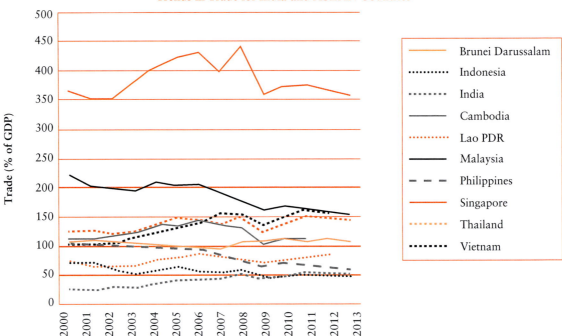

FIGURE 1.6
Trends in Trade for India and ASEAN Countries

Source: Drawn based on Direction of Trade Statistics (DOTS), IMF.

Quarterly growth of world trade was approximately constant in 2013 and the first quarter of 2014. Due to the easing of the global crisis, import demand from developed countries are, however, on the rise, implying that world trade is expected to grow faster in the coming months in 2015. Thus, real exports were expected to grow at 4.1 per cent in 2014 (twice the rate of 2013 but below the pre-crisis trend). The trend is expected to continue into 2015 with export growth at 5.1 per cent. Slow growth in large emerging economies has dampened the prospect of even higher growth rates in world trade (UNCTAD, 2014).

The growth rate of export for the ASEAN 10 members between 2012 and 2013 was −9.52 per cent, while that for import was −9.16 per cent. Thus, clearly as far as trade is concerned, the ASEAN members were not able to come out of the crisis legacy even in 2012–13. As far as export is concerned, Brunei, Indonesia and Thailand had negative growth rates of export between 2012 and 2013, while Cambodia, Malaysia, the Philippines and Singapore had positive growth rates for export. In case of imports, Indonesia, the Philippines and Singapore had negative growth rates for this period, while Brunei, Cambodia, Malaysia and Thailand had positive growth rates.[9]

India's merchandise trade stood at US$ 758.62 billion in 2014–15 as compared to US$ 467.12 billion in 2009–10,[10] which means that India has significantly improved its export over the past few decades. Since the India–ASEAN Trade in Goods Agreement was implemented in January 2010, India's total trade with the ASEAN members increased rapidly. It now stands at US$ 77 billion. There is a growing realization that both regions are complementary rather than competitive, and this has given a further boost to trade and economic engagements. As a result, the bilateral trade has increased by more than 90 per cent in the last 10 years (see Table 1.3).

As far as tariff is concerned, all ASEAN countries as well as India have reduced their tariff levels between 2000 and 2010 (see Table 1.4).

4.2 Current Account Balance

While most of the emerging and underdeveloped nations have negative current account balance, that is, a current account deficit, countries like Bangladesh and Iraq are an exception since they have current account surplus in most years and negligible current account deficit in some years. Not only the developing nations, but several

---

[9] Calculated from UNCOMTRADE Database.
[10] Sourced from the Ministry of Commerce and Industry, Government of India.

Economic Outlook and Prospects　　9

TABLE 1.3
India's Trade with EAS Countries in 2013

Country	Total Trade (US$ million)	Share in India's Total Trade (%)	Growth (%)*
Australia	12,122.81	1.59	−21.46
Brunei Darussalam	796.05	0.10	−6.88
Cambodia	154.04	0.02	24.04
China	65,858.98	8.61	0.12
Indonesia	19,598.50	2.56	−3.03
Japan	16,294.82	2.13	−11.98
Lao PDR	89.29	0.01	−46.71
Malaysia	13,427.80	1.76	−6.72
Myanmar	2,182.68	0.29	11.51
New Zealand	891.20	0.12	−10.76
The Philippines	1,810.59	0.24	7.06
Singapore	19,273.03	2.52	−8.68
South Korea	16,679.28	2.18	−3.63
Thailand	9,043.47	1.18	−0.47
Vietnam	8,036.19	1.05	27.92

Source: Ministry of Commerce & Industry, Government of India.
Note: Growth between 2012 and 2013.

TABLE 1.4
Tariff Rate, Most Favoured Nation, Simple Mean, All Products (%)

Country	2000	2001	2002	2003	2004	2005	2006	2007	2008	2009	2010
Brunei		3.8	3.9	3.79	3.73	3.67	3.68	3.7	2.46		2.46
Cameroon		18.04	18.04			18.05		17.74		17.62	
Indonesia	8.43	6.89	6.9	6.9	6.95	6.95	6.95	6.9		6.81	6.72
India		34.6			30.16	19.88		17.35	12.45	14.03	
Lao PDR	9.5	9.63			9.65	9.71	9.71	9.71	9.71		
Myanmar		5.5	5.5	5.5	5.5	5.6	5.6	5.6	5.6		
Malaysia		8.34	8.33	8.36		7.32	7.18	7.18	6.79	8.6	
The Philippines	7.6	7.3	5.72	4.74	6.27	6.27	6.26	6.26	6.25	6.26	6.26
Singapore		0.02	0.02	0.02	0	0.02	0	0.02	0.09	0.09	0
Thailand	18.42	16.06		15.35		11.92	11.93	9.74	9.74	10.42	
Vietnam		16.46	16.4	16.81	16.82	16.81	16.81	16.81	10.79		9.77

Source: World Development Indicators, World Bank, Washington, DC.

developed nations witnessed a deficit in their current account balance (for example, Italy and United States) as well. Israel, on the other hand, is a good example of decreasing current account deficit over time. Of the ASEAN countries, Singapore, the Philippines and Malaysia have always witnessed a current account surplus. On the other hand, Indonesia moved from a current account surplus to a current account deficit, while countries like Cambodia and Lao PDR generally have current account deficit all along. Vietnam showed improvement in its current account balance (Table 1.5) (World Bank, 2013).

4.3 Foreign Exchange Reserves

Massive accumulation of foreign exchange reserves by many countries started in the mid 1990s and has accelerated in recent years. It has been driven by the emerging market countries but it is not limited to these countries. Indeed, with the exception of the developed world and of the Latin American countries, the phenomenon is very general, including oil exporting Africa. It has been most spectacular in Southeast Asia and in particular in China. Indeed, at the end of 2006, the seven East Asian countries — ASEAN plus China and Korea — held a total of more than US$ 1500 billion, of which US$ 1000 billion alone are owned by China. The foreign reserves for emerging economies have been increasing at a much rapid rate, compared to that of developed nations (see Figure 1.7). As of 2013–14, China's foreign exchange reserve was about US$ 300 billion, while that of Indonesia and the Philippines was between US$ 50 and 100 billion. India and Singapore had substantially higher foreign exchange reserves (about US$ 150 and 250 billion, respectively). Thailand and Malaysia were the two countries, which had exceptionally low foreign exchange reserves (see Table 1.6).

TABLE 1.5
Current Account Balance (in US$ Billion) for ASEAN+6 Countries

Country	2005	2006	2007	2008	2009	2010	2011	2012
Australia	−430.00	−450.00	−640.00	−521.20	−490.00	−440.00	−410.00	−640.00
Brunei Darussalam	40.30	52.30	48.30	69.39	39.80	0.00	0.00	0.00
China	1320.00	2320.00	3530.00	4205.70	2430.00	2380.00	1360.00	1930.00
Indonesia	2.78	109.00	105.00	1.26	106.00	51.40	16.90	−240.00
India	−100.00	−93.00	−81.00	−309.70	−260.00	−550.00	−630.00	−910.00
Japan	1660.00	1710.00	2120.00	1593.60	1470.00	2040.00	1190.00	609.00
Cambodia	−3.10	−2.30	−4.20	−8.20	−7.80	−7.70	−7.10	−12.00
Korea	186.00	141.00	218.00	31.97	328.00	294.00	261.00	433.00
Lao PDR	−1.70	0.75	1.39	0.78	−0.61	0.29	−2.10	−4.10
Myanmar	5.82	7.94	13.80	12.47	9.86	15.70	−14.00	0.00
Malaysia	200.00	262.00	298.00	389.14	318.00	270.00	335.00	186.00
New Zealand	−80.00	−79.00	−93.00	−102.20	−30.00	−34.00	−48.00	−70.00
The Philippines	19.80	53.40	71.10	36.27	93.60	89.20	69.70	71.30
Singapore	269.00	361.00	463.00	288.38	335.00	620.00	653.00	514.00
Thailand	−76.00	23.20	157.00	22.11	219.00	99.50	41.30	−14.00
Vietnam	−5.60	−1.60	−70.00	−108.20	−66.00	−43.00	2.36	90.60

Source: World Development Indicators, World Bank, Washington, DC.

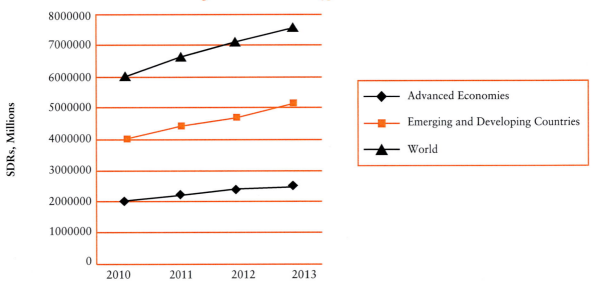

FIGURE 1.7
Foreign Reserves of Three Types of Economies

Source: International Financial Statistics, IMF (Various Issues), Washington DC.

TABLE 1.6
Foreign Exchange Reserves (US$ Millions), 2013–14

Country	Foreign Exchange Reserves
Cambodia	5,415
Indonesia	107,678
Lao PDR	846
Malaysia	131,865
Myanmar	8,278
The Philippines	80,733
Singapore	277,967
Thailand	168,207
Vietnam	32,490

Source: IMF, 2014.

5. Level of Economic Development

5.1 Per Capita Income

The world per capita income, proxied by per capita GDP, declined sharply during the 2008-09 global financial crises. Before that, it showed an increasing trend (see Figure 1.8). ASEAN's average GDP per capita was US$ 3,600 in 2011. Income levels among ASEAN countries are hugely diverse. So, the trend in per capita GDP measured in constant 2005 US$ is plotted in line diagrams in Figure 1.8 for select ASEAN countries for which data is available for the complete period. Except Brunei, all other member countries of ASEAN witnessed an increasing trend in per capita GDP over time (see Figure 1.9). Singapore's per capita GDP was the highest among all the members at US$ 36,897 (at constant 2005 price) in 2013, followed by Brunei Darussalam and Malaysia. This confirms that these three are among the wealthiest nations of the ASEAN members. India's per capita income increased at around 1 per cent annualized rate during the three decades prior to the initiation of its liberalization policies in early 1990s. However, the rate of increase in per capita income picked up after this period. It almost doubled from US$ 609 in 2002–03 to US$ 1164 in 2010–11, averaging 13.7 per cent growth over these eight years peaking at 15.6 per cent in 2010–11 (see Figure 1.10).

5.2 People below Poverty Line

A declining trend in the number of persons below the poverty line can be seen for most countries in the world. For example, China had a record high poverty level of 363 million of poor people in 2002, but this declined to 157 million in 2009. East Asia and Pacific countries as a whole reduced their number of people below the poverty line from 523.11 million in 2002 to 250.9 million in 2010.[11] India, Nigeria, South Asia, Sub-Saharan Africa, Bangladesh, and Indonesia still have substantial levels of poverty. The top performing countries that have been able to reduce poverty sharply are Russia, South Africa, Chile, Mexico, Malaysia, Argentina and Uruguay,

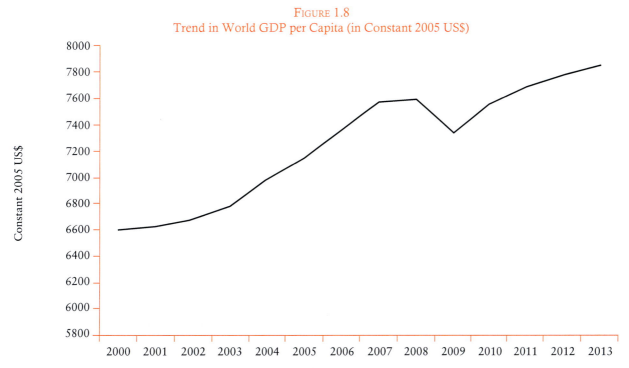

FIGURE 1.8
Trend in World GDP per Capita (in Constant 2005 US$)

Source: World Development Indicators, World Bank (Various Issues), Washington, DC.

---

[11] This data has been sourced from the World Bank's World Development Indicators (WDI) Database. Available at http://databank.worldbank.org/data (accessed 16 February 2015).

FIGURE 1.9

GDP per Capita (Constant 2005 US$) for ASEAN Economies

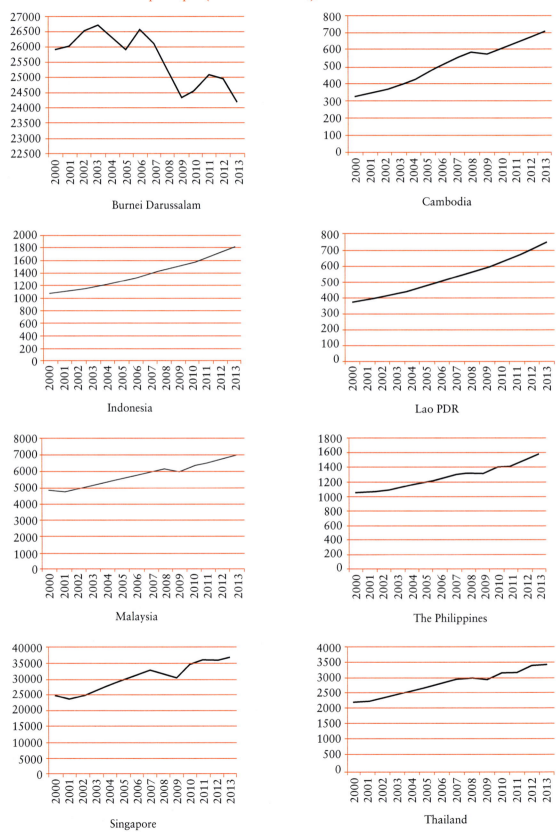

Source: World Development Indicators, World Bank (Various Issues), Washington, DC.

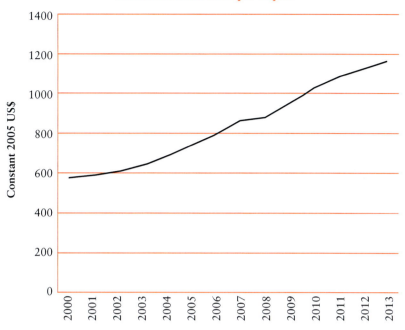

FIGURE 1.10

Trends in India's GDP per Capita

Source: World Development Indicators, World Bank (Various Issues), Washington, DC.

among others. Using the Human Development Index (HDI) we can see that Norway tops the list indicating that it is the most developed nation in the world, followed by Australia and Switzerland with the Central African Republic being at the bottom of the list. Countries, such as Bangladesh, India, China, and Nepal, which have high poverty but low rank in HDI.

The World Bank in 2010, using its older 2005 methodology, estimated that about 400 million poor people lived in India, as compared to 1.29 billion people worldwide (less than $ 1.25 (PPP) per day). The World Bank revised its methodology for poverty calculations in May 2014. According to this new methodology, the world had 872.3 million people below the new poverty line, out of which 179.6 million people lived in India. So, India with 17.5 per cent of the world's population had 20.6 per cent of the world's poor population in 2013.

5.3 Human Development Index

Singapore, Thailand, Indonesia and Vietnam showed significant improvement in world ranking in the Human Development Index (HDI) (see Table 1.7) between 2012 and 2013, while Brunei maintained its same rank. On

TABLE 1.7
ASEAN Countries' HDI Rankings of 2012 and 2013

Country	HDI Rank (2012)	HDI Rank (2013)
Brunei	30	30
Cambodia	138	136
Indonesia	121	108
Lao PDR	138	139
Malaysia	64	62
Myanmar	149	150
Philippines	114	117
Singapore	18	9
Thailand	103	89
Vietnam	127	121

Source: United Nations Development Programme (UNDP).

the other hand, Myanmar and the Philippines showed deterioration. Singapore entered the top ten's list in HDI in 2013. India is somewhere in the lower middle part of the HDI. In 2013, India's rank was 135 out of 187 countries.

5.4 Poverty Gap and Inequality

The poverty gap decreased for all the countries in the ASEAN in the five years between 2008 and 2013, with Malaysia and Thailand having the lowest poverty gap. As far as inequality is concerned, for Malaysia, Indonesia and Lao PDR inequality has increased between 2008 and 2013. For all other countries in the region, inequality has decreased. India also has a very high level of inequality (Gini index of 33.9).[12]

6. Concluding Remarks

The latest edition of the IMF's *World Economic Outlook*, predicts that the developed countries have left the worst behind them and are on a path to recovery. It posits that this is good news to the emerging market economies as the demand for their exports will increase. However, it remarks that full recovery of these countries will take more time. As far as Asia, especially Southeast Asia, is concerned, the OECD reports that Southeast Asia is expected to fully recover from the effects of the global financial crisis in the medium term (next five years). The same cannot be said about India and China. Both these countries are showing signs of a more gradual recovery. However, according to the latest reports, India's GDP growth has partially recovered to about 7.5 per cent in the first quarter of 2015. Thus, there appears to be a clear sign that the economies of the ASEAN region plus India are on a road to recovery as well.

We have remarked that there was a time lag between the downturn of developed countries and the emerging economies during the financial crisis. What the two reports mentioned earlier point out is that there will be a lag between the upturns as well. Further, this should be read in tandem with what we have mentioned — that the recovery from the global financial crisis is turning out to be much more drawn out than the two crises prior to it, the Asian crisis of 1997 and the depression of 2000–01.

The main factor in this prolonged recovery and the lagged response of emerging market economies is the contagion associated with globalization. Though the major source of growth in Asia remains domestic demand, outside factors, especially those in Europe and North America are increasingly exerting their influence on the performance of this region. It appears that these effects have become stronger during the financial crisis, compared to the earlier two crises,[13] and will become even stronger as globalization progresses.

Therefore, the main macroeconomic challenge for these economies should be to combat this contagion. If the advanced economies recover strongly, there is every chance that investment flowing into Asian economies from these countries during their recessionary period will reverse. The twin options open to these economies then would be to increase returns on assets and simultaneously reduce risk associated with investments. Both monetary and fiscal tightening appears to be a good option under the circumstances. However, it should not be forgotten that these economies still depend substantially on domestic investments to fuel their growth and domestic investments may be crowded out in a bid to attract foreign investment. To ensure that this does not happen, extra sops need to be given to domestic investments.

Another important method of combating the contagion will be to define an economic subregion within the larger context of globalization by systematically facilitating trade and investments among the countries in the region to an extent that goes much beyond what is true for the rest of the world. South and Southeast Asia can be such an economic subregion. The only problem in this respect is the pull of gravity. Being in the low-to-middle income category, these countries have an inherent vulnerability in increasing their engagement with nations that have greater size as well as levels of economic development. For instance, most major trading partners of all these countries are either in North America or Europe. The doors of contagion from these countries are therefore wide open.

---

[12] Ibid.

This 'pull of gravity' from the point of view of economic size and development can, to an extent, be combated by concentrating on the distance aspect. Lowering transport and transaction costs among these economies to a much larger extent than what has been achieved with the rest of the world can clearly help. And, this is the crux of India–ASEAN economic cooperation. While the Free Trade Agreement (FTA) between the ASEAN countries themselves and between India and the ASEAN countries are a step in the right direction, much more remains to be done. The investment agreement and the infrastructure agreement that are planned between India and ASEAN will without any doubt take this much further.

But, the main issue remains implementation and ensuring effectiveness. The signing of an agreement does not automatically ensure that it is effective. Is trade taking place through the FTA route? Is the reduction in tariff too small compared to the loads of extra paperwork that needs to be dealt with to take advantage of the reduced tariff? Is poor connectivity between countries acting as a hindrance?

Furthermore, are the right goods being targeted for tariff reduction? Are the goods for which tariff is relaxed tariff-elastic? Recent evidence shows that most of the goods for which tariff was relaxed in the India–ASEAN FTA have insignificant tariff elasticity, meaning that their imports are not expected to respond significantly to tariff reductions (Bhattacharyya and Mandal, 2014). Tariff negotiations before the signing of an FTA have their own logic. That logic may not coincide with the economic logic of the agreement, that is, the incremental impact of the negotiation on the volume of trade. The next few chapters attempt to answer some of these questions and discuss the policy priorities that need to be focused in these directions.

---

[13] The Asian crisis was, of course, of South Asia's own making; so, the question of contagion does not arise for many of the economies being discussed here. But, countries like India were virtually insulated from it due to its 'closed door' policies at that time.

2
Trends and Patterns of Merchandise Trade

India's engagement with ASEAN has gained momentum since the 1990s with the initiation of India's 'Look East Policy' and a conscious translation of the trade policy objective of diversifying its trade partners. While the former has led to an evolution of this bilateral relationship from India becoming a sectoral partner of ASEAN in 1992 to a dialogue partner in 1996 and finally a Summit partner in 2002, the latter is reflected in growing volumes of bilateral trade over the last two decades. The ASEAN–India bilateral trade has increased from US$ 2.76 billion in 1992 to US$ 9.28 billion in 2002 and US$ 75.92 billion in 2012.[1] The growing trade volumes have led to an institutionalized trade relationship as reflected in the ASEAN–India FTA (AIFTA). The FTA, the framework agreement for which was announced in 2003, was finally signed in 2009 and became effective on the 1 January 2010.

The institutionalization of the ASEAN–India relationship is also a reflection of the acceptance of regionalism as an alternative to the increasingly slow moving multilateral Doha Development Agenda (DDA).[2] The near stagnant levels of intra-regional trade in South Asia coupled with ASEAN's interest in drawing upon India's economic dynamism provides further rationale for a stronger ASEAN–India economic integration. The global financial crisis of 2008–09 and the slowing down of the growth process in the advanced economies have also made it imperative that intra-Asian economic linkages must be strengthened. Furthermore, ASEAN's FTA agreements with the other East Asia Summit (EAS) founding members added to regional compulsions as any further delay in India's FTA initiative would have prevented India from acquiring the legitimate right to participate in the emerging regional economic architecture.

Given the background, this chapter examines the trends in ASEAN–India trade in goods, both in the bilateral and regional context. The analysis helps us understand the extent of India's integration in regional supply chains, implications of prior implementation of other trade agreements and emerging mega-regional agreements in Asia as well.

1. TRENDS IN ASEAN–INDIA BILATERAL TRADE

The trends, pattern and structure of trade between ASEAN and India are analyzed here. A pre- and post- FTA analysis is undertaken to examine the impact of AIFTA, if any, on bilateral trade. The exports, imports and trade balance are examined in the years 2000, 2005, 2009 and 2013 as reference time points to observe if ASEAN–India trade has been on an upward trajectory since the beginning of the decade or if the increase is owing to the implementation of the FTA. The last two years are indicative of the immediate pre-FTA and completion of the first phase of tariff elimination time points, while the years 2000 and 2005 provide a relatively longer comparative perspective.

1.1 Trade Volumes and Rates of Growth

India's exports to ASEAN increased from US$ 2.91 billion in 2000–01 to close to US$ 10 billion in 2005–06 and then to US$ 25 billion in the first year following the implementation of the FTA in 2010. Similarly, the import volume increased from US$ 4.15 billion to close to US$ 11 billion in 2005–06 and then to US$ 30 billion in 2010. In 2013–14, exports and imports have further increased to US$ 33.28 and US$ 41.61 billion, respectively.[3] The exports and imports have hence registered a consistent increase in volume over the last decade.

---

[1] Data sourced from UNCOMTRADE.

[2] The progress at the 2013 Bali Ministerial with regard to the 'limited deliverables' now seems to be in the doldrums given India's stiff resistance to accept the trade facilitation deal without a corresponding concession on food security issues.

[3] Data has been sourced from the Export–Import Databank, Ministry of Commerce and Industry, Government of India.

The annual percentage increase in exports to and imports from ASEAN has fluctuated with the periods of 2010–11 and 2011–12 showing rather high growth rates of over 40 per cent, followed by a decline in the subsequent year. The imports show an increase of 38 per cent in 2011–12, following the start of the FTA implementation. While the increase in exports could be due to the implementation effect of the FTA, the decline in 2013 would not necessarily support the idea. The same can be stated for imports.

The growing trade between India and ASEAN has, however, been in favour of ASEAN with India incurring a deficit vis-à-vis the region. Imports have grown more rapidly than exports and the trend has continued to post the implementation of the FTA as well. The trade deficit that India registered vis-à-vis ASEAN in 2012 was eight times the level in 2000–01. Even though the trade deficit in 2013–14 has fallen relative to 2012–13 levels, it continues to be large.

1.2 Trade Shares

Despite the increasing trade volumes, ASEAN's share in India's exports has been consistently around 10 per cent since 2004–05 with the exception of the year 2011–12, when the share increased to 12 per cent, probably as an immediate after effect of the initiation of the AIFTA implementation, after which it settled to around 10 per cent in the following years. Similarly, the share of imports from ASEAN to India's total imports has been in the 8 to 9 per cent range throughout the last decade and a half. Overall, the share of ASEAN in India's total trade has been close to 10 per cent through the last decade. The AIFTA does not appear to have resulted in any distinct break in the trade trends over the last decade and a half.

ASEAN, with a little over 10 per cent share in India's total exports in 2013–14, was at rank five, following the European Union with a share of 16 per cent, North America (13.85 per cent), West Asia–GCC (15.38 per cent) and Northeast Asia (13 per cent) in that order. Regarding imports, the picture is largely the same in 2013–14 as it was in 2009–10, with ASEAN occupying around 9 per cent share in India's total imports at rank four following other regions like the West Asia–GCC (22 per cent), Northeast Asia (18 per cent), the European Union (11 per cent) in that order. The implementation of the AIFTA in 2010 has not altered ASEAN's ranking among the regions that India trades with. At the start of the decade ASEAN with a share of 8 per cent of India's total imports was at rank three, following West Asia–GCC and Northeast Asia. With about the same share in India's total imports, ASEAN has in the last decade, lost a rank in the overall order of all the regions with Northeast Asia gaining the most.

1.3 Share of ASEAN Countries

Among the ASEAN countries, Singapore and Indonesia, with a share of 2.64 and 2.56 per cent, rank among the top ten trade partners of India. Indonesia, Malaysia and Singapore are the largest source countries for India's imports in 2013–14, and the same was in 2009–10 and also at the starting of the decade 2000–01. For exports other than these countries, Vietnam has emerged among the top destinations for Indian exports in 2013–14, with a share that is more than that held by either Malaysia or Indonesia. From among the other three, while Indonesia and Malaysia occupy almost equal shares in total exports to ASEAN, Singapore garners almost three times as much as exports of the other two economies. With Singapore, India has maintained in the last five years a trade surplus, even though with Indonesia, Malaysia and Thailand it has had a trade deficit. The magnitude of trade deficit is largest with Indonesia.

1.4 India's Share in ASEAN Exports and Imports

India's share in ASEAN's exports and imports has increased relative to that at the start of the decade. While the share has doubled between 2000 and 2013, the change has been only marginal post the implementation of the FTA in 2010. Overall, India's share, at less than 3 per cent of ASEAN's total trade, remains small. In terms of total trade, India is ASEAN's 7th largest trading partner. The topmost trading partner for ASEAN is China with almost six times as much share as India.

Member countries that show an increase in India's share in their exports relative to the pre-FTA shares include Lao PDR, Malaysia, Thailand and Vietnam. The increase in post-FTA shares though is rather small. India has the maximum export share in Indonesia's export. Also, in ASEAN, India ranks among the top 10 trade partners for Brunei (rank 3: share 7 per cent), Indonesia (rank 7: share 4.6 per cent), Malaysia (rank 9: share

3.08 per cent), and Singapore (rank 10: share 2.6 per cent). Other than Brunei, China is the largest trading partner for all the ASEAN member countries.

1.5 Trade Intensity Index

The value of the trade intensity (TI) index[4] is more than one for ASEAN and all member countries except Thailand, the Philippines, Lao PDR and Cambodia (see Table 2.1). Among the member countries, the TI index is the highest for Myanmar, followed by Brunei Darussalam. For all ASEAN member countries with a greater than unity TI index in 2009, as also for ASEAN, there has been a decline in the value of the TI in the following year, that is at the end of the first year of AIFTA implementation. Subsequently, the TI index retains about the same value or registers a further decline. The AIFTA, therefore, does not appear to have positively impacted on trade intensity of India vis-à-vis the ASEAN.[5]

1.6 Regional Trade Introversion Index

The trade pattern analysis is further supplemented by calculating the regional trade introversion (RTI) index, which unlike the TI index, provides information on the intra-regional trade bias of a region relative to its trade with the outsiders. The index[6] has a range of [−1, +1]. The RTI index is calculated for ASEAN and ASEAN plus India in order to examine the differential intra-regional trade bias when the region is defined as inclusive of India. The RTI index for the two regions is calculated at two points in time: immediately prior to the implementation of the ASEAN–India FTA and for 2013, that is, post of the implementation of the FTA (see Table 2.2). It is observed

TABLE 2.1
India's Trade Intensity with ASEAN Countries

Partner	2000	2005	2009	2010	2012
ASEAN	1.24	1.46	1.59	1.40	1.40
Brunei	0.08	0.40	3.23	1.02	2.25
Cambodia	0.36	0.29	0.25	0.24	0.25
Indonesia	1.83	2.04	2.64	2.36	2.20
Lao PDR	0.73	0.25	0.31	0.29	0.87
Malaysia	1.35	1.10	1.50	1.15	1.27
Myanmar	6.73	7.72	6.65	4.68	3.62
The Philippines	0.37	0.53	0.53	0.42	0.44
Singapore	1.40	2.20	1.89	1.75	1.71
Thailand	0.89	0.84	0.89	0.86	0.90
Vietnam	1.08	1.01	0.98	1.11	1.03

Source: ARIC, ADB
Notes: As ADB data is on annual basis, the year 2009 has been included as immediately prior to the implementation of the FTA and 2010 as the year immediately after.

---

[4] Trade intensity (TI) index is the ratio of trade share of a country/region to the share of world trade with a partner. An index of more than one indicates that trade flow between countries/regions is larger than expected, given their importance in world trade. The index is calculated as:

$$TII_{ij} = \frac{t_{ij}/T_{iw}}{t_{wj}/T_{ww}},$$ where t_{ij} is the dollar value of total trade of country/region i with country/region j, T_{iw} is the dollar value

of the total trade of country/region i with the world, t_{wj} is the dollar value of world trade with country/region j, and T_{ww} is the dollar value of world trade (Refer, ADB, ARI for Technical Notes).

[5] Interestingly, the EHP with Thailand and the Singapore CECA shows a similar trend.

[6] Regional Trade Introversion Index = (HIi − HEi) /(HIi + HEi), where HIi = (Tii/Ti) / (Toi/To) and HEi = (1 − Tii/Ti) / (1 − Toi/To). Here, Tii ≡ is exports of region i to region i plus imports of region i from region i, Ti ≡ is total exports of region

Table 2.2
RTI Index

	ASEAN-5*	ASEAN + India
2009	0.70	0.58
2013	0.62	0.45

Notes: *ASEAN includes Indonesia, Malaysia, the Philippines, Singapore and Thailand and **Outsiders includes world except 5 ASEAN countries (Indonesia, Malaysia, the Philippines, Singapore and Thailand).

that the ASEAN has an RTI index value of 0.70 and 0.62 in the two time periods. However, on addition of India to the region, the RTI value falls to just around 0.58 in 2009 with a further decline to 0.48 in 2013. This implies that over the two reference years, ASEAN's tendency to trade within the region has marginally declined and further that the tendency to trade within the region inclusive of India is lower than the tendency for the ASEAN5 (that includes Malaysia, Singapore, Indonesia, the Philippines, and Thailand[7]) to trade among themselves and this tendency falls further in 2013. Clearly, India's inclusion leads to a decline in intra-regional trade bias for the region and the implementation of the AIFTA is yet to make a positive impact on the trade tendencies.

2. TRADE PERFORMANCE: SECTOR-WISE ANALYSIS

2.1 Top 20 Export Sectors

Of the top 20 sectors that together contribute about 85 per cent of India's total exports to ASEAN, mineral oils and mineral fuels (HS-27) is the top ranking export sector at all three reference time points. In 2013–14, it accounted for around 30 per cent of total value of India's exports to ASEAN. The composition of the top 20 sectors in 2013–14 is relative to the composition in 2009-10, that is at the time of implementation of the AIFTA since the implementation of the FTA only changes to the extent of the addition of four new sectors: HS-88 (Aircraft, spacecraft and parts thereof); HS-09 (coffee, tea, mate and spices); HS-75 (nickel and articles thereof); and HS-03 (fish and crustaceans, molluscs and other aquatic invertebrates). Of these four sectors, HS-03 is also among the top 10 export sectors with a share of 4 per cent in total exports from India to ASEAN. The highest annual growth rate is observed for the sector HS-88, followed by HS-03, HS-09 and HS-73 in that order. Sectors that have been eliminated from among the top 20 over the same period include HS-99 (miscellaneous goods), HS-72 (Iron and Steel), HS-74 (copper and articles thereof), HS-76 (Aluminium and articles thereof), and HS-38 (miscellaneous chemical products). Ten of the top 20 sectors have experienced over 10 per cent CAGR since the implementation of the AIFTA in 2010 (see Table A2.1).

2.1 Top 20 Import Sectors

As regards imports, three sectors HS-74 (copper and articles thereof), HS-73 (articles of iron and steel), and HS-80 (Tin and articles thereof) are new additions in 2013–14 relative to 2009–10 among the top 20 sectors that together contribute 91 per cent of the total imports from ASEAN. The maximum CAGR since the implementation of the AIFTA is registered by the sector HS-40 (rubber and articles thereof), followed by HS-87 (vehicles other than railway or tramway rolling stock, parts, and accessories thereof) and HS-39 (plastics and articles thereof) each, with over 20 per cent CAGR between 2009–10 and 2013–14. Other sectors with over 10 per cent

i to the world plus total imports of region i from the world, Toi is exports of region i to outsiders plus imports of region i from outsiders, To is total exports of outsiders plus total imports of outsiders, Tw is total world exports plus imports.

[7]The value of the RTI index for ASEAN and ASEAN+India remains unchanged with variations in the definition of ASEAN as ASEAN7 (5+Cambodia and Vietnam) or with ASEAN8 (5+Brunei, Cambodia and Vietnam) and the outsiders is all countries other than the ASEAN10. The varying regional composition is in accordance with the availability of data.

CAGR include sectors HS-29 (organic chemicals), HS-44 (wood and articles thereof) and HS-76 (aluminium and articles thereof).

2.2 Commodity-Wise Exports: HS-6 Digit

Of the top 100 commodity exports that together contribute about 78 per cent of India's total exports to ASEAN, the maximum number of commodities belong to sectors such as HS-29 (organic chemicals) and HS-72 (Iron and Steel). Both these sectors have eight commodities each in the top 100 commodity exports to ASEAN. These are followed by HS-89 (ships, boats and floating structures) and HS-87 (vehicles other than railways and tramways rolling stock and accessories thereof) with seven commodities each and HS-84 (nuclear reactors, boilers, machineries, and mechanical appliances) and HS-27 (mineral fuels and mineral oils) with six and five commodities in the top 100, respectively.

Of the top 100, 42 commodities in 2013–14 are new additions and were not exported in 2009–10.These commodities account for 27 per cent of the total export value from India to ASEAN (see Table A2.2). Tariffs for these commodities are down to zero in most of the ASEAN5 countries. While it may be difficult to ascertain whether the entry into the top 100 exports is purely due to the AIFTA preferences, it is possible as at least some of these commodities (almost 7 per cent of the total) did not have an initial revealed comparative advantage in 2009. Gains, for this set of commodities spread across various sectors, could therefore be entirely or largely on account of the FTA preferences.

Another set of 37 commodities from among the top 100 has registered an over 10 per cent CAGR since 2009–10 (see Table A2.3). All these commodities have an initial RCA greater than one and tariffs down to zero on account of AIFTA. Again a part of the large gains could be on account of the AIFTA preferences.[8]

2.3 Commodity-Wise Imports from ASEAN

In 2013–14, of the top 100 imports that contribute about 80 per cent of total imports from ASEAN, the maximum number of commodities (15) belong to the sector HS-85 (electrical machinery and equipment and parts thereof) followed by HS-84 (machinery and mechanical appliances) with 13, HS-29 (organic chemicals) with 11, HS-39 (plastics and articles thereof) with 8 and HS-89 (ships, boats and floating structures) with 5 commodities, respectively. However, 31 of the top 100 commodities are new and were not being imported in 2009–10. The maximum number of new import commodities belong to sectors HS-39 (plastics and articles thereof) and HS-85 (electrical machinery and equipment and parts thereof) (see Table A2.4).

This set of new imports includes the commodity HS-090411, that is, pepper neither crushed nor ground, which is classified as a special product under the AIFTA and has undergone a gradual cut in tariffs to 60 per cent in 2013 from 70 per cent in 2010. The reduction by 10 per cent has led to an immediate effect in terms of the commodity now being imported from ASEAN. The commodity undergoes a further and final reduction in the tariff level of another 10 per cent by 2019. The schedule of lower and gradual reduction in tariff over a longer period has been included in the AIFTA for five special products, categorized as such, keeping in view the plantation farmers' livelihood concerns. Therefore, it is imperative that the remaining period of tariff adjustment be used for implementation of productivity enhancement schemes for these products so as to be able to successfully combat the competitive pressures arising from these new imports.

The maximum number of commodities that have, since the implementation of the FTA, registered a CAGR of 10 per cent or more belong to sectors HS-85 (electrical machinery and equipment and parts thereof), HS-84 (machinery and mechanical appliances), HS-29[9] (organic chemicals) and HS-39 (plastics and articles thereof). Included in this set of high growth commodities are HS-090111 (coffee neither roasted nor decaffeinated), and HS-151190 (refined palm oil and its fractions), both classified as special products under the AIFTA. Concerns

---

[8] It is also to be noted that the initial tariffs for both sets of commodities are low and in the range of 0–10 per cent in most cases.

[9] Anti-Dumping Duty (ADD) has been levied on imports from this sector originating in Singapore and Thailand, among other countries (Refer CBEC ADD notifications).

regarding the productivity levels of these commodities must be addressed as even small tariff cuts have led to a significant increase in imports of these commodities. Also included in this set is commodity HS-850440 (static converters) of the sensitive track with duty reduction to 6 per cent from a base rate of 10 per cent (see Table A2.5).

Overall for imports, maximum change in terms of growth and addition of new products since the implementation of the AIFTA has been found to be concentrated in four sectors that include organic chemicals (HS-29); machinery and mechanical appliances (HS-84); electrical equipment; parts thereof; sound recorders and reproducers, television image and sound recorders and reproducers, and parts and accessories of such articles (HS-85); and HS-39: plastics and articles thereof (HS-39).

3. ASEAN–INDIA FTA: TRADE LIBERALIZATION FEATURES

Starting from January 2010, the AIFTA aimed at elimination of tariffs for about 4,000 products at the HS 6-digit level. Of these 4,000 products, 3,200 products were scheduled to have duties reduced by end of the year 2013, while duties on the remaining 800 products would be lowered to zero or near zero by end of 2016. Tariff lines are divided into four broad categories, that is, Normal Track, Sensitive Track, Special Products,[10] and Highly Sensitive Lists and Exclusion List, according to the intensity of tariff reduction or elimination commitments. Normal Track products are further divided into two sub-groups, namely, Normal Tracks 1 and 2. The tariff elimination schedule under each track is presented in Table 2.3a and for special products it is presented in Table 2.3b.

The sensitive track is such that it allows for duties on items with MFN applied tariffs of more than 5 per cent to be reduced to 5 per cent with a normal track-2 schedule. This can be maintained for up to 50 tariff lines. For remaining products from tariff lines beyond 50, duties on products with MFN applied tariff rates higher than 5 per cent will be reduced to 4.5 per cent upon entry into force of the Agreement for ASEAN6[11] and five years from entry into force of the Agreement for CLMV countries. The AIFTA preferential tariff rate for these tariff lines are to reduce to 4 per cent eventually. Applied MFN tariff rates on four per cent of the tariff lines placed in the Sensitive Track (as will be identified) will be eliminated by 31 December 2019 for Brunei Darussalam, Indonesia,

TABLE 2.3a
AIFTA Tariff Elimination Schedule

ASEAN 6		CLMV		India	
NT-1	NT-2/SL	NT-1	NT-2/SL	NT-1	NT-2
Jan. 2010–Dec. 2013 (2018**)	Jan. 2010–Dec. 2016 (2019**)	Jan. 2010–Dec. 2018	Jan. 2010–Dec. 2021	Jan. 2010–Dec. 2013 (2018**)	Jan. 2010–Dec. 2016 (2019**)

Source: Ministry of Commerce & Industry, Government of India.
Notes: NT: Normal Track; SL: Sensitive List **To the Philippines.

TABLE 2.3b
AIFTA Tariff Elimination Schedule for Special Products

	Base Rate	2010–19	January 1 2014
CPO	80	37.5	60
RPO	90	45	70
Coffee	100	45	75
Black Tea	100	45	75
Pepper	70	50	60

Source: Export–Import Databank, Ministry of Commerce & Industry, Government of India.
Note: Figures in parentheses indicate tariff rates as of December 2013.

---

[10] Specified only by India in AIFTA. The five commodities comprising this set constitute about 0.3 per cent of its tariff lines.

[11] Special arrangements apply for Thailand. See http://commerce.gov.in/trade (accessed 16 February 2015).

Malaysia, Singapore,[12] and Thailand, and India, 31 December 2022 for the Philippines and 31 December 2024 for Cambodia, Lao PDR, Myanmar and Vietnam.[13]

The goods included in the highly sensitive list (HSL) are divided into three categories, and will undergo reduction in tariff by 50 per cent in case of the first two and 25 per cent in the third category and are to be achieved by December 2019 by Indonesia, Malaysia and Thailand, December 2022 by the Philippines and December 2024 by Cambodia and Vietnam. The AIFTA also specifies an exclusion list that shall be subject to an annual tariff review with a view to improving market access.[14]

The schedule of tariff reduction commitments undertaken by the AIFTA members varies significantly among them. Singapore with 100 per cent tariff elimination coverage is followed by Cambodia (88.4 per cent), Brunei (85.3 per cent), the Philippines (80.9 per cent), Lao PDR (80.1 per cent), Malaysia (79.8 per cent), Vietnam (79.5 per cent), Thailand (78.1 per cent) and Myanmar (76.6 per cent). Indonesia offers the lowest tariff elimination coverage at 48.7 per cent (Fukunaga and Isono, 2013).

As regards the Rules of Origin (RoO) for AIFTA, the twin criteria of value addition whereby AIFTA content is not to be less than 35 per cent of the *fob* value and a change in tariff sub-heading (CTSH) of the Harmonized System is to be fulfilled to avail the tariff concession.

4. ASEAN–India FTA: An Assessment

The phased implementation of ASEAN–India FTA (AIFTA) started in 2010 through partial liberalization with respect to Malaysia, Singapore and Thailand. For the remaining ASEAN members, it is expected to come into force by 2016 after the countries complete their internal requirements. In other words, India, Malaysia, Singapore and Thailand under the AIFTA have completed the tariff liberalization with respect to the products in their Normal Track 1.

The computable general equilibrium (CGE) modelling framework of the GTAP is one of the best possible ways to analyze *ex ante* the economic consequences and trade implications of multilateral and bilateral trade agreements. With the help of GTAP8 database, we analyze the direction of possible impacts of AIFTA on trade, factor demand (especially, employment), prices and welfare, with particular reference to India. The database used here is the latest version (ver. 8.0) of the GTAP database, which has 2007 as the base year. This has been updated to reflect the world economy in 2010. The database is compiled for bilateral exports and imports and tariffs inclusive of other flows for 129 regions across the world and for 57 tradable commodities of the world. Various simulations using this database were done, and accordingly, the 129 regions of the database have been aggregated into 23 regions. Similarly, the 57 sectors have been aggregated into 36 sectors for all the simulations conducted.

We take up a practical approach by considering unemployment closure since it is expected that the wages in India will remain downward inflexible. Sikdar and Nag (2011) considered the full employment model, thereby allowing wages to remain flexible. In contrast to the earlier work, the CGE simulations in this study show that unskilled workers in the region gain significantly as the ASEAN–India FTA implementation moves towards full liberalization. India's trade with ASEAN will rise between 37 to 53 per cent as the agreement unfolds. India is likely to benefit from the FTA as more of the smaller countries from the region liberalize their trade with India. Price reduction on number of goods imported into India will be less, compared to ASEAN countries, where Indian companies need to reduce prices on a larger number of goods to get a better market penetration. ASEAN members can afford to sell larger number of goods in India at relatively higher prices as India will offer huge demand. These lead to major Terms of Trade gain to ASEAN members. As a result, bilateral trade deficit will remain unfavourable to India. However, as the prices of the endowments will remain downward inflexible, factors of production including labour will get major boost due to increase in domestic production activities. Welfare results show that there are major gains in India through endowment effect. Trade cost reduction along with trade liberalization will add to this endowment gain for India. The study concludes that bilateral trade

---

[12] Modality for Sensitive Track does not apply to Singapore (ASEAN–India: Trade in Goods Agreement, http://commerce. gov.in/trade [accessed 16 February 2015]).

[13] Ministry of Commerce, Government of India. See http://commerce.gov.in/trade (accessed 16 February 2015).

[14] Refer, www.asean.org.

deficit of India is bound to rise and we should not have a myopic view towards the trade deficit. The ASEAN FTA is expected to increase economic activities within India, leading to more employment and income generation. The aggregate welfare of India will be substantially higher in case of full liberalization vis-à-vis partial liberalization.

Trade between countries across the world has grown rapidly over the last few decades. This growth in trade has largely been due to the worldwide drop in average import tariffs on goods. In spite of this drop in trade tariffs, trade has not grown and diversified uniformly across the world. The trade share of least developed countries continue to lag behind those of high income countries and their trade basket is still largely made up of low value added primary products. This has led to a shift in focus towards non-tariff barriers of trade, which are now thought to be the primary obstacles to trade between the countries. In the wake of reduced tariff barriers across the world, cross-border inefficiencies or trade costs are often cited as more important determinants of trade between countries. Thus, we turn to examine the welfare implications of reduced trade costs between India and ASEAN. We consider three different reductions (25 per cent, 20 per cent and 10 per cent) in trade cost with respect to goods entering India from ASEAN. Thus, the total trade cost is made up of cost of exports from individual ASEAN countries plus the cost of imports in India. The country and product specific trade costs associated with movement of goods from the ASEAN countries to India is calculated and converted into their corresponding ad valorem or tariff equivalents for all sectors considered in the present study and for all of India and the ASEAN countries.

Using this data on tariff equivalents, the impact of reduced trade costs (25 per cent, 20 per cent and 10 per cent) on welfare of India and the ASEAN countries are estimated. The impacts on welfare of other non ASEAN countries are also closely examined. Two main scenarios are simulated:

(*a*) A reduction in trade costs (25 per cent, 20 per cent and 10 per cent)
(*b*) A reduction in trade costs (25 per cent, 20 per cent and 10 per cent) along with trade liberalization between the countries.

Here, the trade liberalization scenario refers to partial liberalization (tariff elimination for products in normal track, tariff reductions for the sensitive track products and no change in tariffs for products in the exclusion list) involving all ASEAN members — a scenario which will represent the status of the FTA as of 31 December 2021. This simulation is done in two stages — first of all, a scenario of partial liberalization is simulated involving India and the three ASEAN members, namely, Malaysia, Singapore and Thailand. Secondly, using this scenario as the base/initial situation, a further simulation is carried out, whereby all other ASEAN members eliminate tariff on all normal track products, reduce tariff on their sensitive track products, while keeping the tariffs on their exclusion list as before. Table 2.4a presents the estimated welfare effect of the FTA with reduced trade costs on ASEAN partners.

TABLE 2.4a
Welfare Effect of the FTA with Reduced Trade Costs on Partners (US$ million)

Country	Only Trade Liberalization Involving All Countries	Reduction in Total Trade Cost* before Entering Indian Market			Trade Liberalization Plus Reduction in Trade Cost* before Entering Indian Market		
		10%	20%	25%	10% Reduction in Trade Cost	20% Reduction in Trade Cost	25% Reduction in Trade Cost
India	1463.5	224.0	461.0	565.9	1686.6	1930.3	2040.2
Malaysia	−67.7	51.0	96.7	121.3	−18.6	25.4	49.2
Singapore	−59.8	64.8	131.9	167.8	1.6	67.3	102.6
Thailand	−116.6	21.8	42.2	52.5	−99.7	−81.2	−71.7
Cambodia	−1.6	−0.4	−0.7	−0.9	−2.03	−2.4	−2.7
Indonesia	809.7	24.0	48.3	58.8	881.0	918.2	934.3
Lao PDR	0.49	−0.04	−0.08	−0.1	0.5	0.5	0.46
The Philippines	13.8	0.8	1.6	1.9	11.7	12.7	13.1
Vietnam	147.0	0.99	1.9	2.4	152.0	155.4	156.9
Rest of ASEAN	142.2	4.9	9.97	12.4	151.0	159.6	163.7

Source: Sikdar and Nag (2014).
Note: *Reduction of export cost from individual ASEAN countries and import cost at the entry point of India.

India has positive welfare gain both from trade liberalization as also reduction in trade cost and as such the highest gain to the country is when trade liberalization occurs uniformly with the entire ASEAN region as per the scheduled tariff commitments alongside a 25 per cent reduction in trade cost. In all the scenarios, India's welfare gain is on account of employment benefits and allocative efficiency gains. Terms of Trade remains negative throughout, implying that in spite of reduced trade cost and elimination of tariff barriers, the import prices for products in India remain higher compared to the export prices India offers to the ASEAN countries. Prices of the imported intermediate goods in India will remain high even after trade liberalization and reduction of trade cost due to high domestic demand in India. Hence, in production processes, substitution between capital and labour will allow a major gain in employment in most of the productive sectors in India.

Among the ASEAN countries, Malaysia, Singapore and Indonesia have notable positive welfare gains, when trade costs are reduced and obviously these gains are highest when trade costs are lowered to 25 per cent along with the countries lowering the tariff barriers. While Indonesia experiences an increase in positive gains owing to all of improved allocative efficiency, endowment and terms of trade, Singapore and Malaysia actually start earning positive gains compared to the negative gains they had when the countries just lowered the tariffs applied to the bilateral trade. This improvement in welfare position is due to improved terms of trade. Thailand continues to face welfare loss, but with reduced trade cost, the magnitude of loss comes down primarily due to terms of trade improvement. The other countries of the region do not display much extra welfare gain when trade costs are reduced along with tariff barriers.

Table 2.4b shows the welfare implication of the trade liberalization and reduced trade cost between India and the ASEAN region on other countries in East and South Asia. As seen from Table 2.4b, China, Japan and Korea in East Asia are most hit by the improvement in trade facilitation. All of them earn negative welfare and this loss deepens as trade liberalization is accompanied by reduction in trade costs. Worsening terms of trade is the main reason for welfare loss to these countries. In South Asia, it is Pakistan and Sri Lanka, which experience welfare loss, again due to the worsening terms of trade. Thus, most of East and South Asian countries are likely to be hit negatively as trade opens up and trade costs come down between India and ASEAN.

Thus, India's trade with the ASEAN increases consistently, with imports rising more than exports and the trade basket gradually becoming more intensive in secondary rather than in primary products. It can be argued that the AIFTA will provide more internal benefit to India as it unfolds gradually. However, the bilateral trade deficit of India will be bound to rise and we should not have a myopic view towards the trade deficit only. The ASEAN FTA is bound to increase economic activities within India leading to more employment and income generation. With reduction in trade cost alongside tariff liberalization, the employment gains to India will increase further.

TABLE 2.4b

Welfare Effect of the FTA with Reduced Trade Costs on Other East and South Asian Countries (US$ million)

Country	Trade Liberalization Involving All Countries	Reduction in Total Trade Cost* before Entering Indian Market			Trade Liberalization Plus Reduction in Trade Cost* before Entering Indian Market		
		10%	20%	25%	10% Reduction in Trade Cost	20% Reduction in Trade Cost	25% Reduction in Trade Cost
Hong Kong	−22.6	−1.9	−3.8	−4.7	−24.7	−26.8	−27.9
China	−152.7	−22.2	−44.0	−56.0	−176.6	−200.3	−212.8
Japan	−312.6	−7.4	−14.3	−17.8	−323.8	−334.4	−339.8
Korea	−139.0	−3.5	−6.9	−8.7	−144.1	−149.1	−151.6
Mongolia	1.12	0	0	0	1.13	1.14	0.15
Taiwan	−88.5	−1.4	−2.9	−3.7	−90.8	−93.1	−94.2
Rest of East Asia	1.11	0.02	0.01	0.01	1.15	1.16	1.17
Bangladesh	1.8	0.08	0.16	0.22	1.95	2.09	2.2
Pakistan	−22.2	−0.8	−1.6	−1.98	−23.0	−24.2	−24.6
Sri Lanka	−0.94	−5.7	−11.6	14.1	−6.6	−12.4	−14.8
Rest of South Asia	−1.6	−2.8	−5.6	−6.8	−4.3	−7.1	−8.3

Source: Sikdar and Nag (2014).

Note: *Reduction of export cost from individual ASEAN countries and import cost at the entry point of India.

5. India's Integration in Regional Supply Chains

Athukorola (2013) has analyzed the evolution of the East Asian trade and production networks including those of the ASEAN6 and the changes therein post global financial crisis. The study has highlighted the asymmetry in trade patterns in terms of the increased trade in parts and components driving the rapidity of intra-regional integration for East Asia and ASEAN6, whereas a similar rapid pace of integration in final products in intra-regional trade has not been evident. In fact, the region's intra-regional trade in parts and components is dependent on its extra-regional trade in final goods. In this context, it is relevant to analyze if the increasing trade integration that is evident for India and ASEAN is a reflection of its integration into the ASEAN production networks or is India emerging as an alternative market for the region. To examine the former proposition, we follow the list of commodities identified as parts and components by Athukorola (2013)[15] and match the Indian imports and exports with this list so as to identify the share of component trade that is taking place or evolving between India and ASEAN. The analysis is undertaken at three time points, namely, 2005, 2009 and 2013, accounting thus for the period well before the initiation of the AIFTA implementation in 2010, immediately preceding the FTA implementation and completion of implementation with regard to NT-1 for some countries in 2013.

Our observations from this exercise reveal that out of the top 100 imports, the number of commodities classified as components are 13, 14 and 21 in 2013, 2009 and 2005, respectively. Correspondingly, the share of total imports cornered by component imports is 4.8 per cent, 6.1 per cent and 16.96 per cent of that contributed by the top 100 commodities in 2013, 2009 and 2005, respectively. In case of exports to ASEAN, the commodities that can be classified as component exports are even fewer. Therefore, it may be fair to say that India is apparently not yet integrated into the intra-ASEAN regional production networks.[16] India may be evolving more as a market for ASEAN products. This is significant in the post-global financial crisis period, when slower growth of the NAFTA and the European Union regions has implied falling demand for final goods and China, in a process of its own growth reorientation may not be able to be the substitute market in place of the contracting advanced markets.

6. Mega Regional Trade Agreements in Asia

In the regional context, the evolving mega regional trade agreements like the Regional Comprehensive Economic Partnership (RCEP) and TPP reflect an important development, while presenting the region with some beneficial alternatives pose some difficult challenges as well.[17] The RCEP is a regional comprehensive economic partnership agreement among the 16 members of the East Asia Summit (EAS) that includes the 10 ASEAN countries and its FTA partners, namely, China, Japan, Republic of Korea, Australia, New Zealand, and India. RCEP was launched in November 2012 and is expected to conclude by 2016. The RCEP is a comprehensive agreement aimed at deeper integration inclusive of goods, services and investment liberalization. The TPP, a US-led[18] initiative includes some of the ASEAN countries, namely, Vietnam, Malaysia and Singapore as members. The initiative, now in its final rounds of negotiations, is aimed at achieving WTO plus provisions in areas like goods, services, investment, IPR, competition, SPS, TBT, dispute resolution, trade remedies, customs procedures and government procurement, labour standards, environment, e-commerce, telecom and financial services.

Even though common membership between the RCEP and the TPP suggests competition, this would only be limited given the huge differences in the agenda of the two agreements. The RCEP is accommodative of development differentials among member nations and allows for step by step liberalization and open accession

---

[15] The list is comprehensive in that it covers the entire spectrum of manufacturing trade.

[16] It may be noted that the index of supply chain connectivity for India has improved, though not very significantly, between the years 2006 and 2012. Refer ISCC Database, ARTNeT, UNESCAP.

[17] The Trans-Atlantic Trade and Investment Partnership (TTIP), launched in 2013 between the United States and the European Union aims at trade liberalization and behind the border and other non-tariff barriers elimination with a 'high standard' compatibility in trade governance. The agreement will have likely implications for Asia given its membership and trade coverage. However as the ASEAN or India are not members, the agreement is not included in the discussion in this section.

[18] The TPP that began as a four-member FTA with Brunei, Chile, New Zealand and Singapore now includes eight more countries, namely, the United States, Australia, Canada, Japan, Malaysia, Mexico, Peru and Vietnam.

according to the level of preparation. The TPP is an agreement among relatively more open and like-minded economies with a far more ambitious agenda beyond liberalization to include regulatory compatibility, facilitating investment and foster a business climate. Notwithstanding the differences, the spill-over effects of the TPP on the RCEP will be evident in terms of the higher standards that may be followed and expected by the common members. While not necessarily a hindrance, this would require an accelerated pace of economic liberalization from the non-TPP members of the RCEP like India.[19] The TPP could, in fact, be the push factor for the region to bring the RCEP to an early conclusion. At present, centred around the ASEAN, the success of the RCEP is to a large extent a function of the credibility of the ASEAN objective of creating an integrated economic community by 2015 and the reconciliation among its FTAs with the other RCEP members. While the former involves further liberalization in the services and FDI sectors alongside overcoming the internal development differentials among ASEAN member nations, the latter demands grappling with the not so easy task of overlapping rules and differential rates and timing of tariff elimination of the 'plus one' FTAs. A big challenge for the TPP though would be the extent to which member states' interest in aligning with slow growing US economy is sustainable.

Petri et al. (2011) have presented estimates of benefits generated by the competitive tracks of mega regional agreements, namely, the TPP and an 'Asian track' over the period 2010 to 2025 by conducting simulations using a CGE model. India is not considered a member of the Asian track. Initial welfare gains for the world economy are predicted to be small and are expected to increase substantially over time. For TPP, gains of small economies like Vietnam, Malaysia and New Zealand are closer to one per cent of GDP. The Asian track implies major gains for China, Japan and Korea and at a later stage for other members. With respect to trade the TPP will have only half as large an effect as the Asian track owing to lower initial tariffs. Economies that are members of both agreements are the biggest winners and capture 14 per cent of trade gains as against the 6 per cent that others do. The extent of trade diversion is maximum for China under TPP and close to 1/4th per cent of GDP for India. Trade creation gains are larger than trade diversion losses for both TPP and Asian track. Petri et al. (2010) also have used a CGE model to estimate the benefits of AEC+ formations, indicating these to benefit bilateral partners like India.

Using a global gravity model,[20] we undertake an estimation of the trade effects of the ASEAN–India FTA, RCEP and TPP. The gravity model is estimated with log exports as the dependent variable with traditional independent variables that include country pair GDP, distance and dummy variables for contiguity, common language and colonial linkages. The model is further augmented with binary dummy variables to estimate trade creation and trade diversion effects of the mega regional agreements. Estimation is undertaken for the year 2011.[21] Interestingly, our results show the mega regional agreements to be trade creating for members as well as stimulating trade with non-members. The potential trade creation effects appear to be larger in case of the RCEP relative to the TPP, possibly on account of the relatively lower scope for tariff reduction in the case of the latter.

Baldwin (2014) has indicated that the discriminatory impact of tariff cuts will be small as the tariffs among member nations are already low. The higher tariffs for these countries cover areas where trade is only modest and political compulsions may not allow any significant reduction in these specific areas, for example, tariffs on Japanese rice or US dairy products. In the non-tariff areas like telecom, IPR rule setting by the TPP or TTIP may actually resemble unilateral liberalization making discrimination difficult. However, for the developing Asian nations, single standards may allow access to a larger set of countries and spill-over benefits of trade creation,[22] though less than that for member nations, it would call for undertaking prior costs to adhere to these standards. Many in Asia may not have the resources to undertake costly reforms in the near term making it necessary, therefore, that the RCEP negotiations be accelerated towards formulating 'suitable to Asia' market access rules.

---

[19] The other challenge would be in terms of competition through preferential access to China under the RCEP, a prospect that India has otherwise resisted.

[20] The gravity model database is provided by the ARTNeT, UNESCAP.

[21] Latest year for which data for all variables is available. Also, RCEP discussions had begun by 2011 and AIFTA was well into implementation with respect to NT-1.

[22] Or, what may otherwise be referred to as minimum trade diversion.

7. Conclusions and Policy Recommendations

In this chapter, the ASEAN–India bilateral trends in trade have been analyzed at four reference time points, that is, 2009, the year immediately preceding the FTA, 2013 to observe the consequences of completion of first phase of FTA implementation, and 2000 and 2005 for a relatively longer comparative perspective prior to the FTA. Our results show that the AIFTA does not appear to have resulted in any distinct break in the trade trends in the previous decade. Exports and imports have registered a consistent increase in volume over the last decade. Trade continues to be in favour of ASEAN. The share of ASEAN in India's total trade has been close to 10 per cent through the last decade. The implementation of the AIFTA in 2010 has not altered ASEAN's ranking among the regions that India trades with. ASEAN member countries that show an increase in India's share in their exports relative to the pre-FTA shares include Lao PDR, Malaysia, Thailand and Vietnam. The AIFTA is yet to make a positive impact on trade intensity among member countries, and in fact leads to a decline in intra-regional trade bias.

New commodity exports since the AIFTA implementation contribute 27 per cent of total export share in 2013–14 and some of these commodities (with almost 7 per cent of the total) did not have an initial revealed comparative advantage in 2009. Gains for this set of commodities spread across various sectors, could therefore be entirely or largely on account of the FTA preferences. The import patterns reflect the realization of *a priori* fears with respect to special products as the set of new imports since the AIFTA implementation includes the commodity HS-090411, that is, pepper neither crushed nor ground, which is classified as a special product under the AIFTA and has undergone a gradual cut in tariffs to 60 in 2014 from a base rate of 70 per cent. Commodities like HS-090111 (coffee neither roasted nor decaffeinated), and HS-151190 (refined palm oil and its fractions), both classified as special products under the AIFTA and HS-850440 (static converters) of the sensitive track have registered a double digit growth since the AIFTA implementation.

Trade patterns show a very small share of component trade, and hence, do not seem to reflect India's integration in regional supply chains in any significant manner, in a very short run, despite the AIFTA.[23] While India could be emerging as the alternative market for ASEAN, particularly in the post-global financial crisis scenario, it would also need to upgrade its manufacturing abilities and participate in regional production networks as these constitute an integral component of intra-Southeast Asian trade.

Finally, given the reality of mega-regional agreements in Asia, both ASEAN and India will have to accelerate the pace of their economic reform processes in order to participate in and benefit from their trade creation possibilities. For ASEAN, this would entail consolidation of the ASEAN Economic Community by the target date of 2015 and ensure thereby a stable centre for the RCEP. India will also have to undertake major reforms so as to overcome competitive pressures from China, a country with which India has resisted a formal trade agreement so far, as also from members common to the RCEP and the more advanced TPP.

7.1 Recommendations

While to a small extent AIFTA preferences may have some importance. Efforts should, therefore, be made to enhance harmonization of customs procedures and other trade facilitation (TF) measures that will impact positively on intra regional trade. At present, TF measures in AIFTA lack specificity. Targets should be set in this respect and periodically monitored.

Schemes for enhancement of productivity and competitiveness of plantation crops need to be implemented to reduce future losses for these products as they undergo further duty reductions under the AIFTA.

There is need for research and policy focus on ways and means for advancing India's participation and integration in regional production networks. Policy measures in the direction of developing manufacturing sector competitiveness supplemented with further liberalization of trade and investment climate and developing necessary infrastructure and trade logistics need to be formulated.

If RCEP, as envisioned, is finalized by 2015, it will, in all likelihood, imply higher levels of tariff elimination and NTBs. Lessons from AIFTA should be used as inputs into prior preparation for the RCEP in terms of identification of sensitive commodities as also NTMs with barrier effects.

---

[23] The caveat is that the analysis of post-FTA data has not been done. This study is based on the transition period.

Finally, while AIFTA may has accorded India a legitimate space in the evolving Asian regional architecture along with the other 'ASEAN plus one' FTA signatories, it is important that FTAs be carefully designed for deriving economic benefits. Both, *ex ante* evaluation of comparative advantages and periodic monitoring of progress and sector-wise impact studies will go a long way towards making FTAs useful economic instruments.

APPENDIX

TABLE A2.1
Sectors among Top 20 Exports Sectors with >10% CAGR since 2009–10

HS Code	Description
27	mineral fuels, mineral oils and products of their distillation; bituminous substances; mineral waxes
2	meat and edible meat offal
29	organic chemicals
84	nuclear reactors, boilers, machinery and mechanical appliances; parts thereof
71	natural or cultured pearls, precious or semiprecious stones, precious metals, clad with precious metal and articles thereof; imitation jewellery; coin
72	iron and steel
10	cereals
87	vehicles other than railway or tramway rolling stock, and parts and accessories thereof
52	cotton
30	pharmaceutical products
12	oil seeds and olea; fruits; misc. grains, seeds and fruit; industrial or medicinal plants; straw and fodder
39	plastic and articles thereof
73	articles of iron or steel

Source: Export–Import Databank, Ministry of Commerce and Industry, Government of India.

TABLE A2.2
New Export Commodities in 2013–14 Relative to 2009–10

HS Code	Description
20629	other edible offal of bovine animals, frozen
30389	other frozen fish incl hilsa, dara, seer, pomfret
30617	other shrimps and prawns: frozen
30741	cutle fish and squid live fresh/chilled
30749	cuttle fish and squids excl live fresh/chilled
40210	milk and cream in powder, grnls or other solid forms containing fat not exceeding 1.5% by wt
90421	fruits of the genus capsicum or of the genus pimenta: dried, neither crushed nor ground
90422	fruits of the genus capsicum-crushed or ground
90931	seeds of cumin: neither crushed nor ground
100199	other wheat and meslin
120242	groundnut, not roasted or otherwise cooked, whether or not shelled or broken-in shelled whether or not broken
210111	extracts essences and concentrates of coffee
230990	other preparations of a kind used in animal feeding
271012	light oils and preparations
271320	petroleum bitumen
290919	other acyclic ethers and thr halogenated, sulphanated nitrated or nitrosated derivatives
293499	other heterocyclic compounds
410719	other whole hides/skins
481159	other paper and paperboard cotd impregnated covered with plastics (excl. adhesives)
520524	single yarn of combined fibres measuring=125 dctx(>52 but <=80 mtrc no)
540233	textured yarn of polyesters
551511	fabrics of polyester stpl fibers, mixed mainly or solely with viscose rayon staple fibers
560749	other cordge etc. of polyethilene/polypropylene
630510	sacks and bags for packing, made of jute or of other textile based fibres of hide no.5303
720810	flat-rolled products in coils not further worked than hot-rolled with pattern in relief
720839	flat-rolled products in coils of thickness of
720918	flat-rolled products in coils not further worked than cold-rolled (cold reduced) of thickness

(Table A2.2 continued)

(*Table A2.2 continued*)

HS Code	Description
721914	flat-rolled products in coils of thickness
730820	towers and lattice masts
750210	nickel, not alloyed
750512	bars, rods and profiles of nickel alloys
800110	tin not alloyed
841480	other pumps, compressors etc.
842139	other filtering/purifying machinery and parts for gas
848710	ships or boats propellers and blades therefor
851770	parts
870190	other tractors
871000	tanks and other armored fighting vehicles, motors, fitted with weapons and parts of such vehicles
880240	aeroplanes and other aircraft, of an unladen weight exceeding 15,000 kg
890120	tankers
890510	dredgers
902214	other, for medical, surgical or veterinary uses :

Source: Export–Import Databank, Ministry of Commerce and Industry, Government of India.

TABLE A2.3
Commodity Exports in 2013–14 with >10% CAGR since 2009–10

HS Code	Description
20230	boneless
70310	onions and shallots fresh or chilled
100590	other maize (corn)
100630	semi/wholly miled rice w/n polished/glazed
120740	seasamum seeds w/n broken
230649	other residues of rape or colza seeds
230690	oil cake and other residues resulting from extraction of other oil-seed and olegnsfruts
271019	other petroleum oils and oils obtained from bituminous minerals etc.
290124	unstrd buts-1 3-diene and isoprene
290220	benzene
290243	polxylene
300410	mdcmntscntngpencllns/drvtvsthrofwth a pencllnc acid strctr/strptmycns or thrdervtvs put up for rtl sale
300420	medicaments containing other antibiotics and put up for retail sale
300490	other medicine put up for retail sale
320416	reactive dyes and preparations based thereon
320417	pigments and preptens based thereon
390210	polypropylene
401120	new tyres used on buses/lorries
410799	other/hides/skins including sides
482390	other articles of paper pulp paperboard cellulose wading or webs of cell fibres
520100	cotton, not carded or combed
520523	single yarn of combined fibres measuring < 232.56 but >=192.31 dctx(>43 but <=52 mtrc no)
540710	woven fabrics obtained from high tenacity yarn of nylon or other polyamides, or of polyesters
710239	others
711319	articles of other process materials w/n pltd or clad
720230	ferro-silico-manganese
720719	other products contng by wt
721049	other products of iron/non-alloy steel otherwise pltd/cotd wth zinc
840710	air-craft engines
843149	other machine parts of hdg no. 8426,8430/8439
848180	other appliances :
870321	vehicle with spark-ignition internal combustion reciprocating piston engine of cylinder capacity <=1000cc
870322	vehicle with spark-ignition internal combustion reciprocating piston engine of cylinder capacity >1000cc but not >1500cc
870899	other parts of vehicles of hdg 8701-8705
871120	motor cycle etc. with reciprocating piston engine of cylinder capacity >50 cc to 250 cc
880330	other parts of aeroplanes or helicopters
890690	other under hdng 8906

Source: Export–Import Databank, Ministry of Commerce and Industry, Government of India

30 ASEAN–India Development and Cooperation Report 2015

TABLE A2.4
New Import Commodities in 2013–14 since 2009–10

HS Code	Commodity Description
71360	pigeon peas (cajanus cajan)
90411	*pepper neither crushed nor ground*
230990	other preparations of a kind used in animal feeding
270112	bitumns coal w/n pulverized but not aglomerated
271012	light oils and preparations
280470	phosphorus
283650	calcium carbonate
290516	satrtdoctnl (octyl alchl)and ismrs thereof
290531	ethylene glycol (ethanediol)
300220	vaccines for human medicine
382370	industrial fatty alcohol
390190	othrpolymersofethyline in primary forms
390230	propylene copolymers
390421	other polyvinyl chloride non-plasticized
390799	other polyesters (saturated)
400219	other styrene-butadiene rubber carboxlated styrene-butadiene rubr(xsbr)
401110	new pnmtc tyres of a knd used on motor cars(incl station wagons and racing cars
710231	non-industrial diamonds unworked/simply sawn cleaved or bruted
711319	artcls of othr prcs mtl w/n pltd or clad
732690	other articles of heading 7326
740819	other wire of refined copper
741110	tubes and pipes of refined copper
750210	nickel, not alloyed
840991	parts suitable for use solely/principle with spark-ignition internal combustion piston engines other than parts for aircraft engine
841490	parts of air/vacuum pumps, compressors and fans
850780	other accumulators
852580	television cameras, digital cameras and video camera recorders:
852871	not designed to incorporate a video display or screen
854140	photosensitive semicndctr devices, semiconductor devices, inc photovoltaic cells when assembled in modules/ made up into panels; light emitting dio
870840	gear boxes
880240	aeroplanes and other aircraft, of an unladen weight exceeding 15,000 kg

Source: Export–Import Databank, Ministry of Commerce and Industry, Government of India.
Note: Italics: special products.

TABLE A2.5
Import Commodities with >10% CAGR since 2010

HS Code	Commodity Description
90111	*coffee neither roasted nor decaffeinated*
151190	*refined palm oil and its fractions*
270119	other coal
290230	toluene
290250	styrene
290711	phenol (hydroxybenzene) and its salts
291532	vinyl acetate
291612	esters of acrylic acid
291614	esters of methacrylic acid
291736	terephthalic acid and its salts
310210	urea whether or not in aqueous solution
382490	chemical products
390110	polyethylene having a specific gravity below 0.94
390720	other polyethers
390740	polycarbonates

(Table A2.5 continued)

(*Table A2.5 continued*)

HS Code	Commodity Description
400121	natural rubber in smoked sheets
400122	technically specified natural rubber (tsnr)
440341	dark red/light red meranti and meranti bakau
440399	other wood in rough
470329	bleached or semi-bleached non-coniferous chemical wood pulp sulphate
710239	others
720421	waste and scraps of stainless steel
760120	aluminium alloys
800110	tin not alloyed
841480	other pumps, compressors, etc.
841510	window/wall types self-contained air conditioning machines
841590	parts of the air conditioning machines etc.
847130	portable digital automatic data processing machines,weighing
847150	digital proccessing units excluding of sub hdngs 847141 and 847149,wh/not cont one/two types of unit,like storage/input/output units
847170	storage units
850440	*static converters*
851712	telephones for cellular networks or for other wireless networks
851762	machines for the reception, conversion and transmission or regeneration of voice, images or other data, including switches
851770	parts
852872	other, colour
852990	othe parts of hdg 8525 to 8528
854231	processors and controllers, whether or not combined with memories, converters, logic circuits, amplifiers, clock
854239	other
890520	floating/submersible drilling/production platforms
980100	project goods
999300	*special transactions and commodities not classified according to kind

Source: Export–Import Databank, Ministry of Commerce and Industry, Government of India.
Note: Italics: special products and Bold and italics: sensitive sectors.

3
Services Trade Patterns and Key Policies

Trade in services has gained more importance in recent years as advances in technology have resulted in new means of providing services across borders. While there is little doubt that services trade is an essential ingredient to economic growth and sustainable development, it is widely accepted that it can only make such positive contribution if appropriately liberalized and implemented across countries.

Services have become an important component of the global economy where the growth of services trade in many countries across the world has outpaced the merchandise trade. ASEAN and India are no exception. The services sector has already become an important source of both output and employment in ASEAN and India. While India and some of the ASEAN member countries are services-driven, a large part of ASEAN has an equally fast growing manufacturing sector. The structural asymmetries in production and trade may tend to suggest that the opportunities for two-way services exports among ASEAN countries and with India in particular are substantial. Nevertheless, an efficient services sector is not only crucial for the performance of the ASEAN economies but also critical to its competitiveness.

ASEAN has been negotiating the ASEAN Framework Agreement on Services (AFAS) and has undertaken a series of reforms to facilitate services trade flow in the region. India, on the other hand, has been driving the South Asia Agreement on Trade in Services (SATIS). While ASEAN and India have complementarities in services trade, deeper cooperation in services trade would eventually strengthen the regional integration in services. In this chapter, we analyze the services trade patterns in India and ASEAN and discuss the key policies in order to strengthen the services trade flow between them.

1. TRENDS IN SERVICES TRADE

Over the last two decades world exports in services has registered remarkable growth. Services trade volume has increased from less than US$ 1 trillion in 1990 to over US$ 4.5 trillion in 2012 (see Table 3.1). ASEAN as a region, however, registered a relatively modest increase in services exports over the same period, and currently stands at US$ 281 billion (see Figure 3.1). Today, India contributes to 3 per cent in world services export, increased from about 1 per cent in 2000 (see Table 3.1). ASEAN, on the other hand, shares 6 and 7 per cent of world services export and import, respectively. Several services sectors export from ASEAN and India faced deceleration during 2008 global financial crisis. Recovery in the initial years after the financial crisis was rather slow, but improved 2012 onwards.

TABLE 3.1
Services Trade Volume and Share
(Volume in US$ billion and share in %)

	Value	Share*	Value	Share*	Value	Share*	Value	Share*	Value	Share*
	2000		2009		2010		2011		2012	
Services Export										
World	1521.35		3547.68		3891.66		4364.41		4458.62	
ASEAN	68.92	4.53	167.35	4.72	202.39	5.20	237.77	5.45	255.63	5.73
India	16.69	1.10	92.54	2.61	116.95	3.01	138.75	3.18	146.44	3.28
Services Import										
World	1519.39		3420.68		3741.05		4177.65		4279.61	
ASEAN	87.92	5.79	189.71	5.55	226.09	6.04	264.96	6.34	278.79	6.51
India	19.19	1.26	80.15	2.34	114.46	3.06	124.73	2.99	128.84	3.01

Source: Calculated based on UNCTAD Stat.
Note: *Share in world.

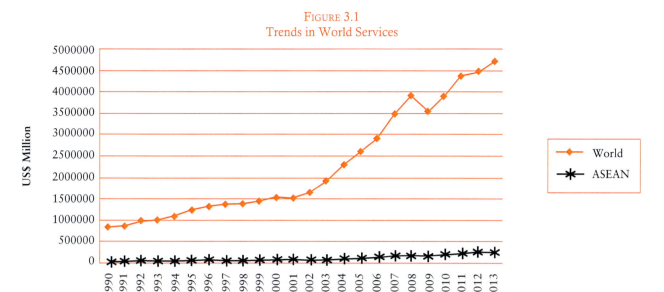

FIGURE 3.1
Trends in World Services

Source: UNCTAD, Geneva.

Singapore occupies the top position in services exports, followed by Thailand, Malaysia, Indonesia, and the Philippines (see Figure 3.2). India is also a leading services exporter in the world.[1] However, not all services trade in India and ASEAN are globally competitive. While Singapore is one of the best performing countries in the services trade, particularly in maritime services, Myanmar, a country that has started reforming only few years back, has almost all tradable services uncompetitive. Overtime, India has become a leading services exporter and has been successful in internationalizing its services, such as information and communication technology (ICT), professional services, among others. In India, software services alone contribute to 45.8 per cent share in total services export in 2013-14, but only grew by 5.4 per cent (GoI 2014).

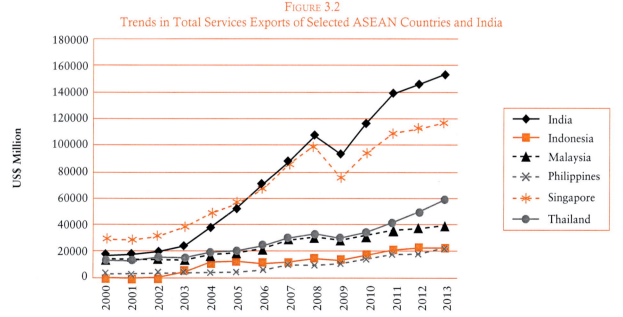

FIGURE 3.2
Trends in Total Services Exports of Selected ASEAN Countries and India

Source: UNCTAD, Geneva.

---

[1] In commercial services trade, India was the sixth largest exporter with 3.4 per cent share of world exports and seventh largest importer with 3 per cent share of world imports in 2012 (GoI 2014).

The services sector's expansion has been attributed to demand as well as supply factors. On the one hand, demand for many services is highly income elastic, that is, as people grow richer, their consumption of services such as tourism, education and health expands more rapidly than their demand for manufactures and agricultural products. The leading role of services sector in the economic output, and growth of services trade exceeding merchandise trade, point towards the emerging potential of trade in services between ASEAN and India.

We investigate the possible contribution of key services sectors towards growth in exports of services for these economies — Indonesia, Malaysia, the Philippines, Singapore and Thailand (ASEAN 5) and India during 2000–2013 and compare those with the growth in exports of similar services overall. We note that for ASEAN 5 the strongest growth in exports was registered for personal, cultural and recreational services (nearly 24 per cent CAGR), followed by computer and information services (20 per cent CAGR), construction (15 per cent CAGR) and travel (13 per cent CAGR).[2] The world however, registered strongest export growth in computer and information services over the same period (15 per cent). Similar to ASEAN 5, India too registered strongest growth in personal, cultural and recreational services, followed by computer and information services. We compound annual growth rates (CAGR) for services exports for ASEAN 5, India and the world in Table 3.2. We also present export growth for the aforementioned services for the ASEAN 5 economies and India, juxtaposed against world trends, in Figure A2.1.

2. COMPARATIVE ADVANTAGE IN SERVICES TRADE

To understand the pattern of services trade specialization in selected ASEAN countries and India, we attempt to measure the comparative advantage through the Revealed Comparative Advantage (RCA) index following Balassa (1965).[3] Table 3.3 shows the estimated RCA scores for Indonesia, Malaysia, the Philippines and

TABLE 3.2
CAGR for Exports in Services, 2000–2013

Category	CAGR (%)	Category	CAGR (%)
Communications		*Computer and Information*	
ASEAN 5	0.09	ASEAN 5	0.20
India	0.10	India	0.22
World	0.10	World	0.15
Construction		*Transport*	
ASEAN 5	0.15	ASEAN 5	0.09
India	0.07	India	0.18
World	0.10	World	0.08
Personal, Cultural, and Recreational Services		*Other Business Services*	
ASEAN 5	0.24	ASEAN 5	0.11
India*	0.43	India*	0.17
World	0.08	World	0.11
Travel			
ASEAN 5	0.13		
India	0.14		
World	0.07		

Source: Calculated based on UNCTAD Stat, UNCTAD.
Note: *Only for 2004–13.

---

[2] Data sourced from BOPS, IMF.

[3] The RCA index is defined as the ratio of two shares. The numerator is the share of a country's total exports of the commodity of interest in its total exports. The denominator is the share of world exports of the same commodity in total world exports. RCA index takes a value between 0 and $+\infty$. A country is said to have RCA in that commodity if the value of the RCA index exceeds unity. The mathematical expression is as follows: $(\Sigma_d x_{isd} / \Sigma_d X_{sd})/(\Sigma_{wd} x_{iwd}/\Sigma_{wd} X_{wd})$, where s is the country of interest, d and w are the set of all countries in the world, is the sector/category of interest, x is the commodity export flow and X is the total export flow. The numerator is the share of good i in the exports of country s, while the denominator is the share of good i in the exports of the world. We draw our data from the UNCTAD database titled 'Value,

TABLE 3.3
Revealed Comparative Advantage (RCA) for Selected Countries and Sectors

Sector	2009	2010	2011	2012	2013
India					
Transport	0.61	0.54	0.63	0.60	0.59
Travel	0.49	0.51	0.53	0.50	0.48
Communications	0.80	0.53	0.49	0.45	0.55
Construction	0.28	0.18	0.25	0.26	0.35
Computer and information	6.53	6.12	5.76	5.70	5.50
Other business services	1.17	1.17	1.29	1.21	1.14
Personal, cultural and recreational services	0.60	0.33	0.28	0.59	0.87
Indonesia					
Transport	0.95	0.76	0.83	0.83	0.83
Travel	1.73	1.70	1.59	1.46	1.66
Communications	2.97	2.68	2.87	1.88	1.53
Construction	1.44	1.22	1.09	1.56	1.70
Computer and information	0.18	0.12	0.18	0.15	0.15
Other business services	0.76	1.02	1.08	1.29	1.30
Personal, cultural and recreational services	0.73	0.74	0.87	1.02	0.94
Malaysia					
Transport	0.78	0.74	0.70	0.59	0.60
Travel	2.23	2.34	2.26	2.18	2.13
Communications	0.74	0.87	0.74	0.88	0.85
Construction	1.03	1.28	1.26	1.45	1.28
Computer and information	0.94	0.83	0.87	0.89	0.83
Other business services	0.58	0.61	0.70	0.79	0.75
Personal, cultural and recreational services	2.87	0.41	0.50	0.52	0.58
The Philippines					
Transport	0.54	0.46	0.42	0.43	0.36
Travel	0.86	0.77	0.74	0.88	0.86
Communications	1.22	0.86	0.91	1.05	0.96
Construction	0.23	0.34	0.11	0.25	0.21
Computer and information	2.97	2.51	2.36	1.86	1.60
Other business services	1.87	2.14	2.19	2.09	1.70
Personal, cultural and recreational services	0.39	0.34	0.38	0.48	0.54
Thailand					
Transport	0.96	0.83	0.69	0.60	0.54
Travel	2.16	2.40	2.69	2.76	2.86
Communications	0.53	0.53	0.50	0.36	0.36
Construction	0.51	0.54	0.44	0.37	0.63
Computer and information	0.01	0.01	0.02	0.01	0.00
Other business services	0.90	0.76	0.61	0.59	0.49
Personal, cultural and recreational services	0.33	0.42	0.25	0.19	0.15

Source: Calculated based on UNCTAD Stat.

Thailand along with that of India for services categories including transport, travel (including tourism), communication, construction, computer and information, other business services, and personal, cultural and recreational services.

From observing Table 3.3, it is easy to deduce certain obvious patterns of services trade specialization for the countries being studied here. Starting with India, the RCA scores for two of its services sectors (from our present selection), namely, computer and information and other business services, have been greater than one for all

shares and growth of services exports and imports by service-category, annual, 1980–2013'. Accordingly, the statistics used correspond to the concepts and definitions from the IMF Balance of Payments Manual, fifth edition (BPM5, 1993). UNCTAD states that for those countries and territories who present their figures according to the Sixth edition of the Manual (BPM6, 2009), data were adjusted to fit the BPM5 concepts.

five years between 2009 and 2013. Significantly, computer and information has the RCA scores that are more than any category of service for any of the countries being discussed. This suggests India's leading position with respect to computer and information services and its potential for trade in services in this particular category. As per definition, this category includes hardware and software-related services and data-processing. The other segment of services in which India registers a revealed comparative advantage is other business services. However, this is a very broad category that covers diverse activities like merchant and trade-related services, operational leasing services, and miscellaneous business, professional and technical services (such as legal, advertising, consulting, accounting, R&D and others). Hence, the potential for trade in services for subcategories cannot be readily ascertained and policy recommendations based on such estimates may not be possible.

Similarly, for Indonesia, three services categories have scored the RCA greater than one for all five years, namely, travel, communications and construction. Communication services include postal, courier and telecommunications services between residents and non-residents. Indonesia also shows increasing competitiveness in other business services category (RCA>1 for the last four years since 2010). Given that both communications and other business services encompass diverse sub-categories, the extent of trade liberalization undertaken for each of these sub-categories holds key to assessing trade competitiveness based on RCA scores. We discuss various facets of trade liberalization under multilateral trading arrangements, such as the WTO and ASEAN, for some of these economies in the following sections. In the case of Malaysia, travel and construction have demonstrated trade competitiveness for the period under consideration based on the RCA scores. Much like India, the Philippines also seems to be competitive in computer and information and other business services. However, relevant subcategories may not show convergence in this regard, and hence, suggest scope for further disaggregated analysis. Thailand demonstrates comparative advantage (RCA>1) only for travel.

3. General Agreement on Trade in Services (GATS) Commitments — India, Malaysia, Thailand and Indonesia: A Comparative Analysis

India and ASEAN member countries like Singapore, Malaysia, Thailand, the Philippines and Indonesia have large services sectors. Singapore is a high income economy with veritable strengths in the service sector. While we study ASEAN–India services trade, we choose to limit our discussion of Singapore on the grounds of disproportionate sector specific strengths controlling for size and concentration of resources. Instead, we focus on other emerging markets of the ASEAN community that provide potential trading opportunities in services based on complementarities and comparative advantage. In general, according to the World Bank's Services Trade Restrictiveness Index (STRI), some ASEAN countries and India are very restrictive under Mode 4 of services trade but having variations in Mode 1 and Mode 3 (Table 3.4).

In the group, India is most restrictive and Cambodia is least restrictive in STRI. Therefore, we go into details of GATS commitments by India, Malaysia, Thailand and Indonesia to ascertain the barriers to services trade. As India has signed India–ASEAN Services Trade Agreement recently, which was held up due to technical issues concerning certain subsectors, the already concluded India–Malaysia CECA provides a window for understanding the extent of mutual agreements possible in services between India and ASEAN and the nature of

Table 3.4
Services Trade Restrictiveness Index (STRI)

Country	Overall	Mode 1	Mode 3	Mode 4
Cambodia	23.70	42.95	18.73	75.00
Indonesia	50.00	11.22	56.47	70.00
Malaysia	46.10	32.49	46.52	90.00
The Philippines	53.50	27.56	57.59	80.00
Thailand	48.00	65.99	44.03	100.00
Vietnam	41.50	23.16	38.43	60.00
India	65.70	70.75	69.34	70.00

Source: World Bank STRI Database.

---

[4] We do not, however, cover India–Singapore CECA.

commitments made so far.[4] We begin with the GATS commitments. While horizontal commitments indicate a country's overall posture towards trade in services, our choice of sectors and sub-sectors is largely directed by our estimation of revealed comparative advantage for these economies. We believe an assessment of current GATS commitments would help us understand the nature of existing trade barriers. We specifically focus on market access commitments under Mode 3 of services trade, which suggests the commercial presence of foreign suppliers and the extent to which this is allowed indicates relative 'openness' of a specific sector for a particular country. Mode 3 encompasses opportunities for foreign suppliers of services to establish, operate or expand a commercial presence in the form of a branch, agency or wholly-owned subsidiary. Mode 3 is, therefore, the principal mode for entry into domestic markets by foreign suppliers and inevitably attracts restrictions of varying degrees imposed by national governments. We also look into national treatment obligations in some sectors. For easier comprehension, we supplement this section with Table 3.5 illustrating market access commitments (under GATS) in Mode 3 and Mode 4.

Even as India has promoted liberalization of its services in many areas, it has been by and large cautious about its Mode 3 and Mode 4 commitments at the WTO. Exceptions are made only for categories of business visitors (managers, executives and specialists) and professionals, who are granted entry for temporary stay for a period ranging from 90 days to five years depending on the category. However, in so far as Mode 3 is concerned, India in its horizontal commitments has assured a limitation on national treatment in order to facilitate preferential access to foreign services suppliers, who offer the best terms for transfer of technology in case of collaboration with public sector enterprises (PSEs) or government undertakings.

Under the WTO, India's requests profile gives a glimpse into India's core interests. At the same time, requests received by India tell us about barriers to service trade faced by other countries in India. The Government of India's Ministry of Commerce gives a brief profile of such requests. India has been asked to take commitments with regard to transparency in domestic regulations, simplify procedures, eliminate differential treatment of foreign suppliers of services and facilitate the movement of natural persons under the Mode 4. The categories of professionals on which commitments have been sought include intra-corporate transferees, contractual service suppliers and specialists (tradespersons, associate professionals, professionals and managers).

At the same time, India has made request to others to take full commitments with respect to the category of independent professionals, de-linked from commercial presence. India has also sought a liberalized visa system from other countries to ensure the fulfillment of horizontal and sectoral commitments undertaken like multiple entry visas for professionals and allow inter-firm mobility to professionals. It is well known that India's longstanding interests are in Mode 4 (cross-border mobility of its large number of highly skilled individuals). However, India, at present, has a growing interest in Mode 3 in areas related to computer, professional, health and tourism services.

3.1 Professional Services

The key professional services areas as per Central Product Classification (CPC) include legal, accounting, architectural services, engineering services, integrated engineering services, urban planning and medical services. India has so far committed to engineering services, integrated engineering services, medical services and architectural services. Sub-sector specific commitments are broadly in line with India's horizontal commitments. While Modes 1 and 2 are not restricted for most subcategories, Mode 3 has seen partial opening up and India has so far strongly reserved its commitments under Mode 4. In professional services, Mode 3 restrictions have been partially modified in the case of services such as engineering, integrated engineering, medical, and architectural, where it is required that foreign service providers can only enter through an Indian collaboration upon approval by FIPB. Under Mode 4, work permits are allowed only for senior management staff, specialists and business visitors.

In case of Malaysia, horizontal commitments refer only to Mode 4, where it has no commitments either for MA or NT, except for categories like senior management, specialists and business visitors. If we go into the sub sector specific commitments, it is apparent that Malaysia has stricter restrictions than India. Mode 3 can only be supplied by natural persons (market access limitation) for most professional services including engineering services, architectural services and medical services. Only in the integrated engineering services are locally incorporated joint ventures allowed.

Thailand's horizontal market access commitments for Mode 3 allow for limited liability company, registered in Thailand, wherein equity participation can go up to 49 per cent of foreign registered capital, and the number

TABLE 3.5
Market Access Commitments (under GATS) in Mode 3 and Mode 4

	Market Access							
	India		Malaysia		Thailand		Indonesia	
GATS	Mode 3	Mode 4	Mode 3	Mode 4	Mode 3	Mode 4	Mode 3	Mode 4
Accounting	Unbound	Temporary business visits	Partial (30%)	Unbound	Partial (49%)	Unbound		
Architectural	None		Natural person	Unbound	Partial (49%)	Unbound	JVs allowed conditions apply	Unbound
Engineering	None		Natural person	Unbound	Partial (49%)	Unbound		
Integrated engineering	None		Partial (30%)	Unbound				
Legal			Natural person	Unbound	Partial (49%)	Unbound		
Medical	Partial (74%)	Temporary business visits	Natural person	Unbound				
Computer and related services	None		Partial (30%)	Unbound	Partial (49%)	Unbound		Technical experts
Telecom	Full conditional upon licenses		Partial (30%)	Unbound		Unbound	Partial (35%)	Limited no. of technical experts
Financial services	Partial (26% for insurance; 49% in banking)		Insurance (Partial 30%)	Unbound	Partial (25%)	Partial		Technical advisor/ expert
Higher education	None				Partial (49%)	Unbound		
health care	Partial (74%)		Partial (30%)	Unbound				
Tourism	Full (100%)	Temporary business visits; Foreign language tour guides allowed	Partial (30%)	Unbound	Partial (49%)	Unbound	Partial (100% in selected provinces)	Senior Staff
Audio visual	Partial	Temporary business visits	Partial (30%)	Unbound	Partial (49%)	Unbound		
Construction	None		Partial (30%)	Unbound	Partial (49%)	Unbound		
Transport	None	Air transport: Temporary business visits; Maritime Transport: Unbound; Maritime auxilliary services: None	Maritime (Partial 30%)	Unbound	Maritime (Partial 49%)	Unbound		

Source: Integrated Trade Intelligence Portal (I-TIP) — WTO.

of foreign shareholders must be less than half of the total shareholders of the company. However, NT under Mode 3 Thailand is 'unbound', suggesting that Thailand is free to impose NT barriers. The professional services that are listed for commitment under Mode 3 include legal, architectural and engineering services, where commitments are 'none', suggesting full market access. In sharp contrast, Indonesia, however, is more closed off in terms of service sector commitments. So far, Indonesia has not undertaken any horizontal commitments under GATS. Professional services like engineering, architectural, industrial services are some of the service sectors that have some sort of guidelines for trading opportunities. It is apparent that in these sectors only joint operations through representative office is allowed. Joint ventures when permitted are strictly monitored through domestic regulations.

3.2 Computer and Related Services

As per the revised offers to the WTO in 2005, computer and related services appear to be the most liberalized service sector in India, where India has undertaken full commitments in Modes 1, 2 and 3. In Mode 3, India has offered full market access, except that the establishment would only be through incorporation and there would be no NT discrimination. For Malaysia, in computer and related services, under Mode 3 locally incorporated joint ventures with Malaysian firms are allowed for subcategories like consultancy services and database services. However, there are no market access restrictions for software development services. Thailand, on the other, allows full market access under Mode 3 in computer and related services. National treatment restrictions, however, remain, when equity participation exceeds 49 per cent. In case of Indonesia, the service trade regime appear more restrictive in computer and related services as well, where market access is limited to joint operation only, and even joint ventures are not allowed. It may be noted that Indonesia has not undertaken any commitments in computer and related services under Mode 2 (unbound).

3.3 Telecommunications

In telecommunication-related services, India has allowed market access in Mode 3, wherein foreign equity participation is limited to 49 per cent, conditional upon FIPB approval. However, the number of telecom licenses in general would be predetermined. In the case of Malaysia, foreign equity shareholding under similar conditions is restricted to 30 per cent and such capital can only be invested in companies that have already obtained licenses. In Thailand, market access under Mode 3 is allowed with foreign equity participation up to 40 per cent (and that the service provider has to be a Thai registered company). In Indonesia, the telecom sector is highly protected with domestic companies as sole service providers. However, foreign equity participation can go up to 35 per cent. We may also note that there are scopes of domestic regulations in this sector even under Mode 2. For example, Thailand requires all traffic to be routed through gateways in Thailand. India, however, has unconditional market access in Mode 2 (none) in telecom services.

3.4 Financial Services

Financial services that include both insurance and backing has high market access limitations in all countries under discussion. In India, foreign banks can operate only through wholly-owned subsidiaries (under strict regulations of the Reserve Bank of India [RBI]), while in insurance foreign equity participation is capped at 26 per cent. In the case of Malaysia, banking services by foreign banks is restricted except for Labuan Territory and that such services can be provided through branch level operations of subsidiaries. However, foreign insurance companies can operate through domestic insurance companies and equity shareholding cannot exceed 50 per cent. According to the US Department of State Investment Climate Statements 2012, this equity cap for foreign participation in the insurance sector has been raised to 70 per cent. In sharp contrast to that of India, the banking sector in Malaysia is more liberalized over the insurance sector. In Thailand, foreign equity participation in Mode 3 for both the banking and the insurance sector is limited to 25 per cent. Indonesia is by far the most protected market among the group with respect to financial services, where foreign participation is discouraged in both banking and insurance.

3.5 Education and Health

In educational services, countries are more likely to undertake commitments in the category of higher education services, where services are more of tradable variety with uniform standards. However, Malaysia and Indonesia have not undertaken any commitments in this sector at the WTO. India has allowed market access through Mode 3 in higher educational services, subject to domestic regulations. Thailand has not undertaken any commitment in educational services beyond its horizontal commitments. In hospital services, equity ceiling for foreign participation (joint ventures) remains at 74 per cent in India and 30 per cent in Malaysia. It appears that neither Thailand nor Indonesia have liberalized their hospital services sector for foreign participation.

3.6 Tourism

Tourism is a potential and important service sector in Southeast Asia. India is also among countries that have high stakes in tourism. Malaysia allows joint venture operations with foreign participation in tourism (30 per cent cap on foreign investment). However, certain NT restrictions remain in so far as the Malaysian tourism sector is concerned. Thailand has offered its horizontal commitments in case of tourism as well that allow market access in Mode 3 through limited liability company registered in Thailand (49 per cent cap on foreign investment and the number of foreign shareholders must be less than half of total shareholders of the company). Indonesia, on the other hand, allows 100 per cent capital investments by foreign investors in tourism in selected provinces. However, entry barriers take the form of NT regulations, where foreign investors are required to fulfill norms like higher paid-up capital and that investments may be undertaken in luxury and business categories of hospitality services only. In tourism (Mode 3), India is relatively open with no ceiling on foreign participation (subject to FIPB approval and prior collaboration), while in Mode 4 India has not undertaken any commitment (unbound).

3.7 Audio-Visual Services

In audio–visual services, India has offered commitments in the subcategory of 'motion picture or video distribution services' and allows Mode 3 operations only through branch offices and has a stipulation of limited number of titles per year. For the same subcategory, that is, motion pictures, Malaysia allows foreign participation through locally incorporated joint ventures (aggregate foreign share holding cannot exceed 30 per cent). In the other subcategory covering broadcasting services, Malaysia allows for Mode 1 and Mode 2 services and the market access (MA) stipulations for Mode 1 include 20 per cent of screening time and in some cases dubbing. Mode 3 in this case would be technically infeasible. In the case of Thailand, Mode 3 in audio-visual category (both direct video production and distribution services; and broadcasting services) complies with Thailand's horizontal commitments regime. Indonesia, apparently, does not offer any commitment in the audio-visual category.

3.8 Transport

In transport services, countries are often more willing to engage in trade in services in the maritime transport sector over other sub-sectors like road, rail and air transport. In maritime transport, India favours domestic shipping companies and grants them the first right of refusal. Malaysia allows market access in maritime transport to foreign investors with an equity cap of 30 per cent. However, Thailand is yet to open up its maritime transport sector for foreign investors (unbound). In the case of Indonesia, in this category foreign participation is restricted to owner's representative offices only for port based activities and cargo handling.

3.9 Construction

In construction and related engineering services, India prefers full market access for foreign participants through local incorporation. Nevertheless, as in other sectors, foreign investment in Mode 3 is subject to approval of the foreign investment regulator (FIPB). Malaysia follows its standard norm of 30 per cent cap on foreign shareholding in locally incorporated joint ventures in the construction and related services as well, while Thailand extends its horizontal commitments to the construction sector. The scope of foreign participation in the construction sector in Indonesia is further limited, given that it is only allowed under joint operation through representative offices.

4 Services Trade Commitments under India–Malaysia CECA

The Comprehensive Economic Cooperation Agreement (CECA) was signed by India and Malaysia in 2010 (and came into force on 1 July 2011). On trade in services, this Agreement clearly laid down its objective towards liberalizing and promoting trade in services in accordance with the Article V of the GATS, including mutual recognition of professions. Here, we discuss schedule of specific commitments of India and Malaysia in trade in services. As discussed in the previous section, we emphasize on Mode 3 market access (and Mode 4 commitments, wherever significant). In terms of horizontal commitments, India has assured FDI in services subject to sector specific limits (as per FDI regulations) and has allowed business visitors and intra-corporate transferees (managers) in all sectors. Similarly, Malaysia seeks to carefully monitor mergers and acquisitions although permission in such cases has been assured. Approvals are important for foreign investments of over 30 per cent in shareholding in Malaysian firms.

4.1 Professional Services

(a) Beyond horizontal commitments, in professional services Malaysia has market access commitments in Mode 3 with cap on shareholding of 30 per cent for architectural, engineering, urban planning and landscaping related services. However, India allows greater market access in Mode 3 with equity cap at 51 per cent (implying foreign ownership) for architectural, engineering, integrated engineering, urban planning and landscaping, and medical and paramedical services.

(b) As per horizontal commitments in Mode 4 professional services, India has made a distinction between contractual service suppliers and independent professionals for categories of services bearing similar CPC codes. While contractual services by Malaysian agencies is allowed in engineering, integrated engineering, architectural, computer-related and management consultancy (excluding legal consultancy) services, independent professionals are allowed in accounting and book-keeping services in addition to services categories listed for contractual supply by agencies based in Malaysia. However, Malaysia apparently has committed more in terms of horizontal commitments in Mode 4. First of all, no distinction has been made between contractual supply and independent professionals and includes additional services like urban planning, landscaping, specialized medical services (such as the services of pharmacists, nurses, physiotherapists and paramedics), technical testing and analysis services, R&D services, waste water management, and scientific and technical consulting services.

4.2 Commercial Services

(a) In computer and related services, India and Malaysia have granted each other full market access (none in commitments as per schedule) in Mode 3.

(b) In telecommunications, higher education and private hospital services, India has committed to a higher foreign equity cap (51 per cent), allowing foreign management ownership in these services. Malaysia has, however, raised limits for these services above GATS commitments of flat 30 per cent cap to 49 per cent in case of India–Malaysia CECA.

(c) In R&D and construction services, India has higher limits of foreign equity holding — 70 and 74 per cent, respectively. In both these services, however, Malaysia allows 51 per cent foreign equity shareholding. For construction, Malaysia has made a higher commitment in India–Malaysia CECA over that in the GATS (30 per cent foreign equity cap).

(d) In transportation services, Malaysia allows 49 per cent foreign equity in freight services, while in the case of maritime services, this is allowed for both freight and passenger services. India also allows 49 per cent foreign equity shareholding in maritime services as per the CECA.

(e) In tourism services, both India and Malaysia allow 51 per cent foreign equity shareholding under the CECA.

(f) In audio-visual services, they have committed in motion pictures, and both India and Malaysia have stuck to their GATS commitment levels.

5 ASEAN Integration in Services

The ASEAN member states have a set a goal for them to integrate into what they call an ASEAN Economic Community (AEC) by 2015. The ASEAN Leaders adopted the ASEAN Economic Blueprint at the 13th ASEAN Summit on 20 November 2007 in Singapore towards the establishment of the ASEAN Economic Community (AEC) by 2015. The understanding is to create a barrier-free trade zone for both goods and services. In services, the Blueprint had set out targets to substantially remove all restrictions on trade in services for four priority services sectors, air transport, e-ASEAN (ICT and e-commerce), health care and tourism, by 2010 and the fifth priority sector, logistics services, by 2013. The scope of e-ASEAN may be understood in terms of the need to liberalize trade in ICT products and services towards building capacities for internet connectivity and narrowing of digital divide as well as for e-governance across ASEAN nations.[5] The Blueprint has also called for removal of all restrictions on trade in services for all other service sectors by 2015. However, progress in services liberalization has been rather slow.[6] Therefore, the 2015 deadline in all likelihood is going to be missed.

The benefits of free trade in services are potentially very high. According to the *ASEAN Integration in Services 2013* report, increasing investments in the services sector in ASEAN will promote the development of a sound and modern financial, telecommunications, distribution and transport sectors for economies in the region (World Bank–ASEAN Secretariat 2014). ASEAN will also benefit from technology flows, know-how and management skills from the free flow of services in the region. In addition, trade in services is expected to keep pace with the economic growth of the region. It also suggests that the key to realize these benefits will be a well-managed and progressive liberalization of the services sector by ASEAN, which will lead to the expansion of productive capacity and economic development. As of now, Singapore, the Philippines and Malaysia have become significant exporters of modern services in sectors such as professional services and information and communication technology, the BPOs, higher education and health tourism.[7]

5.1 Institution (The AFAS Framework)

After setting up of ASEAN Free Trade Area or AFTA in 1992, ASEAN member countries signed the ASEAN Framework Agreement on Services (AFAS) in 1995, mandating progressive negotiations on the liberalization of trade in services. The AFAS is based closely on the provisions of the GATS.[8] Subsequently, the AEC Blueprint mandates liberalization of trade in services in ASEAN, through actions, targets and timelines to create a single market and production base called ASEAN Economic Community. AFAS has been implemented through the following institutional channels:

(*a*) The Coordinating Committee on Services (CCS)
(*b*) The Coordinating Committee on Investment (CCI)
(*c*) The Air Transport Sectoral Negotiation (ATSN) of the Air Transport Working Group (ATWG)
(*d*) The Working Committee on ASEAN Financial Services Liberalisation under AFAS (WC-FSL/AFAS)

The CCS has been the core mechanism to negotiate on the trade in services under AFAS and worked with emphasis on seven priority sectors: air transport, business services, construction, financial services, maritime transport, telecommunications and tourism. In 1999, air transport and financial services were separated from the CCS process. Since 2001, services incidental to manufacturing, agriculture, fishery, forestry and mining and

---

[5] Refer the 'e-Asean Framework Agreement' (signed in 2000).

[6] The ASEAN Heads of State and Government decided to establish an ASEAN Free Trade Area or AFTA in 1992. According to ERIA (2012) Report the average Common Effective Preferential Tariff (CEPT) for ASEAN-6 is virtually zero and for CLMV it is 2.6 per cent (2010).

[7] For details, see the *ASEAN Integration Monitoring Report* (2014).

[8] The AFAS provides the enabling framework for setting out the broad parameters that enables that enables Member States to progressively improve market access and provide national treatment to services suppliers of ASEAN Member States. All AFAS rules are consistent with international rules for trade in services as provide for under the GATS Agreement of the WTO.

quarrying have also been separated from CCS. Currently, there are six sectoral working groups under the CCS, namely, business services, construction, health care, logistics and transport services, telecommunication and IT services, and tourism sectoral working groups, and a caucus on education services.

AFAS requires member countries to enter into negotiations on measures affecting trade in specific service sectors, and the results to be listed in schedules of commitments. The initial rounds of negotiations were undertaken on a three-year cycle for each round of negotiations. In the first four rounds (1996–98, 1999–2001, 2002–04, and 2005–07), liberalization of the services sector was undertaken based on parameters agreed for each respective round. Liberalization thresholds for subsequent rounds of negotiations are based on the AEC Blueprint. The 7th and 8th Packages of AFAS commitments under CCS have been completed (in 2009 and 2010, respectively) in line with these requirements.[9] The Blueprint had concrete stipulations to begin with. Additionally, the Blueprint also mandates zero restrictions for Modes 1 and 2, with exceptions only in case of bona fide regulatory reasons (such as public safety), which are subject to agreement by all member states on a case-by-case basis; and progressive removal of other Mode 3 market access limitations by 2015. The targets set by the Blueprint on foreign (ASEAN) equity participation in Mode 3 are illustrated in the Table 3.6.

6. AFAS AND GATS: A COMPARATIVE ANALYSIS

Having discussed the AFAS Framework and the AEC Blueprint targets, we present a brief comparison of GATS and AFAS commitments for market access in Mode 3 for Malaysia, Thailand and Indonesia. This would help us in understanding the depth and extent of commitments made by these countries under AFAS. We illustrate the nature of the commitments undertaken under GATS and AFAS in a tabular form (see Table 3.7). The sectors chosen include accounting, engineering, medical, paramedical and architectural services under professional services category; and computer and related services, telecommunication, maritime transport, tourism, health care services, and educational services. The nature of commitment is categorized as 'None', 'Unbound', domestic supply ('Domestic SS'), and the equity cap on foreign shareholding (marked as '%'). If a country has made assurances of full market access (unregulated/unconditional) then we tick (✓) 'None'; if it has not committed to any binding commitments then we tick 'Unbound'; if it has explicit preference for supply by a natural person then we tick 'Domestic SS'; and in case a country has a stipulated foreign equity participation limit we indicate its maximum permissible value under '%'. If a sector is not listed in country specific schedules we skip all options.

Given strict compartmentalization (with minimum qualification) of a country's commitments, we have resorted to generalizations — it is only natural that 'None' implying unregulated market access (in this case in

Table 3.6

Targets on Foreign (AMS) Equity Participation in Mode 3 as per AEC Blueprint

Sectors	Targets
Priority sectors	51 % (by 2008)
Air transport	70 % (by 2010)
e-ASEAN	
Health care	
Tourism	
Logistics	49 % (by 2008)
	51 % (by 2010)
	70 % (by 2013)
Other sectors	49 % (by 2008)
	51 % (by 2010)
	70 % (by 2015)

---

[9] The 5th Package onward, all the previous AFAS and GATS commitments were consolidated into a single comprehensive schedule along with new/improved commitments made under the subsequent packages. These commitments, however, concern the CCS process and exclude commitments made in financial services, air transport, and services incidental to manufacturing, agriculture, fishery, forestry, and mining and quarrying.

Table 3.7
Commitments under GATS and AFAS: A Comparison

Malaysia	GATS				AFAS			
	None	Unbound	Domestic SS	%	None	Unbound	Domestic SS	%
Professional services								
Accounting				30	✓			
Engineering			✓					30
Medical			✓				✓	
Paramedical							✓	
Architectural			✓					30
Computer and related services				30	✓			
Telecommunication				30				70
Maritime transport				30				51
Tourism				30				70
Healthcare services				30				70
Education services								51

Thailand	GATS				AFAS			
	None	Unbound	Domestic SS	%	None	Unbound	Domestic SS	%
Professional services								
Accounting				49				49
Engineering				49				49
Medical								
Paramedical								
Architectural				49				49
Computer and related services				49				49
Telecommunication							✓	
Maritime transport				49				49
Tourism				49				49
Healthcare services								49
Educational services				49				49

Indonesia	GATS				AFAS			
	None	Unbound	Domestic SS	%	None	Unbound	Domestic SS	%
Professional services								
Accounting								51
Engineering								49
Medical								
Paramedical								
Architectural								51
Computer and related services								49
Telecommunication				35				49
Maritime transport								60
Tourism								70
Healthcare services								70
Educational services								49

Source: Integrated Trade Intelligence Portal (I-TIP) — WTO and AFAS

Mode 3 trade in services) would be rare under GATS and/or AFAS. 'Unbound' commitments in Mode 3 is also much less likely for the class of services selected and given that countries have agreed to obligatory commitments under either of the multilateral agreements. Some countries would choose to explicitly indicate if a service can solely be provided by domestic suppliers. Most ASEAN countries by now have allowed foreign entry in services; however, limits vary in a significant manner. Moreover, the limits of foreign equity shareholding in various sectors are often different for GATS and AFAS. While in committing limits under GATS countries usually indicate a threshold value, improvements under AFAS suggests willingness towards deeper integration among ASEAN economies.

6.1 Assessment (Based on AFAS Commitments)

Total intra-ASEAN exports in services have more than doubled between 2005 and 2011 (see Figure 3.3). In the case of individual sectors, significant growth in trade in services during the same period is evident (see Table 3.8). We have selected transportation, travel, communication services, construction services, computer and information services and personal, cultural and recreational services. These sectors broadly cover those under the four priority sectors as identified by the AEC Blueprint, except for health care services for which information was not readily available.

7. Conclusions and Way Forward

Total intra-ASEAN exports in services have more than doubled between 2005 and 2013. In the services trade, the AEC Blueprint had set out targets to substantially remove all restrictions on trade in services for air transport, ICT and ecommerce, health care and tourism, and logistics services. Most ASEAN countries have allowed foreign entry in services, but limits vary in a significant manner. Moreover, the limits of foreign equity shareholding in various sectors are often different for GATS and AFAS. Under the GATS, countries usually indicate a threshold value in terms of commitments. However, improvements under AFAS suggest willingness towards deeper integration among ASEAN economies.

There has been some progress in services trade liberalization in the ASEAN.[10] Sectoral coverage of AFAS increased from the 5th to the 7th Package.[11] Liberalization commitments range from moderate to high among ASEAN members. However, liberalization commitments in Mode 3 are low; indeed, a number ASEAN countries have been facing challenges as higher commitments on foreign equity kick in, resulting in the delays in the conclusion and implementation of AFAS packages. Progress in the financial services is also relatively modest; similarly, for air transport services.

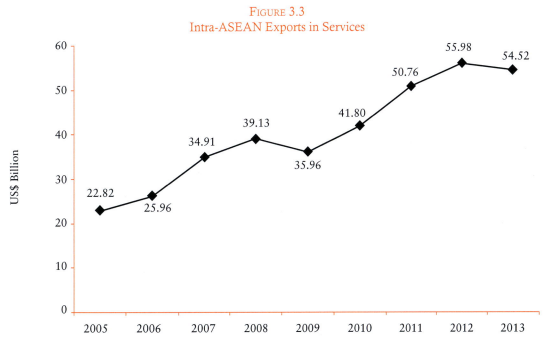

Figure 3.3
Intra-ASEAN Exports in Services

Source: ASEAN Stats, ASEAN Secretariat, Jakarta.

---

[10] This refers to the Mid-term Review of the Implementation of AEC Blueprint. ERIA was requested by the ASEAN Economic Ministers to undertake the Mid-Term Review of the Implementation of the AEC Blueprint (MTR). The analysis on trade in services in this report is based on a background study (Dee 2012).

[11] The ERIA report has not gone into assessing further progress in the subsequent packages due to delayed disclosure of such documents in the public domain.

TABLE 3.8
Intra-ASEAN Exports in Services (Selected Sectors), 2005–13

Category	2005	2006	2007	2008	2009	2010	2011	2012	2013
	(US$ million)								
Maintenance and repair services n.i.e.	499.75	495.81	599.56	823.26	879.70	878.17	887.19	1033.17	1169.37
Transport	4883.69	4888.69	6341.01	8587.17	5671.52	6688.48	7889.47	8547.46	8860.65
Travel	12247.68	14073.03	19264.17	19938.38	19297.29	23174.58	28813.71	30792.66	28071.26
Construction	509.58	729.33	984.55	1205.42	948.36	754.98	829.34	1061.26	1416.84
Insurance and pension services	410.95	463.54	621.19	776.23	739.09	818.94	774.40	1360.73	1237.56
Financial Services	398.25	407.40	629.70	630.90	647.49	1130.75	1234.90	1267.59	1433.03
Charges for the use of intellectual property n.i.e	126.78	151.20	195.97	259.22	419.98	365.05	413.04	459.15	499.28
Telecommunications, computer, and information services	790.77	973.02	1283.17	1366.71	1436.38	1550.48	1900.27	2171.70	2032.25
Other business services	2797.16	3569.67	4738.75	5252.88	5564.03	6030.00	7542.29	8792.69	9169.22
Personal, cultural, and recreational services	104.87	155.11	162.54	214.10	225.74	265.81	321.80	342.29	367.88
Government goods and services, n.i.e.	52.56	49.93	87.58	76.92	125.68	139.48	157.84	148.03	264.11

Source: ASEAN Stats, ASEAN Secretariat, Jakarta.

The very recent *ASEAN Integration Monitoring Report, 2014* assesses service sector integration in ASEAN as mixed and modest. Overall, there has been progress in meeting sectoral commitment targets until the 8th Package of AFAS. However, while in terms of commitments of AFAS often goes beyond GATS commitments or Doha Round offers, the Report suggests that this rarely leads to changes in the regulations that are applied in ASEAN member states. Therefore, AFAS possibly retains stronger assurances of unlikely roll-back in commitments compared to the GATS, which ensures threshold obligatory commitments on the part of its members.

Under the WTO, India's requests profile gives a glimpse into India's core interests. At the same time, requests received by India tell us about barriers to service trade faced by other countries in India. This is true for ASEAN countries as well. India has been asked to take commitments with regard to transparency in domestic regulations, simplify procedures, eliminate differential treatment of foreign suppliers of services and facilitate the movement of natural persons under the Mode 4.[12] However, India, at present, also has a growing interest in Mode 3 in areas related to computer, education, health and tourism. These are the sectors where barriers on the ASEAN side exist in terms of domestic regulations. The prospect that India could gain in-roads into ASEAN markets (market access) depends on streamlined and favourable domestic regulations in ASEAN countries. India has often faced barriers in terms of different levels of openness (market access) offered by countries on Mode 3 and Mode 4. This has implications for commercial operations that involve presence of personnel from abroad for execution of projects.

Therefore, India has made a request under GATS to take full commitments with respect to the category of independent professionals, de-linked from the commercial presence. India has also requested others to follow a liberalized visa system by ensuring the fulfillment of horizontal and sectoral commitments that were undertaken, such as multiple entry visas for professionals and allowing inter-firm mobility to professionals. India has long-standing interests in Mode 4 (cross-border mobility of its large number of highly skilled individuals). We stress that one crucial bottleneck for ASEAN–India trade in services concerns skilled labour mobility. Negotiating for recognition of academic and professional qualifications is a complex and time-consuming process given the wide divergence in the levels of development among ASEAN countries and absence of comprehensive or single MRAs for a broad range of professional categories among ASEAN members. However, both India and ASEAN should make attempts at sealing MRAs mutually in such sectors, where ASEAN has successfully completed MRAs. This could significantly improve prospects of cross-border movements of professionals from either side.

---

[12] The categories of professionals on which commitments have been sought include intra-corporate transferees, contractual service suppliers and specialists (tradespersons, associate professionals, professionals and managers).

4
Investments, Prospects and Challenges

The ASEAN region has remained robust in the past few years posting a remarkable growth amidst the presence of major global economic shocks. The region has been able to maintain consistent growth in its productive capacities domestically as well as at units located in countries other than the ASEAN. FDI flows into ASEAN increased from an all-time high of US$ 114 billion in 2012 (up 17 per cent year-on-year compared to 2011) to US$ 120 billion in 2013, indicating about 8.6 per cent as ASEAN's share in total global FDI inflows in 2013. (UNCTAD, 2014).

ASEAN region has contributed significantly to the overall FDI flows of India (approx. 12 per cent during 2000 to May 2014). Total FDI inflow to ASEAN has seen a fourfold increase — from US$ 21.81 billion in 2000 to US$ 114.08 billion in 2011 with Singapore, Indonesia and Malaysia leading the member states.[1] FDI has also been on the rise from India. India's outward FDI flow to ASEAN in 2010 was US$ 2.58 billion, an increase of 221.6 per cent from US$ 811.18 million in 2009, which accounted for 3.4 per cent of the total FDI into ASEAN in 2010.[2] Chapter 3 of this Report reveals that India enjoys its comparative advantage in the service sector such

FIGURE 4.1
Top Foreign Direct Investing Countries in ASEAN (2011–13)

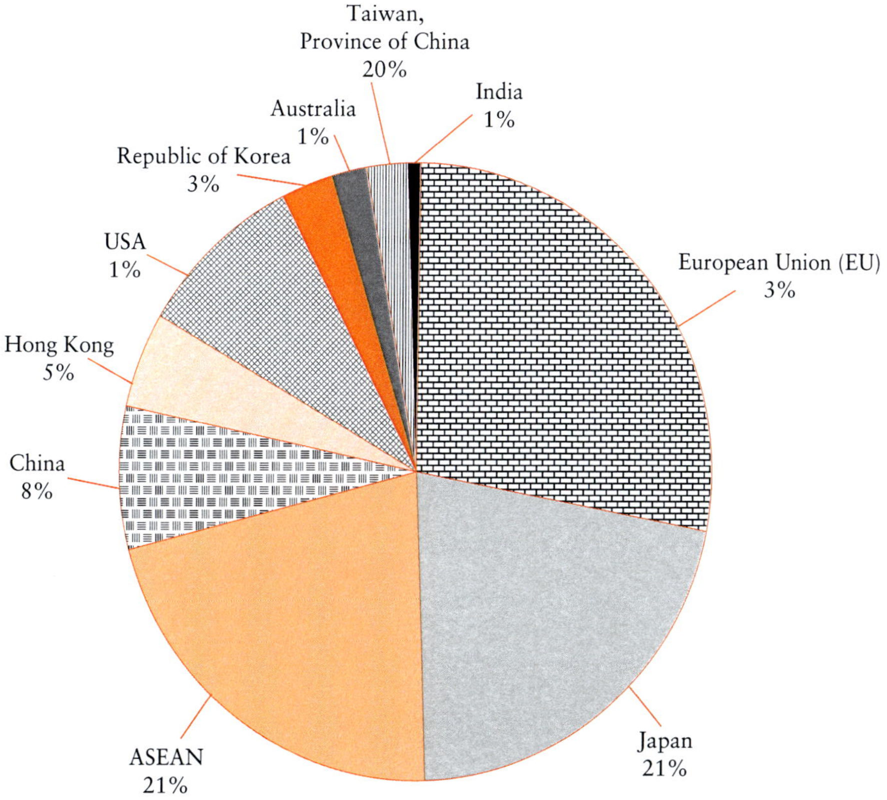

Source: Drawn based on UNCTAD Stat., Geneva.

---

[1] *ASEAN Secretariat News.* 2013. 'Latest ASEAN Statistics Show Progress towards 2015 Integration', 17 September.
[2] Based on FDI statistics, Department of Industrial Policy and Promotion (DIPP), Government of India.

as computer and IT services, whereas ASEAN has revealed comparative advantages in construction and transportation services.[3] In the area of finance and insurance services, both are competing on equal level. The growing realization that both regions (India and ASEAN) are complementary rather than competitive has further boosted trade and economic engagements and interdependence between them. Acknowledging this trend and recognizing the economic potential of closer linkages has seen both sides focused on opportunities for deepening economic relations through encouraging FDI between ASEAN and India.

In this chapter, we talk about the growing partnership between India and ASEAN countries in the area of investment, where significant amount of synergy exists them. We analyze the trends in FDI flows between ASEAN and India, discuss the investment related challenges and suggest policy measures to strengthen the investment relations between them.

1. TRENDS IN FDI BETWEEN INDIA AND ASEAN

Indian investment in ASEAN from 1995 to 2004 totalled US$ 737 million, of which US$ 733 million went to Singapore.[4] However, since 2004, there has been considerable leap in Indian investments, taking advantage of ASEAN's large markets, competent manufacturing capabilities and natural resources. Indian companies have been active in acquisitions all over the ASEAN region. Given India's massive infrastructure requirements and the world-class competencies of ASEAN in construction, there is huge potential to scale up ASEAN investment in India. Singapore and Malaysia are showing the way through ambitious plans in India's construction sector, setting up SEZs and building highways and power plants. Thailand is examining opportunities in infrastructure, tourism, and agro and food processing industries. Table 4.1 presents the major Indian investment in ASEAN.

Singapore has been the major recipient of FDI inflow from India. However, with the increased liberalization and improvement in regulation, the FDI by Indian companies has increased in the ICT, Pharmaceuticals and Engineering sectors. FDI net inflow from India to ASEAN during 2008–10 was US$ 3.94 billion and India's outflows to ASEAN have seen a 200 per cent growth in 2010, showing great scope for expansion. However, in 2011, the net inflow became negative, its share declining to –2.3 per cent. Since 2012 onwards ASEAN has seen a positive net inflow from India, which shows the presence of wider scope that needs to be explored to reap the opportunities. During 2006–11, Indian companies invested an annual average of US$ 1 billion in ASEAN, as compared to US$ 152 million in 2000–05. The key Indian players are Biocon, Cipla, Dr Reddy's Laboratories, HCL Technologies, I-Flex Solutions, Infosys Technologies, Mahindra Satyam, Mphasis, NIIT Technologies,

TABLE 4.1
Major Indian Investments in ASEAN

Sr. No.	Particulars
1	Tata Group has acquired Singapore's NatSteel, South Korea's Daewoo Commercial Vehicles and significant stake in PT Kaltim Prima Coal and PT Arutmin, Indonesia
2	Aptech Ltd has signed an MoU with the Vietnam-based company FPT to open 20 IT and multimedia training centres in Vietnam by 2008
3	Ballarpur Industries has acquired Sabah Forest Industries Ltd, Malaysia
4	Essar Steel is setting up plants in Vietnam
5	The Ruia Group has acquired 30 per cent controlling stake in Industronics Berhad of Malaysia
6	TVS has a manufacturing facility at Karawang, Indonesia
7	Singapore has agreed to allow State Bank of India and ICICI Bank to launch full banking operations
8	Wipro Ltd. has acquired Singapore's Unza Holdings Ltd to expand its software footprint
9	ONGC Videsh has invested in oil and gas exploration in Vietnam
10	Reliance has bought Hualon of Malaysia for backward integration with its textile operations

Source: Confederation of Indian Industry (CII), New Delhi.

---

[3] Refer, for example, Deloitte-FICCI (2013).

[4] Based on FDI data of DIPP, Ministry of Commerce and Industry, Government of India, New Delhi.

Ranbaxy, Strides Arcolab and Tata Group (ASEAN Secretariat 2012). As on 31 March 2013, EXIM Bank of India has provided finance to 5 Indian companies for setting up ventures in Vietnam, with sanctioned amount of ₹1.29 billion.[5]

Indian companies have also been active in investing in the region, through both greenfield and mergers and acquisitions (M&As). FDI equity inflows received from ASEAN countries during April 2000 to May 2014 were around US$ 28 billion, which represented 12.55 per cent of the cumulative FDI inflows worth US$ 223.70 billion, received during this period.[6] The time series behaviour of ASEAN FDI flows to India are reported in Table 4.2. It is pointed out that Singapore is the largest contributor to the ASEAN investment in India, which is followed by Malaysia and Indonesia. Interestingly, Singapore has recorded phenomenal growth as FDI inflows have increased almost 7–8 times in the recent years, compared to its level of early 2000s. Moreover, the country occupied the pie equivalent to 5.6 per cent in 2006, which increased to 17.15 per cent in 2013. Although China is the second largest economy of world, it could not hold the largest pie in India's total FDI inflows. Malaysia and Indonesia are investing more in India, compared to China. However, the share of flows of Indonesia has declined constantly after 2010 due to a rise in domestic investment opportunities in Indonesia.

According to a FICCI Report,[7] during April 2000 to August 2012, the major sectors attracting FDI equity inflows from ASEAN into India is the service sector, which accounts for 28.2 per cent, followed by telecommunication, construction, petroleum and gas, and computer hardware and software sectors. Between 2007 and 2012, Southeast Asian countries initiated 150 projects in India worth US$ 12.2 billion, creating 56,423 jobs (Ernst and Young 2014).[8] From ASEAN, Singapore was the largest investor, followed by Malaysia and Thailand. In 2012, Singapore's DBS Bank invested US$ 94.5 million of fresh capital to boost its Indian operations. The presence of complementarities in factor endowments, economic structure, skills and capabilities has led to the bilateral investment flows between the two regions.

The major foreign companies of the ASEAN countries who invested in India during 2000–10 include Reckitt Benckiser (Singapore), Biometrix Marketing, Dal Singapore Investments, Barclays Bank, Surya Abha Investment, Hindustan Coca Cola Overseas Holdings, Schender Electric, Bharat Coco Cola Overseas Holdings, IP Holding Asia Singapore and Mudajaya Corporation Berhad.

2. Barriers and Challenges to India–ASEAN FDI

Foreign investment in India has faced the challenges of macroeconomic uncertainties, such as a high current account deficit and inflation, as well as delays in the approval of several large FDI projects (UNCTAD 2014). The lower level of foreign investment in India by most of world economies is attributed to poor infrastructure; a high, complex and unclear tax structure; weak regulatory mechanism, etc. (Bedi and Kharbanda 2014). Other factors which impede the investment include restrictive labour laws, absence of centre–state coordination, a dormant Special Economic Zone policy, lack of institutional reform, land acquisition or environmental clearances (WIR, 2014). The variability in labour laws across states leaves room for a large degree of discretion for interpreting these laws, and thereby encourages corruption and rent-seeking activities. Because of this, owners of firms become easy targets for the labour inspectors (Banik 2014).

The infrastructure deficiency of India is well captured as India ranked 85 out of 148 countries for its infrastructure. In its *Doing Business Report 2014*, the World Bank placed India in the 134th position, out of a sample of 189 countries. Enforcing a contract in India takes an average of 1,420 days and involves 46 different procedures. Importing goods takes an average of 20 days and 11 documents. Tax payments have to be made on average 33 times per year and the process takes 243 hours. Even the ranking of India in terms of FDI Regulatory

---

[5] Available at http://www.eximbankindia.in/sites/default/files/Full%20OP/CLMV%20OP%20NEW%20REVISED.pdf (accessed on 22 February 2015).

[6] Refer 'India got ₹1.39 lakh crore in FDI from ASEAN in last 14 Years', *Outlook*, 24 July 2014.

[7] FICCI ASEAN Team, Retrieved from http://www.india-aseanbusinessfair.com/country-profile/ASEAN.pdf.

[8] Available at http://www.ey.com/Publication/vwLUAssets/EY-attractiveness-survey-India-2014/$FILE/EY-attractiveness-survey-India-2014.pdf (accessed 22 February 2015).

TABLE 4.2

ASEAN Countries' Equity Inflows in India (US$ Million)

Country	2000–05	2006	2007	2008	2009	2010	2011	2012	2013	2014*	Cumulative**
Singapore	598.18	629.75	1410.11	3626.23	3038.73	2123.92	4246.53	2844.57	3850.79	3096.02	25464.84
Malaysia	93.41	6.55	4.90	104.31	38.91	43.93	20.87	215.62	111.36	10.33	650.20
Indonesia	25.02	0.37	3.56	5.63	133.61	436.88	0.42	4.69	1.20	0.79	612.16
The Philippines	0.42	0.09	0.15	0.02	0.21	0.34	1.89	25.48	4.62	0.02	33.23
Thailand	24.43	2.84	12.27	2.97	20.71	15.33	10.41	11.25	63.71	7.95	171.86
Myanmar	0.05	0.19	0.00	7.97	0.00	0.00	0.00	0.00	0.00	0.00	8.21
Vietnam	0.09	0.02	0.00	0.00	0.01	0.00	0.02	0.00	0.09	0.00	0.23
China	2.31	0.71	0.25	7.94	41.06	1.03	51.81	136.51	72.30	94.73	408.64
Grand Total	20702.59	11120.94	19283.79	32127.14	26845.55	21076.18	27598.56	22692.02	22448.16	9475.32	213370.24
Shares (%)											
Singapore	2.89	5.66	7.31	11.29	11.32	10.08	15.39	12.54	17.15	32.67	11.93
Malaysia	0.45	0.06	0.03	0.32	0.14	0.21	0.08	0.95	0.50	0.11	0.30
Indonesia	0.12	0.00	0.02	0.02	0.50	2.07	0.00	0.02	0.01	0.01	0.29
The Philippines	0.00	0.00	0.00	0.00	0.00	0.00	0.01	0.11	0.02	0.00	0.02
Thailand	0.12	0.03	0.06	0.01	0.08	0.07	0.04	0.05	0.28	0.08	0.08
Myanmar	0.00	0.00	0.00	0.02	0.00	0.00	0.00	0.00	0.00	0.00	0.00
Vietnam	0.00	0.00	0.00	0.00	0.00	0.00	0.00	0.00	0.00	0.00	0.00
China	0.01	0.01	0.00	0.02	0.15	0.00	0.19	0.60	0.32	1.00	0.19
Grand Total	100	100	100	100	100	100	100	100	100	100	100

Source: Department of Industrial Policy and Promotion (DIPP), Government of India.

Note: *January to April 2014, **Considers the period January 2000 to April 2014

Restrictiveness Index 2013 suggests for restrictive FDI policies in the country as the score in the index is found greater than 0.25 (OECD 2014). Many times, the FDI approvals are kept pending for months that prompts the investor to drop out. All these mark the biggest hurdles for free flow of investment in India.

The ASEAN–India FTA in Services and Investment has been signed recently, but it has faced considerable opposition within the ASEAN bloc with Thailand, Indonesia and the Philippines to individually ratify the deal.[9] Thailand and Indonesia had demanded unconditional access to India's multi-brand retail trading segment, while the Philippines was appeared to be scared of India's information technology (IT) sector (Basu 2014). ASEAN countries hold huge potential for Indian professionals like teachers, nurses, accountants and architects. Some members of ASEAN had been concerned that free movement of professionals will impact their own workforce.[10] Singapore is making substantial investment in India, but the country is very cautious about stability in political and legal terms, security, good labour laws and management, and regarding the factors of production, such as land, for making investments in India.[11] These numerous investment hurdles, prove discouraging for the ASEAN region.

2.1 Recent Policy Initiatives in India and ASEAN

India is carrying out several economic reforms in the form of management of liquidity adjustment facility, marginal standing facility, special attention to the growing non-performing assets of the banks mainly emanating from the big promoters, actively targeting the exchange rate, among others, all signifies the greater interest of the Government to address the recent economic problems. More importantly, the setting up of the Cabinet Committee on Investment, introducing the *force majeure* closure for renegotiation of the stalled projects, providing a helping hand to the small and medium enterprises[12] may contribute in enhancing the investment potentialities of the country leading to the higher economic growth. In the near future, the country has to travel on the ground of reforms. These reforms include reassuring investors, pruning of subsidies, administration streamlining, kicking off a bond market and reforming the financial sector, addressing the fuel shortage by scrapping of coal nationalization, expediting the transition from Central Value Added Tax (CENVAT) and State Value Added Tax (STATEVAT) to a goods and services tax, addressing bureaucratic hassles, clearance system, merging the ministries, tackling the land acquisition issues, clarity on retrospective tax laws, decentralization, adoption of Centre's development vision by states, harmonization between the Centre and State on development issues, boost to investment in infrastructure, push to DTC and others.[13]

Brunei Darussalam has introduced multifold reforms for foreign investment in the form of liberalizing the registration requirements for establishing corporate entities; reduction of corporate income tax to 22 per cent; allowing foreigners a leasehold property for a longer period (99 years instead of 60 years); tax exemption for qualifying projects under pioneer industries and signed Double Taxation Agreements with a number of countries and full foreign equity ownership investment in manufacturing and fisheries activities for export purposes. Cambodia has also launched a package of reforms by streamlining investment procedures, increasing transparency and clarity of regulations and provision of tax incentives for projects related to paddy production. The establishment of the Government–Private Sector Forum by Cambodia is a landmark step for improvement in the business environment of the country.

Indonesia pursued a more open investment policy in various sectors such as construction services, film, technical services, hospital and health care and small-scale electric power plants. Other steps include a tax holiday to new investors in certain industries and locations, identification of further special economic zones, clearer rules and regulations and streamlining of investment approval processes. Lao PDR in 2011 introduced a set of new tax

---

[9] Available at http://indianexpress.com/article/business/economy/india-asean-fta-delayed-by-jan-dhan-yojana-roll-out/ (accessed 22 February 2015).

[10] For more details, see 'Fear of Indian pros holding up services deal: Malaysia'. 2011. *The Economic Times*, 3 March.

[11] For more details, see *The Telegraph*, 22 August 2014.

[12] The SME sector contributed 8 per cent of India's GDP and 45 per cent of total manufacturing exports.

[13] For more details, see *The Economic Times*, 17 May 2014.

rates as an incentive to boost the investment in the country along with further liberalization of manufacturing sector for FDI under the ACIA commitment.

The major initiatives carried out by Malaysia includes liberalization of 27 services subsectors with no equity conditions imposed, including health and social services, tourism services, transport services, business services, and computer and related services. Malaysia created the Special Task Force to Facilitate Business (PEMUDAH) with the aim of simplifying business operations in Malaysia by improving the government delivery system. Myanmar introduced the Special Economic Zone (SEZ) Law in 2011, and designated 24 development zones throughout the country. Other major reforms deals with the greater access of private as well as government land on lease for business entity, the double taxation agreement with Thailand (2012), removal of the dual foreign exchange system, reduction of corporate income tax from 30 per cent to 25 per cent; and removal of commercial tax for export except for teak, natural gas, petroleum, hardwoods, jade and other precious jewellery, and less cumbersome procedural aspect for investment. The Philippines established an 'open sky policy' in 2011 to liberalize the country's aviation industry and ease restrictions on the domestic aviation market. Some other active agenda items of the Philippines includes streamlining and simplifying procedures, registration process and other measures (for example, licensing, registration and issuance of permits) to reduce cost of doing business in the country, restructuring of Board of Investment (2012), access to other markets such as mining and gambling industry.

Singapore's initiatives were to facilitate more effective delivery of e-Government services, and enhance technology neutrality, signing a double taxation agreement with Switzerland, clarity on tax guidelines, removal of a few goods such as air-conditioners, pig iron, sponge iron, refrigerators, rolled steel products and steel ingots, billets, blooms, slabs and firecrackers, among others, from the Control of Manufacture Act (COMA). The average time taken to start up a business in Singapore has been reduced from five days in 2007 to three days in 2012 (World Bank and IFC 2013). Thailand announced a set of measures to boost the investment through reduction of corporate tax from 23 per cent in 2012 to 20 per cent in 2013, double taxation avoidance agreement with Myanmar, and extension of Investment Promotional Zones, among others. Also, promoting outward investment by relaxing approval requirements on foreign exchange regulations has been the key initiative among policy actions. In Vietnam, the package of reforms oriented towards prompt access of natural resources, clarity in the application of investment incentives to expanded projects, regulation of financial markets and banks and investment incentives for wind power projects.

3. Investment Flow between India and ASEAN Countries: Private Sector Engagements

ASEAN and India relations have been strongly driven by very wide economic activities with private sector from both sides playing critical role. While government-to-government engagements in ASEAN and India relations have grown rapidly from a sectoral dialogue partnership in 1992 to a summit level partnership in 2002, the two sides also worked hard to enhance institutional tie-up between the private sectors.

ASEAN and India private sector engagement got a major boost through several bilateral forums providing important stage to deepen business relations. CEOs forums with Indonesia, Malaysia, Thailand and Myanmar provided much dynamism to the private sector engagement. Indian businesses, particularly, have been seeing great opportunities in the CLMV (Cambodia, Lao PDR, Myanmar and Vietnam) region, where the Government of India too has special focus. Several other private sector-led events like Asian Business Summit and ASEAN-India Business Council were part of the efforts to stimulate trade and business-to-business engagement between India and ASEAN.

The growing engagement of private sector in promoting investment led trade is a testimony to this fact. The operationalization of FTA with ASEAN and CECA/CEPA with major countries of the region such as Singapore and Malaysia, have enabled the private sector to further deepen the trade and investment ties.

3.1 India–Singapore Bilateral Investments

Singapore is a major source of FDI for India. The FDI inflows, particularly, increased after the CECA came into effect in 2005. Cumulative FDI from Singapore between 1991 and 2005 was US$ 3.8 billion, accounting for just

3.1 per cent of total inward FDI into India. This made Singapore the 8th largest investor in the Indian economy. In the post-CECA period, FDI from Singapore has increased substantially. Cumulative FDI from Singapore between 2005–06 and 2012–13 was US$ 19 billion. Overall, between April 2000 and May 2014, cumulative investment was US$ 26.4 billion. Singapore accounts for about 10 per cent of India's total inward FDI making it the 2nd largest investor in the Indian economy ahead of the United States and behind Mauritius. Mauritius and Singapore together account for 48 per cent of the FDI inflow into India.

According to Singapore's Economic Development Board, Indian investment to Singapore has also increased manifold in recent years. There has been a phenomenal increase in Indian investment into Singapore, which has risen from just over US$ 351million till 2005 to almost US$ 4 billion in 2010–11 and US$ 1.8 billion in 2012–13, with a cumulative FDI of US$ 25.7 billion, making India the second largest investor in Singapore from Asia after Japan, outstripping China, which is the 11th largest source of FDI into Singapore.[14] Overall, India has emerged as the 6th largest investor in Singapore, behind the United States, the Netherlands, the United Kingdom, Japan and Switzerland.

Singapore is targeting more investment from India in sectors like bio-medical sciences, information communication, infrastructure, natural resources, bio-technology and health services. Punj Lloyd, Fortis Healthcare, Tata Communications, TCS, HCL Technologies, L&T Infotech, Pidilite, and Bilcare are amongst the major Indian investors in Singapore. From India, 19 of the top 20 Indian technology companies have their presence in Singapore. Some have regional or Asian headquarters in Singapore, while others use a 'front office' there to approach the thousands of multinationals with operations in the city-state.

Why are so many Indian companies investing in Singapore? The primary reason is Singapore's low tax rate. Companies in Singapore are exempted from capital gains tax and withholding tax in Singapore, and the government levies only 17 per cent corporate tax making it an attractive investment destination. The country also provides tax exemption on service income, adding the largest foreign business community in Singapore is from India.

3.2 India–Indonesia Bilateral Investments

Indonesia has cumulatively invested US$ 621.31million in India from April 2000 to May 2014[15] and is ranked 22nd in terms of source of FDI inflow into India. India and Indonesia signed a bilateral investment promotion and protection agreement in 2004. On the other hand, the interest of Indian companies in the Indonesian economy has been growing rapidly.

According to the UNCTAD's *World Investment Report 2014*, there was a sharp rise in investments into Indonesia (173 per cent increase) over 2009. This rise continued and 2012 was also a good year for Indonesia with over US$ 19,138 million of FDI coming into the country in 2012. India has substantial investments in Indonesia in the textiles, steel, automotive, banking and resources sectors. Foreign investment from India in Indonesia dates back to the 1970s. In recent years, there has been a new wave of investment focusing on the mining, automotive and banking sectors.

3.3 India–Malaysia Bilateral Investments

Malaysia is now emerging as a major potential investor in India, with investments in power, oil refineries, telecommunication and electronics, and electrical equipment industries, besides highway and other infrastructure development projects. Recently, there has been a surge in Malaysian private sector investment into India. Notable among these are Axiata in IDEA Cellular, Khazanah in IDFC, and TM International in Spice Communications.

FDI from Malaysia from April 2000 to March 2012 was US$ 312 million, placing it at 27th position in India's FDI inflows.[16] However, this figure is understated as the majority of investments from Malaysia are routed through indirect means and the actual FDI pipeline is worth several billion dollars.

Malaysian companies have also invested in many project-related works. For instance, Malaysian construction companies' largest presence outside Malaysia is in India. Malaysian companies have completed 52 construction projects worth US$ 2.34 billion in India, while 35 projects of similar value are under various stages of

---

[14] Data sourced from FDI statistics, Department of Industrial Policy and Promotion (DIPP), Government of India.
[15] Ibid.
[16] Ibid.

implementation.[17] Under a partnership with Malaysian Airports, GMR completed an airport in Hyderabad in 2008, and a second one in Delhi in July 2010. An MoU on cooperation relating to the Provision of Technical Assistance Services on Highway Management and Development was signed in December 2010 during the visit of Indian Minister of Road Transport and Highways to Malaysia. A bilateral Steering Committee has been established to oversee the implementation of this MoU, which will enhance the participation of Malaysian infrastructure companies in the Indian economy.

Indian companies have invested about US$ 2 billion, making it the 7th largest investor in Malaysia.[18] Indian companies that made major acquisitions include Reliance Industries, Ballarpur Industries, Larsen & Toubro and WIPRO. Biocon India, Manipal University and Strides Arcolabs are amongst the companies who have announced fresh investments in Malaysia in the recent times. There are over 100 Indian companies including 60 Indian joint ventures operating in Malaysia. In addition, there are 60 Indian IT companies operating from Malaysia. IRCON International has been actively engaged in the development of railways in Malaysia since 1988, and it is currently executing a double tracking project (Seremban–Gemas) worth over US$ 1 billion.[19] In health care sector, Fortis and Appollo have invested in Malaysia.

3.4 India–Thailand Bilateral Investments

Both India and Thailand are big economies but investment between the two countries does not reflect the size of their respective economies. Thailand is yet to be a major source of FDI for India. Thailand has cumulatively invested US$ 99 million in India in the last 12 years.[20] Thai industries are focusing largely on labour-intensive industries in India. Major areas of Thai investment are marine food, automotive parts and electronic equipment as well as industrial estate development and telecommunications.

Cumulative Indian investment in Thailand from 1991 to date is more than US$ 1 billion.[21] At present, there are 26 joint venture projects in operation producing chemicals, steel wires and rods, rayon fibre, drugs and pharmaceuticals and others.

Many Thai construction companies are also keen to participate in India's National Highways Development projects. India's infrastructure development opportunities have attracted several multinational companies to investment significantly in India. India offers significant opportunities for Thai companies in food processing and agro-based industries, industrial estate development, building of roads and highways, construction and financial sectors.

3.5 India–Vietnam Bilateral Investments

Vietnam is a negligible source of FDI for India. Vietnam has cumulatively invested only US$ 0.14 million in India in the last 12 years.[22] However, Vietnam's economic policies have opened up significant opportunities for Indian investment, both for tapping the growing domestic market and for exports. Its impending entry into the ASEAN preferential tariff regime makes it an ideal springboard for export marketing to the entire region. At present, Indian investment in Vietnam is to the tune of US$ 125 million, mainly in sugar production, edible oil, pharmaceuticals, office furniture and plastic sectors.

However, Indian companies are showing keen interest in Vietnam's rising manufacturing sector, and investments are due to expand exponentially. As of June 2013, India has 73 investment projects with total registered capital of US$ 252.21 million.[23] If investments by Indian companies from third countries are included as well, India has 68 valid projects with an estimated total investment capital of US$ 936.23 million.[24] Several Indian companies in sectors as diverse as oil and gas, steel, minerals, tea, coffee, sugar and food processing have invested in Vietnam.

---

[17] According to the Construction Industry Development Board (CIDB) of Malaysia.
[18] Sourced from the CII FDI Database.
[19] Ibid.
[20] Data sourced from FDI statistics, Department of Industrial Policy and Promotion (DIPP), Government of India.
[21] Sourced from the CII FDI Database.
[22] Data sourced from FDI statistics, Department of Industrial Policy and Promotion (DIPP), Government of India.
[23] Sourced from the Vietnam Foreign Investment Agency.

The Oil and Natural Gas Corporation (ONGC) is involved in a major joint venture offshore oil and natural gas exploration in the southern part of Vietnam. In the coming years, this ONGCVL (ONGC Videsh Limited) investment in the production-sharing contract (PSC) between itself, Petro Vietnam, BP and the Norwegian company, Statoil, will be one of the largest investments (US$ 228 million) of the Government of India anywhere in the world. ONGCVL's share of the PSC is 45 per cent. The Government of Vietnam attaches a lot of importance to this project and the Vietnamese National Assembly has elevated it to the top three projects of national importance.

Vietnam continues to consolidate FDI related policies such as policies on tax, land and service fees, use of Vietnamese workers, technology transfer, among others, to make Vietnam an attractive and competitive investment destination in the region. Vietnam ranks first among ASEAN nations, up three notches in FDI attraction, and is one of the top ten economies of investment attraction (UNCTAD 2013).

3.6 India–Myanmar Bilateral Investments

Following the liberalization introduced by the Myanmar government in 2009, foreign nationals investing in Myanmar are entitled to incentives, benefits and legal guarantees. Among the guarantees offered are the rights to repatriate profits and to withdraw legitimate assets on the winding up of business. The Myanmar Investment Commission has permitted the exploration and development of hitherto restricted sectors like oil, gas and minerals. The country also passed a Special Economic Zone Law in 2010–11, which provides incentives for foreign investors in banking and insurance. Investor friendly Foreign Investment Law was also enacted in November 2012.

In Myanmar, developed countries, such as the United Kingdom, the United States, the Netherlands and France, are major sources of foreign direct investment (FDI). Amongst Asian countries Singapore remains the main source of FDI going to Myanmar. India is the 13th largest investor in Myanmar. Around 98 per cent of Indian investment in Myanmar is in the oil and gas sector with the remaining 2 per cent in manufacturing.[25]

Indian companies having operations in Myanmar include ONGC Videsh (OVL), Jubilant Oil and Gas, Century Ply, Tata Motors, Essar Energy, RITES, Escorts, Sonalika Tractors, Zydus Pharmaceuticals, Sun Pharmaceuticals, Ranbaxy, Cadila Healthcare, Shree Balaji Enterprises, Shree Cements, Dr. Reddy's Lab., CIPLA, Gati Shipping, TCI Seaways, Apollo, and AMRI. In the banking domain, the United Bank of India (UBI) has set up a representative office in Myanmar. Bank of India and State Bank of India have also expressed interest in setting up offices in Myanmar.

Indian investment ranges from oil and gas sector to hydroelectric power, railways, electric power, and others. Other significant Indian investments are US$ 120 million in Kaladan Multimodal Transit Transport Project, US$ 20 million credit line for TATA Motors to set up a heavy truck assembly plant in Myanmar.

In addition to these, India has taken up development projects in Myanmar. The projects are supported by India through line of credits and/or grants. In recent years, India has offered to cooperate on a number of road projects, such as the India–Myanmar–Thailand Trilateral Highway. Other projects include supply of railway equipments, remote sensing, supply of design and equipment for transmission projects and others.

3.7 India–Brunei Bilateral Investments

Brunei witnessed an FDI inflow of US$ 895 million and an outflow of US$ 135 million in 2013 (UNCTAD 2014). The Government of Brunei, through its Wawasan 2035, has set out the directions for its economic goals with a growing emphasis on attracting foreign direct investments as an important driver of growth, focusing mainly on economic activities that bring new knowledge, new industries, new technologies, new markets as well as new business and employment opportunities for its people.

The Indian private sector has not so far made any direct significant investments in Brunei. However, huge potential lies in oil and gas, infrastructure, ICT and construction. Brunei is the 4th largest producer of natural LNG in the world. Japan purchases about 85 per cent of Brunei's LNG, followed by South Korea, which buys

---

[24] Sourced from the CII FDI Database.
[25] Ibid.

about 11 per cent.[26] The Brunei LNG joint venture between Mitsubishi (25 per cent) Shell (25 per cent) and the Brunei government (50 per cent) produces Brunei's LNG.

3.8 India–the Philippines Bilateral Investments

India and the Philippines have to invest huge efforts to boost the bilateral investment. However, only US\$ 4 million in FDI have come from the Philippines from April 2000 till March 2012.[27] Indian investments in the the Philippines are mainly confined to the areas of textiles and IT.

On the other hand, the Philippine investments in India are primarily restricted to telecommunications, reprocessing of waste and human resources development in the field of management education. During the last few years, Indian companies have successfully executed some small and medium-sized projects in the Philippines. Most of these projects were related to the area of power transmission.

3.9 India–Cambodia Bilateral Investments

FDI into Cambodia averaged less than US\$ 200 million from 1995–2005, but surged in 2007 and 2008 to over US\$ 800 million (UNCTAD 2012). In 2009, FDI into the country fell to US\$ 600 million due to the financial crisis, but as the investor sentiments improved, the FDI flow into the country rose to over US\$ 780 million in 2010 and in 2011; Cambodia attracted about US\$ 892 million (ibid.).

Bilateral FDI inflows between India and Cambodia are minimal. India's approved direct investments in joint ventures and wholly-owned subsidiaries in Cambodia amounted to US\$ 9.6 million during 2012–13. Cumulative FDI outflow from India into Cambodia during April 1996–March 2013 was US\$ 24.6 million. Some of the Indian companies present in Cambodia include Kirloskar Brothers, WAPCOS, Essar Group, Angelique International, Tata Steel, Ranbaxy, Glenmark and Futurelinks India, and Bank of India.

3.10 India–Lao PDR Bilateral Investments

FDI has played an important role in the development of the economy of Lao PDR in recent decades. Economic transition of Lao PDR to a market-driven economy has attracted international investors' attention. FDI inflow to Lao PDR has been recorded at US\$ 9.7 billion for the period 2006 to 2010 (ibid.). About 80 per cent of total FDI in Lao PDR goes into the resource sector, particularly hydropower and mining. Major FDI to Lao PDR in recent years comes mainly from the European Union, Thailand, the United States, China, Japan, Vietnam, Korea, Australia and India.

3.11 Private Sector Role in Human Resource Development

Both government and private sector of India have been deeply engaged in capacity building in the ASEAN region. Indian management schools are raring to go to Singapore, while computer-training firms, such as NIIT and APTECH, are already well-established in Vietnam, Malaysia, Cambodia and Indonesia. Manipal Medical College and Delhi Public School (DPS) have set up their branches in Malaysia and Singapore. The Institute of Clinical Research, India, has started operations in Singapore as well.

India's Entrepreneurship Development Institute (EDI) has taken its formidable training expertise to Lao PDR, Cambodia, Vietnam and Myanmar, setting up centres for creating and hand-holding new entrepreneurial energy. India has also decided to set up English language training centres in Cambodia, Laos, Myanmar and Vietnam and implement the ASEAN–India project on education fairs. An India–ASEAN Institute for intellectual property to build human resource capacities and training centres in the ASEAN region is also on the anvil.

The potential in the education sector for bilateral cooperation is large, deriving from India's language capabilities, low delivery costs and high quality of curriculum. Training, skill development and capacity-building ventures can be vigorously expanded. India's strengths in IT education and training need to be leveraged to enhance its presence in the region.

---

[26] Sourced from the CII FDI Database.

[27] Data sourced from FDI statistics, DIPP, Ministry of Commerce and Industry, Government of India, New Delhi.

4. Policy Actions to Strengthen India–ASEAN FDI Flow

Investment growth in India is expected to accelerate with the ambitious and growth oriented recent leadership in the power. Government infrastructure spending continues to contribute considerably to overall investment growth across the Southeast Asia countries. In Indonesia, infrastructure remains a top priority under the Master Plan for Acceleration and Expansion of Indonesia's Economic Development (MP3EI), which calls for investment in infrastructure projects in six economic corridors. In Malaysia, the government's Economic Transformation Programme (ETP) to develop higher value-added industries and infrastructure will continue to support infrastructure spending. Under the Philippine Development Plan, the government plans to increase infrastructure spending to around 5 per cent of GDP by 2016, as it allocates more funds to build roads, railways, airports and bridges to support its goal of inclusive and sustainable growth. Thailand is also aggressively pursuing infrastructure improvements and has recently rolled out ambitious development plans to invest THB 5.5 trillion (Thai Baht) (US$ 179 billion) — 20 per cent of Thailand's GDP — on new roads, rail networks and other projects over the next seven years (OECD, 2013).

Despite the complementarities, FDI between India and ASEAN still faces some considerable challenges. India and ASEAN are significant markets in the world economy and therefore the foremost step should be to identify the potential areas of investment (Table 4.3). For instance, the CLMV countries are highly dependent on agriculture; however, the agro-industries in these regions are highly underdeveloped leaving a significant opportunity for development of agro-based industries. Both the regions should focus on issues such as poor infrastructure, land acquisition, regulatory hurdles and the slow pace of reforms which hinders FDI. Further, Indian companies should endeavor to participate in the projects for CLMV countries, funded by multilateral institutions, such as the World Bank and the Asian Development Bank (ADB). Mutual cooperation is required in a wide range of areas from food and energy security to infrastructure and human resource development. The range of existing complementarities between ASEAN and India are substantial but still not fully exploited. This will require that the ideological and informational blinders are lifted. Moreover, the removal of restrictions for ownership in various sectors such as banking, mining and querying, construction, distribution, hotels and restaurants, etc. offers superb opportunity for both the regions.

While cost and the potential growth are important considerations, what ultimately seals the deal is the accessibility of the market and the ease of operating in that environment. Multinationals are reluctant to enter sectors which have strict ownership limits. Despite the need for better infrastructure in India, Indonesia and the Philippines, FDI in the transport sector is relatively restricted. With respect to manufacturing, Malaysia, Thailand, Vietnam and India are most open to FDI. However, India, despite its massive glut of labour and large market, currently has one of the smallest FDI inflows in Asia (relative to GDP). This is because wages are relatively expensive thanks to the inefficiency of the labour market, access to certain sectors is limited and

Table 4.3
Potential Sectors for FDI in India

Country	Potential Sector for FDI in India
Singapore	Science and technology, logistics infrastructure including Special Economic Zones, drugs and pharmaceuticals and education
Malaysia	Infrastructure Sector, Health care, drugs and parma, biotech, services (consultancy etc.) automobiles, agriculture and food processing, tourism, education, small and medium industries, banking and finance, textiles and garments
Indonesia	Textiles, steel, automotive, banking and resources sectors, computer software, agri-biotech, food processing, plastics, pharmaceuticals light engineering, telecommunications, it products
Thailand	Automotive and auto parts, agro processing and food industry, organic chemicals, natural rubber industry, software industry, yacht building, electrical and electronics, transportation and trading industry, textiles, spa, real estate, gems and jewellery
Myanmar	Agriculture and food processing, forestry, mini hydel power plant, garments and textiles, gems and jewellery, sme industry, metallurgical industries etc.
The Philippines	Pharmaceuticals, steel, textiles, motorcycles and auto-parts, mining and infrastructure, dairy and other agro-based industry etc.
Vietnam	Electricity, high-value manufacturing, electrical part production, steel manufacturing, high technology, entertainment, complex development, seaport construction, hotel development

Source: FICCI ASEAN Team, Individual Country Reports, FICCI, New Delhi.

infrastructure is poor. So, in addition to further liberalizing regulations to attract manufacturing FDI, India in particular needs to create a legal and physical infrastructure that is industry friendly.

The attraction of investment from ASEAN into India largely depends on the policy responses to macroeconomic problems. The policy paralysis experienced by India in the last decade is major setback for global firms. Here, the nation needs to enhance its business environment by reducing corruption and strengthening the rule of law, faster clearances for projects, develop infrastructure, boost manufacturing, simplify the taxation system, ease FDI regulations and increase awareness about its emerging cities, flexibility in the Public–Private Partnership (PPP) contracts through renegotiations, among others.

India has strong comparative advantage in export of computer and information services, other business services such as financial, medical tourism, insurance, etc. and movement of natural persons such as IT professionals and seafarers. Likewise, ASEAN countries have comparative advantage in logistic-related services that can be of great help to India. Complementarities among the two exist in terms of trade in energy, consumer durables and food items (Banik 2014). Addressing the above mentioned competitive sectors coming into the ambit of services sector may enhance the scope of India ASEAN FTA in services and investment.

5. CONCLUSIONS

The ASEAN region has backed itself well on macro fundamentals even in the presence of global slowdown. The region has been very resilient in terms of receiving foreign investment, while posting an 18 per cent growth in the capital inflows particularly when world economies are striving to manage their economic fundamentals. India and ASEAN have elevated their relations to strategic partnership level in 2012. The growing trade and investment relations between the two countries justify further areas for economic collaboration. Singapore being the largest investment contributor to India and having core competence in areas such as air and sea transport, innovation, technology upgradation, etc. sets a clear roadmap for collaboration. Malaysia and Thailand are sound in logistic performance and automatically enhance the scope for further tie-up. The growing middle income class in the region amid more active policy measures in all countries of the region is adding a significant scope for bilateral investment. Major hurdles for investors in both India and the ASEAN continue to be on the fronts of legal environment, poor infrastructure, lack of transparency, regulatory issues and others. The issues for restrictions in ownerships in sectors such as banking, construction, hotel and restaurant, mining and quarrying, etc. need to be considered at par for further investment and economic cooperation. The growth prospects of ASEAN region provide the best avenue for India to encash on the region's service sector potential in which India enjoys a comparative advantage. Besides the Indian target of uplifting its manufacturing sector has great potential for the ASEAN region to exploit.

5
Emerging Production Networks

Global value chains (GVCs) have become an important feature in modern international trade. Activities in the value chain are no longer confined within domestic borders or a single firm. Production now involves multiple countries and multiple firms with complex webs and layers of interaction. Empirical evidence suggests that the emergence of international production networks (IPNs) in East Asia results from market-driven forces such as vertical specialization and higher production costs in the home country and institutional factors such as free trade agreements (see Kimura and Obashi 2011).

Reduced tariffs on manufactured goods under the ASEAN–India FTA have opened up a new opportunity for the expansion of the ASEAN production network to India and vice versa. FDI from Singapore, Malaysia and Indonesia has shown a positive trend in the last few years. India's investment in ASEAN has also gone up. India's import of machinery products from ASEAN grew up substantially. Auto components, telecom equipments, automatic data processing equipments, mechanical and electrical apparatus are the main items imported by India from Southeast Asia.

Here, we discuss India's integration process especially in three sectors, that is, machinery, electrical and optical products and the automobile sector including parts and accessories. Studies suggest that production fragmentation in these sectors is relatively higher than other manufacturing sectors, and hence, there is higher degree of internationalization (see Nag 2012). We have observed significant growth in trade along with marked drop in tariff rates especially in these identified sectors. Special attention on these sectors stem not only from the fact that they are among the key trading sectors between India and ASEAN but this also because these are few important sectors, among others, where internal production network building process, as a result of FTA, carries emphatic impact for small and medium enterprises (SMEs). We also analyze the role of trade agreements in accentuating production network and the role of SMEs.

To understand the trade aspect, in this chapter, we make an attempt to explore trade in value added (TIVA) data prepared by the OECD. Analyzing the degree of foreign value added components in India's gross exports in selected sectors, we identify the emerging trend of IPN in India between 2000 and 2009. As post India–ASEAN FTA data on value added trade is not yet available, the significant opening up in the last few years following the FTA indicates deeper integration.

1. Participation of Asian Countries in International Value Chain

The present study begins with describing the distinction between global value chain and international production network and how these two are interwoven. Kimura and Obashi (2011) have argued that the unprecedented development of international production networks in the region has made East Asia truly the 'Factory of the World' (Backer and Miroudat 2013). They have also observed that the pattern of international division of labour and international trade in East Asia is no longer adequately explained by traditional trade theories as the international division of labour in the region is not by industry, but by the production process. What we observe is the fragmentation of the production process and the formation of industrial agglomerations. The network among different players at various stages of the production process has provided a new dimension in the Asian value chain development. Such networks are well developed in machines and auto component sectors, though they are also present in other industries. Machines typically consist of a large number of parts and components, each of which is produced by diversified technologies and inputs. Machinery industries are thus particularly suited to the fragmentation of production. The networks are initiated by lead firms, who are typically multinational corporations (MNCs) and they play the role of designers and coordinators. These MNCs are not just from Japan or Korea, but are also from the United States and Europe. The ADB (2007) has reported that the increase in intra-Asian trade comes from the vertical integration of production networks among countries and more than 70 per cent of intra-Asian trade is in intermediate goods, while G3 countries are important markets for final goods.

Authukorala (2010) has identified wage differentiation and lowering of trade transaction cost in Southeast Asia as major catalysts in enhancing and expansion of the network to ASEAN including countries like Vietnam and Indonesia. Transaction costs have been reduced because of soft policies such as trade and investment regimes (FTAs and investment promotion) and trade facilitation measures, and hard policies such as the development of airports, seaports, domestic transportation systems, etc. He has also highlighted the importance of the 'second mover advantage', rather than the first mover advantage, as the key determination of production fragmentation and relocation in the region. Foreign investment, which came as part of the first wave, created the foundation for the second wave. Investors during the second wave have received the benefit of supporting industries from the earlier investment and learned from the first wave's experiences. They expanded their operations in neighbouring countries as well. Additionally, the investors in the second wave and particularly the third wave, which invested in Vietnam, enjoy the economic growth of Southeast Asia and benefit from its positive income effect. Needless to say, the investment activity has got accentuated due to proliferation of FTAs in the region in which ASEAN has been actively involved; this also includes India–ASEAN FTA as well.

One of the important aspects that ensues the discussion on global value chains is to segregate the role of various countries in the value chain ladder. Most of the trade databases and statistics available today present a gross analysis in the way that they record most of the items in gross terms and the problem of multiple counting also remains inevitable. As an example, one can see the iPhone's value chain and multiple counting in trade statistics. The iPhone is designed in the United States but before it reaches the final stage of assembly in China, its components are procured, and some assembly operations are done in three countries, that is, Germany, Japan and Korea. Trade statistics take into account the value of the products traded in each stage from one country to other country. Trade data also takes into account the full value, when the final product is exported back from China to the United States despite the case that actual value addition by China is only 3.6 per cent of the total value of the iPhone (Xing 2013). As the global production is increasingly fragmented, the current way of capturing the value of trade is quite misleading.

One of the recent attempts to address needful issue is a new database that has been developed by the OECD, in cooperation with WTO, of trade flow in value-added terms based on a global model of international production and trade networks, better known as TIVA. It extracts data from the Inter-Country Input-Output (ICIO) model that links internationally input-output tables from 58 countries (one of these countries being the 'rest of the world') and accounts for more than 95 per cent of world output. Flows of intermediate inputs across countries and industries come from the Bilateral Trade Database by Industry and End-Use Category (BTDIxE). It allows the analysis of GVCs from a truly global perspective detailing all transactions between industries and countries for several industries. However, the analysis is based on various economic assumptions and hence it provides estimated value added information. Data for five years are available — 1995, 2000, 2005, 2008 and 2009 (see Backer and Miroudot 2013). What this allows us to ascertain is important questions like the position contribution and the nature of involvement of a country in a particular value chain. This database includes emerging economies such as India, Brazil and most of the ASEAN members.

The TIVA database maps the involvement of countries in value chains. This is done by analyzing several indices like Index of Production Stages, Participation Index and Index of distance to final demand. The thrust amid this discussion, however, still centres on comparing and locating the possible production networks between India and ASEAN entities. More specifically, these are explored by focusing on IPN in certain key industries that is, electrical, machinery and automobiles between these entities. A comparative analysis of aforesaid indices is also done for India, ASEAN and other leading Asian economies (like China, Japan and Korea), who are key players in these industries, to find out how they have evolved in regards to the parameter of value addition. Apart from this, the analysis of certain other variables like source country and source industry value addition, foreign component in gross exports and service value addition is carried out to further build on the issue.

2. Analysis of Relevant Indices

To start with, we would like to analyze the engagement of major Asian economies in GVC and how it has progressed over the years. We can compare India's position vis-à-vis ASEAN. It is important to note that the TIVA database provides information till 2009 and hence we are unable to analyze the post-FTA situation. Nonetheless, the information between 2000 and 2009 is important for India as during this time the country has been slowly integrated with the world economy and 2006 MSME development policy has given a boost to SMEs for international exposure. Also, studies by Uchikawa (2011) and Yamashita (2011) have given indication that both forward and backward linkages of Indian industries are growing internationally.

2.1 Participation Index

The immediate question that follows the above discussion is to find out the magnitude of involvement of countries in the value chain. A country's involvement in the production process can be said to have both forward and backward linkages. These could be understood as a country entering the value chains both as a recipient of foreign inputs for the items it exports as well as a supplier of intermediate products which acts as inputs in third countries exports to which it has supplied. To understand this clearly one can look at the 'Participation Index'. The index is expressed as a percentage of gross exports and indicates the share of foreign inputs (backward participation) and domestically produced inputs used in third countries' exports (forward participation). The calculation of the index is based on work suggested by Koopman et al. (2010). The higher the foreign value-added embodied in gross exports and the higher the value of inputs exported to third countries and used in their exports, the higher is the participation of a given country in the value chain. The index is expressed as percentage of gross exports and hence the range of value is 0–100.

Selected Asian countries in Table 5.1 have shown a steady increase in their participation in GVC except in 2009, which we may consider as an exception due to the global financial crisis. But the increase in participation is not homogeneous for all the countries and further translates into either higher use of foreign inputs in own exports or a rise in the contribution of exports to third countries. This is precisely the trend that gets corroborated from Table 1. India, for instance, has witnessed a rise in the participation index from 31.84 per cent to 42.27 per cent over the reference period, but within that rise the share of forward participation index has increased slightly from around 19 per cent in 2000 to 22 per cent in 2008 and then reduced to 20 per cent in 2009. In case of backward participation index, in 2000, it was only 13 per cent but increased to 24 per cent in 2008 and came down to 22 per cent in 2009. This implies that during the last decade India has been integrated more backwardly as increasing amount of foreign inputs are now used in its exports. This is more than our forward linkage in terms of supplying semi finished goods to third country exports. Similar is the case for China, where the overall participation index has increased from around 32 per cent to nearly 46 per cent over the period, but within that there has been significant increase in backward participation index from nearly 18 per cent to around 32 per cent that has contributed significantly to the overall rise in the former. The share of forward participation index on the contrary has remained more or less same during this period with certain fluctuations. Apple's iPhone example above is corroborating the fact that China has come up as the final stage assembler of many products having significant backward linkage. ASEAN's participation index has shown relatively less growth. Backward index is more or less constant, where forward linkage increased marginally. ASEAN's overall participation index has been around 57.63 per cent in 2009, which is higher than India, China and Japan. Korea's international linkage is much higher compared to other selected countries in the Table 5.1. The participation index for Korea has increased from 52 per cent to 65 per cent over the period with the share of backward participation index

TABLE 5.1
Participation in GVC by Asian Countries: Year-wise Participation Index (%)

Participation Index	Year	India	China	ASEAN	Japan	Korea
Total	2000	31.84	32.57	54.96	36.00	52.06
Forward	2000	19.06	13.75	18.38	26.09	19.13
Backward	2000	12.78	18.81	35.47	9.91	32.93
Total	2005	42.78	48.63	61.77	43.39	63.94
Forward	2005	23.27	12.25	23.55	29.64	26.22
Backward	2005	19.51	36.38	36.55	13.75	37.72
Total	2008	46.07	47.62	62.09	50.05	68.40
Forward	2008	22.34	14.35	23.94	30.70	24.98
Backward	2008	23.72	33.27	36.13	19.35	43.42
Total	2009	42.27	46.06	57.63	47.75	65.03
Forward	2009	20.35	13.43	22.45	32.95	24.39
Backward	2009	21.92	32.63	33.14	14.79	40.64

Source: OECD STATS, TIVA Indicators, May 2013.

reaching almost 40 per cent in 2009, compared to 32 per cent in 2000. This reflects the increasing reliance on foreign inputs for own exports for concerned countries. Japan has highest forward linkage which has been around 33 per cent in 2009. Japan derives significant gain from exporting technology based high valued components, which are used in other country's exports.

2.2 Distance to Final Demand

At the next level to gauge the India's engagement in IPN, we need to understand its position in the value chain in different industries. The distance to final demand, an indicator suggested in literature by Fally (2012), gives an idea of this. It tells us about how upstream or downstream a country is located in a particular value chain. A higher value is indicative of the fact that a country is involved in more upstream activities that lie at the beginning of the value chains (R&D, input-oriented activities). Lower value of the index indicates closer proximity to final consumers, and thus, engagement in downstream activities.

Tables 5.2a and 5.2b show the comparative analysis of the index for India, China and some leading Asian countries for the years 2000 and 2009 for certain key industries. We have not included Japan and Korea in this discussion as we have noted from the earlier index that they are in general ahead of most of the Asian countries. Also, selected countries in Tables 5.2a and 5.2b are the close competitors to each other in many industries. A closer examination of Tables 5.2a and 5.2b reveal that China's value has increased in almost all industries between 2000 and 2009 implying its increasing involvement in upstream activities. However, in contrast, India's industries, such as machinery, chemical, electrical and optical equipment, wholesale and retail trade, transport, storage and telecommunication and financial intermediation, have experienced a rise in the index score reflecting their increased engagement in upstream activities in international value chain. On the other hand, a fall in the index score is visible in industries, such as textile, transport equipment and business services, which indicates the move towards the downstream activities. In other words, companies in these industries operating from India are exporting products, which are close to final goods in the value chain. Among the ASEAN members, Vietnam, the Philippines and Indonesia have experienced move towards downstream activities, where Singapore, Thailand and Malaysia have gone ahead with the upstream activities focusing more on technology development and critical component manufacturing. To summarize, countries such as Singapore, Malaysia and Thailand have moved ahead towards upstream activities and have more control on the value chain and this trend is visible in some industries in India too. But, Indonesia, the Philippines and Vietnam are at the lower end of the value chain and mostly concentrating on assembly shop activities. ASEAN FTA has reduced the duties on parts and accessories substantially. Along with this, streamlining the trade facilitation process, investment in infrastructure and

TABLE 5.2a
'Distance to Final Demand Index' Reflecting Country's Position in Industry-Wise Value Chain

Year: 2000	China	India	Indonesia	Malaysia	Philippines	Singapore	Thailand	Vietnam
Food products and beverages	1.82	1.27	1.62	2.27	1.37	1.67	1.68	1.40
Textiles, leather and footwear	2.22	1.64	1.88	1.42	1.25	1.89	1.70	1.41
Wood, paper, paper products, printing and publishing	2.98	2.37	2.98	2.59	2.34	2.51	2.70	2.19
Chemicals and non-metallic mineral products	3.13	2.54	2.76	2.66	2.63	3.10	2.74	2.44
Basic metals and fabricated metal products	3.28	2.52	2.97	3.02	3.06	2.86	2.77	2.86
Machinery and equipment n.e.c	2.23	1.68	2.36	1.52	1.84	1.77	1.97	1.90
Electrical and optical equipment	2.29	1.72	1.87	2.57	2.56	2.44	2.20	2.33
Transport equipment	2.39	1.64	2.07	1.97	2.41	2.63	1.94	2.16
Wholesale and retail trade; hotels and restaurants	2.69	1.92	2.17	2.68	1.95	2.06	1.90	1.86
Transport and storage; post and telecommunications	2.84	1.93	2.27	2.38	1.91	2.51	2.27	2.34
Financial intermediation	2.85	2.39	2.43	3.41	2.46	2.77	2.69	2.32
Business services	2.08	1.69	2.19	2.24	2.02	2.22	2.00	2.68

Source: OECD STATS, TIVA Indicators, May 2013.

Emerging Production Networks 63

TABLE 5.2b
'Distance to Final Demand Index' Reflecting Country's Position in Industry-Wise Value Chain

Year: 2009	China	India	Indonesia	Malaysia	Philippines	Singapore	Thailand	Vietnam
Food products and beverages	2.55	1.35	1.74	2.39	1.30	1.72	1.67	1.30
Textiles, leather and footwear	2.53	1.61	1.54	1.51	1.73	1.99	1.84	1.37
Wood, paper, paper products, printing and publishing	3.64	2.56	2.68	2.82	2.51	2.54	2.74	2.21
Chemicals and non-metallic mineral products	3.41	2.67	2.67	2.83	2.62	3.25	2.87	2.35
Basic metals and fabricated metal products	3.48	2.58	3.30	3.19	3.08	3.00	2.88	2.69
Machinery and equipment n.e.c	2.34	1.73	1.83	1.60	1.57	2.01	2.12	1.52
Electrical and optical equipment	2.55	1.89	1.63	3.08	2.82	3.10	2.39	1.89
Transport equipment	2.34	1.57	1.91	2.08	1.83	1.83	1.96	2.01
Wholesale and retail trade; hotels and restaurants	2.59	2.07	1.84	2.75	2.01	2.41	1.96	1.71
Transport and storage; post and telecommunications	2.97	2.17	2.18	2.54	2.01	2.61	2.39	2.13
Financial intermediation	3.27	2.55	2.03	3.62	2.53	2.48	2.76	2.12
Business services	2.24	1.62	2.07	2.27	2.09	2.42	2.03	2.52

Source: OECD STATS, TIVA Indicators, May 2013.

reduction of trade barriers have helped the ASEAN value chain to spread across the region. Bigger and richer countries in the region are ahead in the value chain leaving basic assembling and non-critical activities to other countries, such as Vietnam and Indonesia. Investment flow within the region has also accentuated the process. Also, due to economic growth, wage rates in Thailand, Malaysia and even in China have increased substantially, which is also one of the major reasons for pushing the basic manufacturing activities towards the countries with lower wage rate.

While discussing industry-wise scenario, it can be mentioned that in production of machinery China is more involved in upstream activities and India is ahead of Malaysia, the Philippines and Vietnam. In case of electrical and optical equipment, Singapore has the highest score in 2009, followed by Malaysia. India has also shown a rising trend and remains close to Vietnam level. In transport equipment, China experienced a fall along with India. India is still not involved in much of upstream activities and is mainly engaged in downstream activities which are more related to final assembly in the production network.

5.3 Index of Production Stages

At this juncture, it is also important to take care of the fact that the participation index discussed earlier only gives an idea of the extent of vertical specialization of a country. This means that it only tells us about the domestic content used in third countries exports or the foreign content used in home countries exports at a particular point. But, it does not give an idea of how 'Long' are the value chains. It might be the case that, for instance, the higher value of forward participation index for a country may be driven by higher share of value added at the final stage. This means that there is a need of certain indicator to throw the light on the longevity of value chains and subsequently to tell how many production stages are involved before a product is finally delivered. One such index suggested in literature and incorporated in the TIVA database is the index of production stages. It measures the length of GVCs in each industry. The index takes the value of 1 if there is a single production stage in the final industry and its value increases, when intermediate inputs from the same industry or other industries are used in the production of the final good or service. This indicator can be further decomposed to reflect domestic production stages and foreign production stages. The index was proposed by Fally (2012) and calculated for the US economy with a single country input-output matrix. Using inter-country inter-industry framework, OECD–TIVA calculate the index of the length of GVCs.

For the selected industries, the index of stages of production is given in the Tables 5.3a and 5.3b. This provides an account of the how long the value chains are for a given industry and how much indigenous or foreign oriented it becomes in terms of the number of production stages driven domestically or internationally. In case

TABLE 5.3a
Index of Number of Production Stages in Selected Countries: Electrical and Optical Equipment Sector

Time	Index of Production Stages in 2000			Index of Production Stages in 2009		
Indicator	Total	Domestic	International	Total	Domestic	International
India	2.42	2.08	0.33	2.51	2.04	0.47
Indonesia	2.48	1.83	0.65	2.41	1.71	0.70
Malaysia	2.47	1.12	1.34	2.62	1.16	1.46
The Philippines	2.50	1.18	1.32	2.65	1.40	1.26
Singapore	2.71	1.41	1.30	2.83	1.33	1.49
Thailand	2.38	1.32	1.06	2.59	1.33	1.26
Vietnam	2.77	1.49	1.28	3.05	1.36	1.69

Source: OECD STATS, TIVA Indicators, May 2013.

TABLE 5.3b
Index of Number of Production Stages in Selected Countries: Transport Equipment Sector

Time	Index of Production Stages in 2000			Index of Production Stages in 2009		
Indicator	Total	Domestic	International	Total	Domestic	International
India	2.65	2.32	0.33	2.61	2.11	0.50
Indonesia	2.22	1.68	0.54	2.31	1.88	0.44
Malaysia	2.58	1.34	1.23	2.69	1.47	1.23
The Philippines	2.72	1.65	1.08	2.80	1.92	0.88
Singapore	2.50	1.81	0.68	2.48	1.46	1.01
Thailand	2.56	1.45	1.11	2.62	1.47	1.15
Vietnam	2.66	1.57	1.09	2.84	1.47	1.37

Source: OECD STATS, TIVA Indicators, May 2013.

of machinery sector, Asia has become the factory of the world and value chain has got elongated during the last decade. A comparison between 2000 and 2009 data reveals that among selected ASEAN members, highest increase is visible for Vietnam. It has increased for other countries as well including that for India. However, in India's final demand index of international stages of production is still quite low. Similar result is observed for electrical and transport equipment. This is important to note that India's index of total production stages is quite close to ASEAN level but it focuses mostly on domestic value addition.

3. ANALYSIS OF VALUE CHAIN IN SELECTED INDUSTRIES AMONG ASEAN AND INDIA

3.1 India

The TIVA country note on India[1] indicates that the country has witnessed a significant move to get itself integrated with GVC. Its domestic value added content for its exports has been around 78 per cent in 2009, which was close to 90 per cent in 1995. Business services, other manufacturing industries, chemical, transport equipment, machinery, electronic equipments and others are the major sectors, which have higher foreign component in their exports. Contributions from many regions in India's gross exports rose during 1995 to 2009, with East and Southeast Asia, Europe and North America increasing their shares by 3.5 per cent, 2.5 per cent and 1 per cent, respectively. India has contributed significantly by providing value added services in other country's exports. In value added terms, over half of India's exports reflect services, which are slightly higher than even OECD in 2009. This has been mainly driven by increasing direct exports of services along with higher service content in manufacturing exports such as machinery, electronics and transport equipment.

Appendix 2 describes the backward linkage in India's exports in selected products. In all these categories between 2000 and 2009, India's domestic component in its exports has come down. In machinery, it has reduced from 84 per cent in 2000 to 77 per cent in 2009. A careful observation reflects that the share of value added

---

[1] Available at http://www.oecd.org/sti/ind/TiVA_INDIA_MAY_2013.pdf (accessed 5 August 2014).

component from the European Union and NAFTA was high in 2000, but it has come down in 2009 with a rising share of East Asia and ASEAN. Partner countries contributed mainly through supplying value added products from sectors such as basic metal and electrical equipments, and providing services such as trading, transport, financial services and business services. In the case of India's exports of electronics and optical equipment, we have observed an increased contribution by East and Southeast Asian countries. These countries are supplying value-added components, which are used in India's exports of electronic products. It is also noteworthy that the contribution of western economies is slowly coming down. The value-added components and services coming from the European Union, which are embodied in Indian exports including products like chemical, basic metals, trading, storage, financial and business services. However, contribution from ASEAN is mostly limited to products not services except trading. In case of transport equipment also similar trend is visible. India is now outsourcing almost 24 per cent of the value added products and services, which are embodied in India's export of automobile and components. The EU's share has slightly decreased and shares of East Asia and ASEAN have significantly increased. It is important to note that share of NAFTA has also increased. Like other sectors, western economies are both supplying products and services, but Asian economies are mostly supplying components, which are embodied in India's exports. More strikingly, in case of manufacturing products (not classified elsewhere),[2] India's exports now contain almost 50 per cent of foreign value added components. All selected regions' contribution including those from ASEAN region experienced a big jump during 2000–09.

Table 5.4 describes country-wise share of value added components and services in India's exports in different sectors. Although, India has become much closer to Southeast and East Asian countries, it is still importing major value added components from European Union and United States for its exports of selected products. Among Asian countries, China and Japan are much above, compared to Southeast Asian countries.

3.2 ASEAN

Table 5.5 explains the foreign value added embodied in major ASEAN members' exports. Intra-ASEAN's trade has helped the region to become more integrated and competitive in other parts of the world. Significant amount of their exports are sourced from other countries in the region. This is very high for Indonesia. We have seen earlier that Indonesia has specialized in downstream activities and hence large portion of its exports originate in other countries and they come to Indonesia at the final stage of production to leverage the advantage of cheap labour. However, in terms of sourcing from India, countries such as Singapore, Malaysia and Vietnam are ahead of other countries in the region. India provides mainly business services, which are required in the

TABLE 5.4
Share (%) of Value Added from Selected Trade Partners Embodied
in India's Gross Exports: Industry-wise Scenario in 2009

Source Countries	Machinery	Electrical	Transport	Manufacturing (n.e.c)
France	0.45	0.47	0.57	1.12
Germany	0.92	0.98	1.09	3.55
Japan	0.65	0.76	0.84	2.66
Korea	0.54	0.61	0.66	1.85
United Kingdom	0.6	0.59	0.69	1.08
United States	2.04	2.04	2.55	4.83
China	1.1	1.28	1.38	6.35
Indonesia	0.26	0.28	0.27	0.66
Malaysia	0.2	0.26	0.23	1.03
The Philippines	0.04	0.07	0.05	0.19
Russia	0.55	0.54	0.55	0.94
Singapore	0.32	0.38	0.41	0.91
Thailand	0.2	0.22	0.26	1.02

Source: OECD STATS, TIVA Indicators, May 2013.

---

[2] This sector is not among the three selected sectors. We have considered it since it has experienced a significant decline in domestic value added component in gross exports during the period of 2000–09.

TABLE 5.5
Share (%) of Foreign Value Added Embodied in ASEAN's Exports in Selected Sectors in 2009

Source Country	Destination Country	Machinery	Electrical	Transport	Manufacturing (n.e.c)
India	Indonesia	0.56	0.59	0.28	0.33
	Malaysia	0.60	0.70	1.23	0.97
	The Philippines	0.74	0.37	0.72	0.30
	Singapore	1.12	1.90	0.85	1.11
	Thailand	0.62	0.43	0.65	0.45
	Vietnam	0.82	0.86	0.63	0.75
Source Region	Destination Country	Machinery	Electrical	Transport	Manufacturing (n.e.c)
ASEAN	Indonesia	66.67	77.07	86.19	88.19
	Malaysia	49.81	49.52	58.93	61.05
	The Philippines	68.39	57.97	70.08	80.63
	Singapore	48.22	47.61	58.66	58.66
	Thailand	60.05	54.00	59.69	68.24
	Vietnam	50.22	44.19	51.14	48.34

Source: OECD STATS, TIVA Indicators, May 2013.

manufacturing process. Apart from this, India also supplies metal products, machinery and other manufactured products. India's engagement in trading, transport, storage and telecommunication are also important for the exports from the ASEAN region.

4. India–ASEAN FTA and Prospect for IPN

It has been argued that as India reduces duties, its industries would get integrated with IPNs in ASEAN. Analysis in earlier sections show that during 2000 and 2009, foreign value added component in India's gross exports from Southeast Asia was not only rising, it was also slowly replacing the European Union and the United States. India–ASEAN FTA is expected to accentuate the process. Between 2010 and 2013, following the FTA process, India has slashed duties especially in the selected sectors substantially. Table 5.6 provides a snapshot of the changes in the preferential rates for three sectors, namely, machinery (HS 84), electrical (HS 85) and automotive (HS 87). In case of HS 84, in 2010 only 104 lines attracted zero duties, which increased to 128 in 2013. In 2010, bulk of the products (1068) under this chapter heading was having 5 per cent duty and now majority (930) of them has come down to only 2.5 per cent. In the 3 per cent category, number of lines increased from 6 to 172. In HS 85, tariff rates of the bulk of the products in 2010 were either 7.5 per cent or 5 per cent. Majority of them also come down to 2.5 per cent. Some products are in 3 per cent and 4 per cent category. The reduction of the tariff in the

TABLE 5.6
Frequency Table of Sector-wise Tariff Rates under India–ASEAN FTA

Tariff Rates	HS 84		HS 85		HS 87	
	No. of Lines on 1-Jan-10	No. of Lines on 1-Jan-13	No. of Lines on 1-Jan-10	No. of Lines on 1-Jan-13	No. of Lines on 1-Jan-10	No. of Lines on 1-Jan-13
0	104	128	146	147	1	1
2.5	0	930	0	331	0	58
3	6	172	0	50	0	0
4	20	7	1	72	0	6
5	1068	0	256	0	0	6
6	43	43	48	48	0	0
7.5	39	21	197	26	64	13
9	21	0	26	0	13	0
20	0	0	0	0	0	6
30	0	0	0	0	12	0
Exclusion list	35	35	20	20	92	92

Source: Calculated and created by the author using the India–ASEAN (5+CLMV) Tariff Schedule.

HS 85 category looks more steady and distributed. In case of HS 87, it is evident from the Table 5.6 that most of the products in this category are in the exclusion list. This corroborates the common view that countries want to achieve high degree of localization in the automobile sector. The other observation revealed from this table is that there seems to be a major one shot decline in the number of those products which attracted higher duties earlier towards the lower category of 2.5 per cent. For all three sectors, India has substantially reduced number of products under higher duty category.

In continuation to the reduction of duties, India's import under these three categories increased significantly in the last few years. India's machinery import jumped leaps and bound after 2009. The imported machineries are used for producing final goods both for domestic as well as international consumption. The rising trade deficit under this category has slightly tapered in 2013 due to a slowing down of imports. In 2013, India's export was around US$ 1.7 billion, and it imported machinery under HS 84 approximately US$ 3.4 billion. India's import of electrical and optical products from ASEAN rose steadily since last one decade. Increased purchasing power due to rising economic growth in India in the post-2000 period has been responsible for higher imports. In electrical (HS 85), India's trade deficit has been rising continuously as India's exports to Southeast Asia has remained more or less stagnant with a slow rising trend. In 2013, India's export was merely US$ 878 million, while it imported goods worth around US$ 4.5 billion. Quite interestingly, in the automobile sector under HS 87, India has accrued small yet positive surplus. A production network in true sense with return trade is visible in this sector. Since the implementation of early harvest scheme under India–Thailand FTA in early 2000, Toyota has started exporting gear box and other critical components from India. India's trade balance in HS 87 has been positive from 2004 onwards. Now, India exports small passenger vehicles, pick up vans, special purpose vehicles and large scale two-wheelers in Southeast region. In 2013, its export was more than US$ 1 billion, while it imported around US$ 414 million.

5. CONCLUSIONS

Developing IPNs depend on a host of conditions ranging from infrastructure, conducive industrial policies, encouragement towards technological innovation, to absorptive capacity of SMEs and end-market competitiveness. Using TIVA database, it has been observed that India is slowly but steadily getting integrated with the industries of Southeast Asia, especially in machinery, electrical and automobile sectors. This also carries some ramifications for Indian SMEs because these industries are closely tied with domestic SMEs. Thus, if SMEs could overcome technological, financial and other barriers, the IPN in these sectors might act as a growth facilitator for them as well. Commenting on the TIVA analysis further, it is observed that so far, in India's exports of above mentioned products (that is, electric, machinery and automobile), contributions of Europe and the United States have been higher than Southeast Asia and China, but the scenario is changing fast. India is mostly importing components and engaging itself in downstream activities. China has moved towards upstream activities, and thereby has better control over the value chain activities. India is ahead of Indonesia, the Philippines and the CLMV countries, but behind Malaysia, Singapore and Thailand in terms of value addition capability in the production system. India's contribution in the global value chain is not only limited to downstream final assembly, but also in various business services, which are required in the manufacturing process. India's engagement in trading, transport, storage and telecommunication are also important for the exports from the ASEAN region. It is noted that in the post-FTA period, India has surged ahead with exports of automobile components, implying its strong presence in ASEAN IPN. On the other hand, in machinery, imports from Southeast Asia are used both in final goods production for domestic consumption as well as for international use. In case of electronic and optical equipment, India is still on the fringe with limited connectivity. India lacks attractiveness in terms of possible investment in these sectors, especially in developing joint ventures with SMEs. Though India is ranked high in terms of adopting new technology, the major skill gap in manufacturing sector is a stumbling block for converting this into a productivity gain. Along with this, as discussed earlier, most SMEs still face certain barriers in the form of lack of financing, exposure to new technology and the ability to conduct small innovation. An effective handholding, proper policy support and awareness about global business strategy can help Indian SMEs to become more connected with emerging international or regional production network.

6

Corridors, Connectivity Challenges and New Direction

An economic corridor is an infrastructure that helps facilitate economic activities. Figure 6.1 shows the stages involved in the development of an economic corridor. A corridor can be national (for example, Leipzig–Frankfurt corridor, Tokyo–Osaka corridor), regional (for example, GMS or CAREC corridors), or even international (for example, submarine telecommunication cables or energy pipelines). Trade facilitation and logistics services are the main catalysts in the development of economic corridor. Economic corridor helps strengthen industrial (or, services) agglomeration over time through establishment of industrial zones (or, SEZs) and facilitates cluster-type development of enterprises.

Economic corridors provide connection between gateways, economic nodes or hubs. The economic corridor approach emphasizes integration of infrastructure improvement with economic opportunities such as trade and investment, and it includes efforts to harness the social and other outcomes of increased connectivity (see De and Iyengar 2014). Economic corridors become successful when corridors connecting gateways (cities) coupled with supporting institutions (logistics) improve the competitiveness of a geographic space (country). The economic corridor approach has gained momentum in Asia with the Asian Development Bank's (ADB) support to the Greater Mekong Subregion (GMS) and later Central Asia Regional Economic Cooperation Programme (CAREC). A major achievement of the GMS Programme is improved transport connectivity in the subregion, particularly in the less-developed areas, as exemplified in the main GMS economic corridors: the East–West, the North–South and the Southern. There are large opportunities for trade, investment and economic growth due to multimodal economic corridors. However, challenges are plenty such as acquisition of land or raising taxes on citizens in highly subsidized economies for development of infrastructure, townships and industrial or economic zones.

India's regional integration with Southeast Asia has been following two major paths: ASEAN–India Transit Transport Agreement (software),[1] and ASEAN–India connectivity (hardware) — Trilateral Highway (TH), Mekong–India Economic Corridor (MIEC). While the first path may lead us in achieving paperless trade, the second one may help us in facilitating seamless trade.[2] India's connectivity with Southeast Asia has been evolving primarily on two structures — national connectivity such as Golden Quadrilateral (GQ) projects, Delhi–Mumbai Industrial Corridor (DMIC), Dedicated Freight Corridor (DFC), etc. and regional connectivity such as the TH, MIEC and others. At the same time, India's regional connectivity with Southeast Asia has been evolving on two pillars: North East India for multimodal and intermodal operations and Southern India for multimodal operation. India's connectivity with Southeast Asia, although lying at present in very initial stage of development, may appear to be a great facilitator of pan-Asian integration in coming years (Bhattacharya et al. 2012).

This chapter presents India's broad proposals on connectivity projects with Southeast Asia and policy recommendations to strengthen connectivity in Asia in general and that between ASEAN and India in particular.

FIGURE 6.1
Stages of Development of Economic Corridor

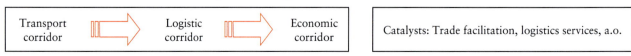

Source: Illustrated by the author.

---

[1] This is presently known as India–Myanmar–Thailand Transit Agreement or Motor Vehicle Agreement.
[2] Refer, for example, *ASEAN–India Eminent Persons Group Report 2012*. Available at http://www.aseanindia.com (accessed 22 February 2015).

1. Economic Links and Role in Production Networks

Economic corridors play a key role in integrating economies across regions. Some of their environmental effects notwithstanding, well-functioning and efficient economic corridors are essential for the development of a region. For example, reducing the costs of transportation, both within and across regions, improves international market access, increases income and reduces poverty. The salutary effect of improving cross-border transport infrastructure in the GMS has been well documented, and better connectivity has helped the subregion reduce poverty.[3] On one hand, economic corridors are meant to fill regional infrastructure gaps, and on the other, promote pro-poor socioeconomic development. They help increase trade flows, create employment and reduce poverty. Box 6.1 presents some economic benefits of an economic corridor.

Why do we need to focus on economic corridors? How do they differ from transport corridors? The literature suggests economic corridors have three specific advantages over transport corridors. First, sustained economic growth increases the demand for infrastructure services — software or otherwise. Improved economic corridors help ease the demand for infrastructure services, generating more output. Second, efficient economic corridor networks are important to regional integration, in both absolute and relative terms, as tariff-based barriers have declined. Economic corridors help facilitate trade and investment, fostering regional integration. Third, better infrastructure (supply links) encourages fragmentation of production, and enhances regional and global trade, expediting regional integration.

Corridor has gained importance, particularly in the 1990s, due to China's involvement in vertically integrated supply chains and large share of international trade in intermediate goods and openness to FDI. If India (or, South Asia) aims to become manufacturing powerhouse through 'Make-in-India', the country needs investment in transport and communications infrastructure for just-in-time delivery (JIT) and opportunities in vertically integrated supply chains.

There is another argument for building regional economic corridor. As the international economy is vulnerable to shocks, there is need to reduce export dependence and increase reliance on regional markets (for example, fruits and vegetables, textile and clothing, and automobile parts). Building regional economic corridors will then increase regional trade, thereby facilitating regional integration process.

Box 6.1

Benefits of Economic Corridors

Economic corridors are meant to serve as a blueprint for enhanced connectivity, increased competitiveness and a greater sense of community in a region. In particular, they have the following specific benefits:

- improving national and regional connectivity by making it faster, cheaper and easier for people and goods to move within and across borders;
- reducing the cost of trade, thus enhancing the competitiveness of national and regional production networks and promoting greater investment;
- promoting greater regional and global integration and, thus, faster economic growth;
- helping reduce poverty by improving poor people's access to economic opportunities, lowering the cost of goods and services they consume, and providing better access to essential infrastructure services such as electricity;
- helping narrow development gaps among regional economies by providing small, poor, landlocked, and remote countries and areas with better access to regional markets and production networks, thereby stimulating investment, trade and economic growth in those areas; and
- promoting greener technologies and a more efficient use of regional resources, such as gas reserves and rivers with hydroelectric potential, by developing cross-border projects that permit regional energy trade.

Source: De and Iyengar (2014).
Note: Illustrated by Manmeet Ajmani.

---

[3] The remarkable progress in Mekong in recent years is reflected in an increase in average per capita income from about US$ 630 in 1992 to about US$ 1,100 in 2006 (World Bank 2007). Edmonds and Fujimura (2008) found a positive effect of cross-border infrastructure on trade in major goods in the Mekong region.

Figure 6.2
Gateways, the Border and Beyond

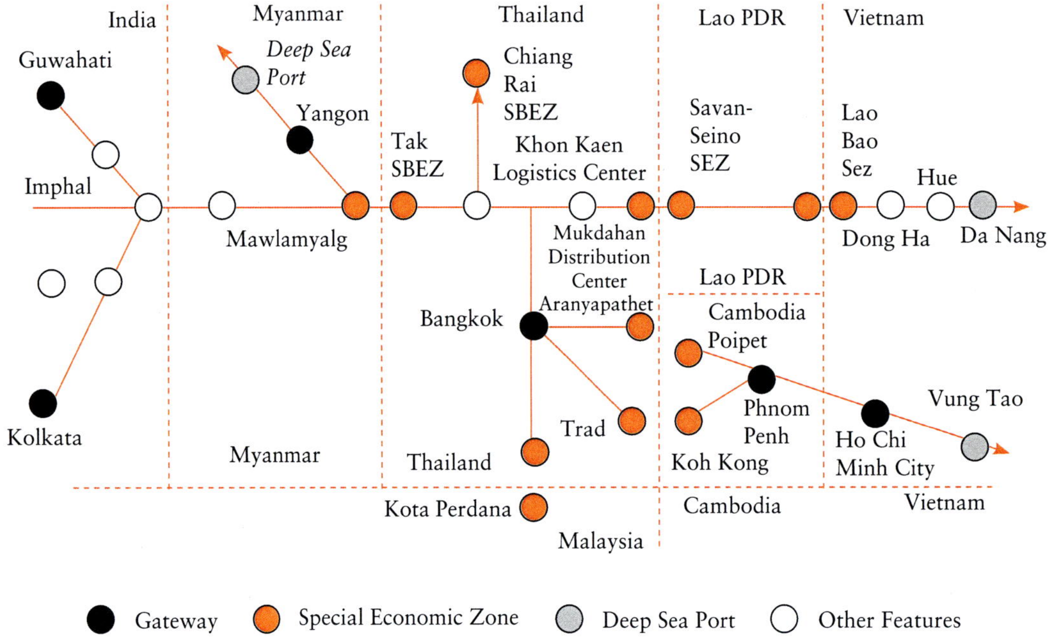

Source: De (2014).
Note: Illustrated by Manmeet Ajmani.

Economic corridors helps strengthen industrial (or, services) agglomeration over time through establishment of industrial zones (or, SEZs) and also helps in dispersion from congested or agglomerated zones to less congested or in periphery areas. Therefore, developed infrastructure in the border region facilitates trade, and regional development through agglomeration of industries.

Compared to GMS, where we have some prominent SEZs and deep sea ports (Figure 6.2), India's North Eastern Region (NER) does not have any operational SEZ at present. Industrial clusters, SEZs and industrial parks in the NER may facilitate investments in industrial and services units.

2. India's Major Corridors with ASEAN

India has been implementing several corridors with ASEAN countries, particularly Myanmar. Some of the corridors are multimodal types and some are intermodals. Corridor like trilateral highway is getting ready, while Mekong–India Economic Corridor (MEC) is yet to be implemented. Here, we present some of the corridors which India has been implementing in ASEAN.

2.1 Trilateral Highway (TH) Corridor

The India–Myanmar–Thailand Trilateral Highway (IMTTH) is a cross-border transportation corridor being financed by the Governments of India, Myanmar and Thailand. This highway links Moreh (in India) with Mae Sot (in Thailand) through Bagan or Mandalay (in Myanmar), which is often termed as the land-bridge between South and Southeast Asia. The alignment of this Trilateral Highway falls within Asian Highways 1 and 2. Shown in Map 6.1, the agreed route of the TH (1,360 km) is as follows: Moreh (India)–Tamu–Kalewa–Yargi–Monywa–Mandalay–NayPyiTaw–Yangon–Thaton–Hypaan–Kawkareik–Myawaddy–Mae Sot (Thailand). Along this corridor, there are two border crossings (India–Myanmar and Myanmar–Thailand), four customs check-points, three international time zones, three customs EDI systems, two different vehicle driving standards and three different motor vehicle laws. Challenge is to reach convergence in standards and procedures along the corridor.

The TH is divided into three phases; the first phase includes 78 km of new roads, upgradation of about 400 km of roads, construction of all-weather approach lanes, rehabilitation/reconstruction of weak or distressed bridges. The entire project is being funded through government resources. Phase-I of the TH was taken up in early 2005.

India assumes responsibility of 78 km of missing links and 58 km of upgradation as part of Phase-I. The Indian government's Border Roads Organization (BRO) had upgraded the Tamu–Kalewa–Kalemyo (TKK) part of the TH (160 km) in Myanmar from the Indian Northeastern border at a cost of Rs. 1.20 billion (about US$ 27.28 million). The Government of India is responsible for maintenance of the TKK part of the TH in Myanmar.

As agreed during the Joint Task Force Meeting on TH, held on 10–11 September 2012 at New Delhi, India is constructing the Kalewa to Yargi portion (132 km) of the TH. The Yargi to Monywa portion of the TH will be constructed by the Myanmar government, whereas the Hpa-An to Mae Sot (Thailand) portion has already been developed by the Thailand government.[4]

Till date, the Tamu and Kalewa friendship road is being constructed with India's assistance (Map 1). About 132 km has been completed and handed over to Myanmar. India has also undertaken the task of repair/upgradation of 71 bridges on the Tamu–Kalewa friendship Road, and upgradation of the 120 km Kalewa–Yargyi road segment to highway standard, while Myanmar has agreed to undertake upgradation of the Yargyi–Monywa stretch to bring it to highway standard by 2016. This project would help in establishing trilateral connectivity from Moreh in India to Mae Sot in Thailand via Myanmar.

Lack of essential institutional support and government commitments are some of the reasons for slow progress of the Trilateral Highway. Deeper regional cooperation among the three countries would speed up the development of the highway. At the ASEAN–India Commemorative Summit 2012, it was decided to extend the Trilateral Highway to Lao PDR, Vietnam and Cambodia in order to add greater momentum to the growing trade and investment linkages between ASEAN and India.[5] The TH is likely to be ready by 2016.[6]

MAP 6.1
Trilateral Highway Alignment

Source: ASEAN–India Centre (AIC), New Delhi.
Note: Drawn by Sachin Singhal.

---

[4] Based on authors' personal communication with the Trilateral Highway Joint Task Force Member.

[5] For further details, see the Vision Statement of the ASEAN–India Commemorative Summit 2012. Available at http://www.aseanindia.com (accessed 22 February 2015).

[6] This date is now changed to 2018 (based on author's own communication with the Ministry of External Affairs (MEA), Government of India.

There is a need to consider new approaches designed to raise its profile, in this case within the economic corridor framework. To make it more inclusive, we should identify link routes connecting other nodes in NER, such as Shillong, Dimapur, Aizawl, Agartala, Nagaon and Dibrugarh. These are the major urban cities in the region, which will become major economic centres along the corridor.

2.2 Delhi–Hanoi Railway Link (DHRL)

Railways can play a positive role in ASEAN–India economic integration, which will promote bulk trans-national movement of goods and services among the neighbouring countries. The needs are five-fold — (a) to link Imphal, the capital of Manipur State of India with India's main railway corridor, (b) to link Imphal with Kalay in Myanmar (about 212 km), (c) to link Thanbyuzayat with Three Pagoda Pass in Thailand (110 km), (d) standardization of the railway tracks in Myanmar and also some parts in India's NER, and (e) to re-establish and renovate railway networks in Myanmar. Indian Railways is actively engaged in harmonization and construction of railway tracks in the north-eastern region of India. Projects for rail connectivity to the state capitals of Sikkim, Meghalaya, Mizoram, Manipur and Nagaland have been sanctioned by the Indian Railways. On 4 January 2014, the first Broad Gauge (BG) train from Guwahati to Tezpur via Rangiya commenced. In March 2015, Lumding-Silchar broad gauge railway line was commissioned. The railway lines between Harmuti–Itanagar and Dudhnai–Mendipathar were completed in part recently. Meghalaya has been brought on Indian Railway map for the first time with commissioning of Dudhnoi — Mendipathar New Line. Itanagar, the capital of Arunachal Pradesh, was connected with Delhi with the flagging off of direct train between Naharlagun and New Delhi recently. Harmuti — North Lakhimpur section has been commissioned for passenger traffic and North Lakhimpur-Murkongselek section has been commissioned for goods traffic. With this, the entire Rangiya — Murkongselek and Balipara — Bhalukpong (510 Km) Metre Gauge line along the North Bank of Brahmaputra has been converted to Broad Gauge.

Indian consulting engineering company, RITES, completed a preliminary study to establish Delhi–Hanoi Railway Link in 2006. The Indian government is planning to develop the DHRL through two possible routes. Both the proposed railway routes will connect Hanoi through Myanmar with different rail links. Route-I will connect Hanoi via Myanmar, Thailand and Cambodia. In Route-II, it is diverted to Bangkok via Ye and the newly constructed portion of Ye and Dawei in Myanmar, and then to Hanoi through Thailand and Lao PDR. In both the routes, the proposed link from Silchar (India) to Thanbyuzayat is common. Although Railways are in service in major parts of these routes, about 238 km are missing links, which have to be built in Myanmar in order to have Delhi–Hanoi railways in operation.[7]

There is a huge investment requirement for the development of railways in Myanmar. According to the feasibility report of RITES, the Jiribam–Imphal–Moreh rail link is estimated to cost US$ 649 million, the Tamu–Kalay–Segyi link in Myanmar US$ 296 million, and the cost of refurbishing the Segyi–Chungu–Myohaung line in Myanmar has been pegged at US$ 62.5 million. Therefore, managing the investment is a big challenge. Tapping the private sector could be a feasible option for a speedy implementation of the project. The Indian government has extended US$ 56 million credit line to the Myanmar government for upgradation of 640 km railway system between Mandalay and Yangon. Similar initiatives should be taken up for renovation of railway network systems in southern (Yangon to Dawei) and northern (Mandalay to Kalay) Myanmar.

The Government of India has been constructing railway lines in Manipur. The Jiribam–Imphal–Moreh rail link (in Indian side) is identified for development and will link India with ASEAN. The 180 km stretch in India from the rail junction at Jiribam (Assam) via Imphal to Moreh is currently under construction. Construction of a 98 km railway line connecting Jiribam to Imphal has already been taken up at the cost of ₹31 billion.[8] Although construction work is being carried out in Jiribum to Tupul section, linking it with Moreh via Imphal (and thereby India with Myanmar and Thailand) depends on how fast the railway system on the Myanmar side is developed simultaneously. The project was initiated in April 2003 and is likely to be completed in 2016 for Jiribam–Tupul section and in 2018 for Tupul–Imphal section. On completion of these projects, there could be possibilities for (i) India–Myanmar–Thailand–Malaysia–Singapore rail link and (ii) India–Myanmar–Thailand–Hanoi rail link.

---

[7] For more details, refer Appendix 2 in De and Ray (2013) for a detailed break up of route lengths and missing links.
[8] According to the Ministry of Railways, Government of India.

MAP 6.2
Kaladan Multimodal Transit Transport Project (KMTTP)

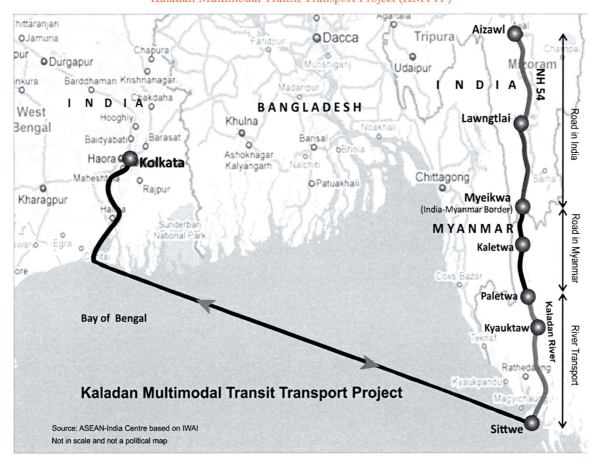

Source: Provide by the author.
Note: Illustrated by Sachin Singhal.

2.3 Kaladan Multimodal Transit Transport Project (KMTTP)

The Kaladan Multimodal Transit Transport Project (KMTTP) in Myanmar envisages connectivity between Indian ports and the Sittwe port in Myanmar and road and inland waterway links from Sittwe to India's northeastern region (Map 6.2). The Kaladan project would provide an alternate route for transportation of goods to northeastern India through Myanmar. KMTTP has two major components — (a) development of the port and IWT development between Sittwe and Kaletwa in Myanmar along Kaladan river, and (b) building a highway (129 km) from Kaletwa to the India–Myanmar border in Mizoram. The components of this project include (a) construction of an integrated Port and Inland Water Transport (IWT) terminal at Sittwe including dredging; (b) development of navigational channel along river Kaladan from Sittwe to Paletwa (158 km); (c) construction of an IWT — Highway transshipment terminal at Paletwa; and (d) construction of six IWT barges (each with a capacity of 300 tonnes) for transportation of cargo between Sittwe and Paletwa. Framework Agreement and two protocols (Protocol on Transit Transport and Protocol on maintenance) were signed by India and Myanmar on 2nd April 2008.

Construction work of the project was started in December 2010. The timeframe for the project has been five years from the date of actual commencement of the project. On the Indian side, construction of 100 km of new road from Lawngtlai on NH 54 to the India–Myanmar border is taken-up under SARDP-NE Phase A. Road from the Border to NH 54 (Lawngtlai) on Indian side in Mizoram is in progress under the Ministry of Road Transport and Highways, Government of India. Construction of integrated port cum IWT jetty at Sittwe is substantially completed. Construction work of IWT terminal at Paletwa has been started in April 2013 and is likely to be completed in 2015–16.

2.4 Mekong–India Economic Corridor (MIEC)

MIEC involves integrating the four Mekong countries, namely, Myanmar, Thailand, Cambodia and Vietnam with India. It connects Ho Chi Minh City (Vietnam) with Dawei (Myanmar) via Bangkok (Thailand) and Phnom Penh (Cambodia) and Chennai in India. The MIEC corridor is conceptualized to be the region around the main highway connecting Vung Tau in Vietnam to Dawei in Myanmar passing through Ho Chi Minh City, Phnom Penh and Bangkok. The highway passes through three borders of (a) Moc Bai–Bavet (Cambodia–Vietnam), (b) Poipet–Aranyaprathet (Cambodia–Thailand) and (c) Sai Yok–Bong Tee (Thailand-Myanmar). There is an existing road from Vung Tau to Bong Tee on the Thailand–Myanmar border, after which there is only an unpaved path to Dawei. In addition to several major cities it covers key towns such as Bien Hoa (in Vietnam), Battambang, Sisophon (in Cambodia) and Chachoengsao, Prachinburi and Kanchanaburi (in Thailand). The major investment will be required for the development of a port at Dawei. This corridor, when completed, is expected to augment trade with India by reducing travel distance between India and MIEC countries and removing supply side bottlenecks. The corridor would provide opportunities to Myanmar, Thailand, Cambodia and Vietnam to build a strong economic and industrial base and a world class infrastructure. The emphasis of the corridor is on expanding the manufacturing base and trade with the rest of the world, particularly with India. The corridor will enable economies of ASEAN and India to integrate further and collectively emerge as a globally competitive economic bloc.

3. FUTURE CONNECTIVITY PROJECTS BETWEEN INDIA AND SOUTHEAST ASIA

India and ASEAN are also in discussions for taking up the connectivity agenda into the next level through new projects.

3.1 Extension of Trilateral Highway

Three new developments in the Mekong (CLMV) region have opened up further opportunities to bring India (South Asia) closer to Southeast Asia without depending too much on existing routes. Three new bridges on the Mekong river are being planned, which would enable road transportation directly to Lao PDR and Vietnam from Myanmar (see De and Ray 2013). In particular, the recently completed Mekong bridge between Xiengkok (Lao PDR) and Kaing Lap (Myanmar) is likely to reduce the travel distance between India and Mekong sub-region. The new route for the extension and/or new highway would be Yangon–Meikhtila–Tarlay–Kenglap (Myanmar)–Xieng Kok–Loungnamtha–Oudomxay–Deptaechang (Lao PDR)–Tay Trang–Hanoi (Vietnam).[9] A part of this proposed corridor follows the same route of TH up to Meiktila in Myanmar. Meiktila to Tarlay and then to Kainglap (Myanmar–Lao PDR border) is a new portion of this corridor. However, a section of Meiktila to Taunggyi to Kyaing Tong to Traley is part of AH 2 and GS corridor. Tarley to Kainglap section (about 60 km) has to be rebuilt. At this place, the new bridge on the Mekong river is being planned. The other side of Kainglap is Xiengkok (Lao PDR), a large part of which is already connected by road with major Lao PDR cities and Vietnam. However, the segment between Xiengkok and Muong Sing needs improvement since it is not an all weather road. While several proposals are underway, there is a need for a consolidated route alignment to bring further clarity on the project. These corridors, when completed, are expected to augment trade in the region by reducing the travel distance between India and Mekong countries and removing supply side bottlenecks. The corridor would provide opportunities to Myanmar, Thailand, Cambodia, and Vietnam to build a strong economic and industrial base and a world class infrastructure. The emphasis of the corridor should be on expanding the manufacturing base and trade with the rest of the world, particularly with India.

3.2 MIEC–SKRL Interlink

ASEAN countries aim to develop the rail linkage in the potential TAR Route Singapore–Kunming Rail Link (SKRL) is one of the ambitious projects of ASEAN countries, covering 3,900 km in Southeast Asia. It links Kunming in the Yunnan Province in China with Singapore, and passes through countries like Myanmar,

---

[9] Another presentation of the same route is Taichang (Lao–Vietnam border)–Muongkhua–Paknamnoy–Oudomxay–Nateuy–Luangnamtha–Muongsing–Xiengkok–Ban Yaa Yee/Xieng lab (Lao–Myanmar Mekong bridge).

Thailand, Cambodia, Vietnam, and Malaysia. However, this project has quite a few missing links, of which Kunming (China) to Lashio (Myanmar), Nam Tok (Thailand)-Three Pagodas Pass (Thailand/Myanmar border) to Thanbyuzayat (Myanmar), and Ho Chi Minh City (Vietnam) to Phnom Penh (Cambodia) are the major ones. To start with, Kunming will be connected with Vientiane in Lao PDR. The section within Lao PDR from the Chinese border to Vientiane is about 421 km. The line will eventually be extended from Vientiane through Thailand and Malaysia to Singapore and reach a total of 3,900 km.[10] Therefore, it is worth linking SKRL with a spur/alternative line with the proposed Dawei port and SEZ. A link with the Dawei port and SEZ would facilitate bulk movement of goods and passengers by railway between India and Southeast and East Asia. Chennai on the other end of MIEC, is well-connected with the Indian railway system.

4. Developing the ASEAN–India Economic Corridor: Policy Framework

With India's FTA with the ASEAN in 2010 and the proposed RCEP, economic integration between India and Southeast and East Asia is set to gain momentum. As was noted in Chapter 5, more fragmentation of production and services between the two regions may happen if the regional economy is adequately supported by cross-border infrastructure facilities, both hardware and software.

Before moving to an economic corridor, ASEAN and India may have to pass through trade corridors. The transformation of the transport corridors into economic corridors will depend on the volume, types and pattern of corridor trade and how it encourages certain level of development in the areas surrounding the corridors. Figure 6.3 illustrates the transformation of corridors in a geographic space. Spatial planning going beyond national policies is needed to support the development of the corridors between ASEAN and India at the same time, development of one area of the corridor is conditional upon the trading conditions along the entire area of the corridor across countries. Building corridor nodes and gateways and linking the nodes along the corridor would help the region moving towards the economic corridor.

Table 6.1 shows the sequencing of the transformation of transport corridors to economic corridors and requisite policies for ASEAN and India. The tasks are primarily three-fold: (a) developing transport corridor, (b) building corridor nodes, (c) linking corridor nodes and gateways and (d) designing and implementing trade facilitation measures.

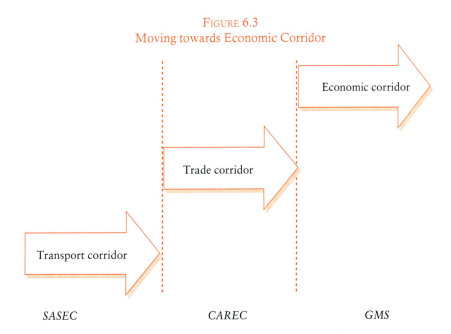

FIGURE 6.3
Moving towards Economic Corridor

Source: De (2014).
Notes: SASEC: South Asia Subregional Economic Cooperation; CAREC: Central Asia Regional Economic Cooperation; GMS: Greater Mekong Subregion.

---

[10] On 25 April 2011, construction was due to start on a new high-speed railway between Kunming and Vientiane in Lao PDR though it was delayed at the last minute.

TABLE 6.1
Corridor Development Policy

Stage	Corridor	Policy	Measure	Role
1	Transport corridor	Trade facilitation	• Integrated trade facilitation • Customs cooperation	• Government; private sector
2	Trade corridor	Trade liberalization	• Border policies; behind-the-border policies	• Government
3	Economic corridor	Economic development	• Corridor value chains; corridor township development; cross-border investments	• Government; private sector

Source: Adapted from ADB (2012).

4.1 Developing Transport Corridor

Soft and hard infrastructure measures along selected corridors aim to accommodate transport activities. For example, all the ASEAN countries and India have adopted trade facilitation programmes in line with regional and global commitments. In particular, they are also signatories of the WTO Trade Facilitation Agreement (TFA), which was signed on 5 December 2013 at Bali, Indonesia. Customs cooperation, bilateral and regional, has been very much active between the countries in the region. On customs cooperation, several important issues have been discussed for implementation such as harmonization of customs clearing procedures and documentation, inter-operability of systems being followed by customs administrations in India and ASEAN countries; preparation of a simplified form for Customs Declaration for trade in goods; harmonization of 8-digit tariff lines and capacity building. Some recommendations are (*a*) accepting the electronic copies of the Certificates of Origin received from importers for clearance of consignments; (*b*) exploring the possibility of having a seven-day working week in case of congestion of consignments at the customs border points and (*c*) considering the possibility of having a single joint customs point for speedy movement of consignments.

We also need speedy reforms for (*a*) improvement of customs operations, including a regional 'single-window' system; (*b*) planning and implementation of a coordinated border management strategy; (*c*) joint customs control, at least at one select post; (*d*) infrastructure development, such as approach road development, installing scanners, among others and (*e*) capacity building and training for customs and border management officers. To operationalize the ASEAN–India economic corridor, both government and private sectors have shared responsibilities. While we need the government in promoting an integrated programme on trade facilitation and customs, private sector's cooperation is required acceding to such measures.

4.2 Building Corridor Nodes

The next level of corridor development will involve improvements in spatial interaction among places located along the corridor. These so-called nodes can be classified into four categories: (*a*) commercial nodes, where major business activity is carried out; (*b*) border nodes, where cross-border movements of goods and services occur; (*c*) gateway nodes, where a corridor ends, and the entry and exit points to the corridor are located and (d) interchange nodes, where two or more corridors intersect.

Premier commercial gateway nodes (such as Kolkata, Delhi, Dhaka, Yangon, Bangkok, among others) are already developed. New SEZs at borders may emerge as new nodes. At the same time, we need to continue with the task of making gateways and nodes more efficient. Special attention shall be paid to introduce border policies as well as behind-the-border policies. Finally, the focus of economic corridor development should be to strengthen and redevelop the gateways, border nodes and development of corridor towns. Examples of production and export quality infrastructure include certification of products and management systems, competence of laboratories related to export, accreditation of laboratories, proficiency testing, metrology and inspection and, in case of food items, inspection systems.

4.3 Linking Corridor Nodes and Gateways

Interaction between nodes along the corridors creates new economic opportunities. Linking corridor nodes would lead towards an enlargement of markets and the creation of industrial or SEZs along the corridor. For the private sector, these activities would facilitate value chains, while for governments, industry associations and multilateral organizations, shall look after the trading infrastructure to ensure that the products originating from different areas along the corridor meet the standards required of domestic or foreign markets. Therefore, trade facilitation has the key role to facilitate trade along the corridor.

Trade in goods and mobility of professionals along the corridors is a major driver for promoting cross-border investment in value chain activities. Support in the form of skill development, trade finance, business support services, e-commerce, public–private sector networking, etc. are eventually required. In parallel, the participation of SMEs is an essential part of the process of converting transport corridors into economic corridors. Noted in the ADB (2012), one proven mechanism is through the integration of SMEs into value-chain activities; another is the promotion of sub-regional business development services along the corridors, supported by a cost-sharing facility with credit guarantee facility. Setting up project development facility (PDF) to promote bankable projects for SMEs will pave the way in making economic corridor development more inclusive.

Improving and modernizing the rural economy lies at the centre of development of ASEAN–India economic corridor by developing road networks linking cities, towns and villages, using new technology in agriculture and increasing output, by developing agro-industry for processing local products supported by micro financing facilities and by building training centres. ASEAN–India economic corridors may provide a framework for cooperation by coordinating policies and signing cooperation agreements.

4.4 Designing and Implementing ASEAN–India Trade Facilitation Mechanism

When it comes to deepening the regional integration process through economic corridors, an exclusive trade facilitation measure has to be implemented and reinforced across the region. Benefits to be derived from implementing the trade facilitation measures are significant. Undoubtedly, trade facilitation will continue to play a key role in deepening ASEAN–India strategic partnership. A comprehensive trade facilitation programme is required to complement the hardware being developed through economic corridor.

Defined broadly, trade facilitation is any policy action (other than cutting tariffs) that reduces international trade costs. Trade facilitation supports modern and effective customs administrations, streamlined and transparent trade processes/procedures, and improved services and information for private sector traders and investors. It often refers to measures reducing/removing non-tariff institutional, administrative and technical barriers to trade. In some studies, trade facilitation has been described not just as tariffs and international transport, but also as an instrument to deal with geography, social and cultural costs (language), logistics performance, etc. 'Narrow' trade facilitation often refers to customs and border procedures. Product standards (SPS and TBT), regulatory differences across countries, etc. are also discussed as part of trade facilitation. Four interdependent elements that constitute the topic of trade facilitation: (*a*) simplification and harmonization of applicable rules and procedures; (*b*) modernization of trade compliance systems; (*c*) administration and standards and (*d*) institutional mechanisms and tools (see Grainger 2011). Trade facilitation and connectivity improvement have become a necessity for trade and development. Trade facilitation helps promote cross-border production networks. With production processes and tasks in production increasingly fragmented across national borders, time-sensitive logistics services along with ICT is the key to facilitate cross-border production networks (Kimura and Kobayashi 2011). Building the economic corridor with investment in other cross-border infrastructure and trade facilitation measures would help the region to improve the efficiency of corridor and supply chain connectivity. Intuitively, a stronger supply chain network would be essential to strengthening the regional value chain.

Table 6.2 presents a list of major trade cost elements negatively affecting the regional trade, of which the high transportation costs, poor institutions, inadequate cross-border infrastructure, and absence of regional transit are major elements penalizing the region's trade and integration. Average time and cost of trading across borders in most of the ASEAN countries and India are relatively high and there is wide variation of performance in the region (Figures 6.4a and 6.4b). Overall, trends in cost to export and import is rising for most of the ASEAN countries, whereas the same in case of time to export and import has been static for most countries in the region. There is divergence in performance in trade facilitation among ASEAN countries and India. One of the critical factors for rise in costs could be inefficient logistics, which also reduces the potential for regional integration. While Singapore port clears the goods very fast, the inefficiency of the port of Yangon negates the benefits of faster handling of cargo in the region. Therefore, much more is needed to close the 'performance gap' in trade facilitation in the region.

TABLE 6.2
Trade Cost Elements Holding Back ASEAN–India Integration

Macro Elements	Micro Elements
• Inadequate infrastructure — national and regional (inadequate and poor stock and link of infrastructure) • Absence of regional transit trade (no regional transit) • High NTMs (complicated and non-transparent) • Lack of harmonization of axle load of vehicle • Poor institutions and governance (no regional mechanism) • Lack of co-ordination at border authorities	• Lack in simplification and harmonization of trade procedures, more particularly at border • Absence of modern corridor management techniques • No fast track lane and priority of goods in transit to cross the border • Lack of standard operating procedures (SOPs) at selected border • Unequal or absence of testing facilities, banks, scanner, etc. • Non-acceptance of customs transit document (CTD) in some border posts

Source: Adapted from De (2014).

FIGURE 6.4a
Trends in Cost to Export and Import

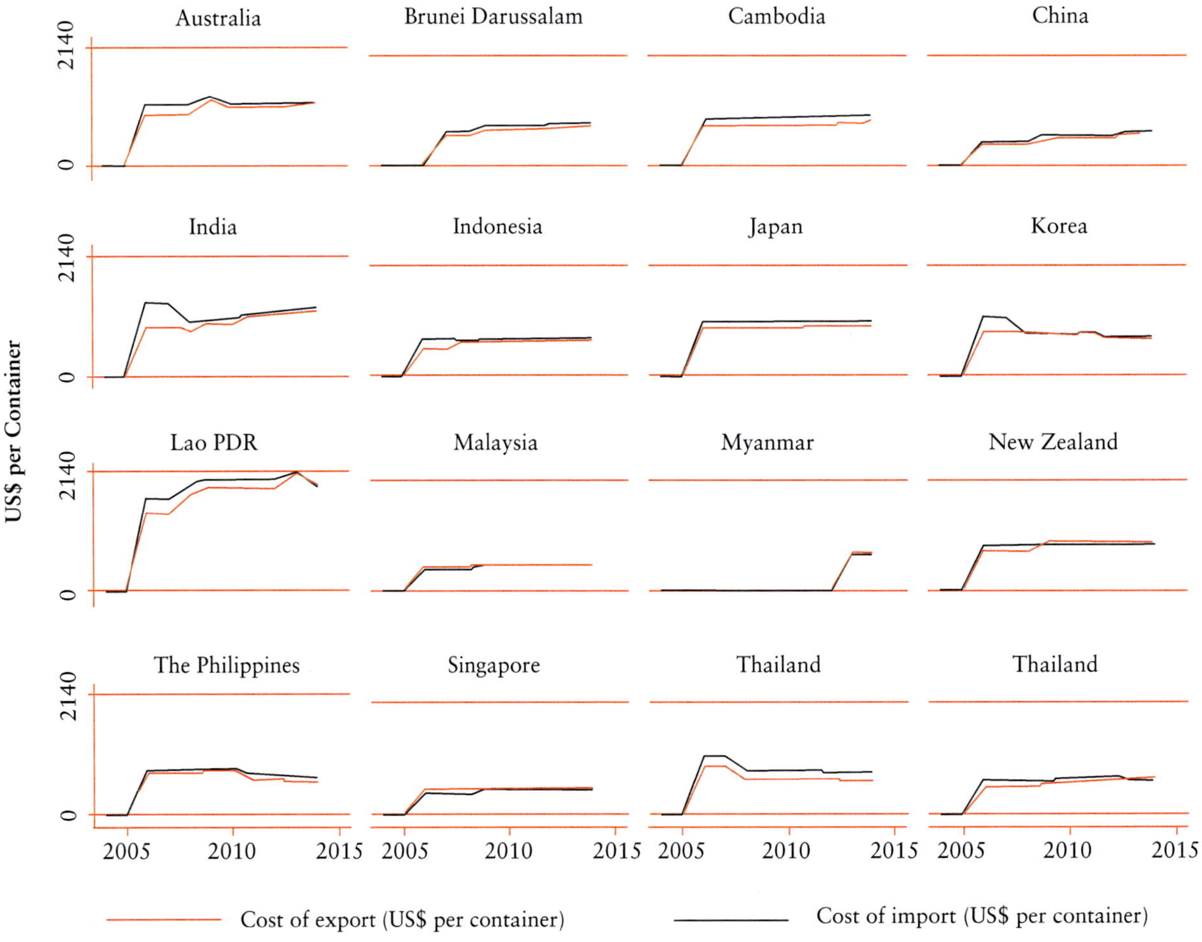

Cost of export (US$ per container)   Cost of import (US$ per container)

Note: Missing values were treated as zero, to have balanced data.

The trade facilitation gap between ASEAN-6 and India has widened rather than narrowed. The gaps existing within ASEAN countries and between ASEAN and India in terms of level of trade infrastructure attainment, therefore, need to be addressed explicitly as a part of the programme of ASEAN–India trade facilitation mechanism. Trade potential will be realized only if we can narrow the trade facilitation gap, not only between them but also with global best practices. Efficient customs and other border management agencies are critical for improving trade facilitation performance.

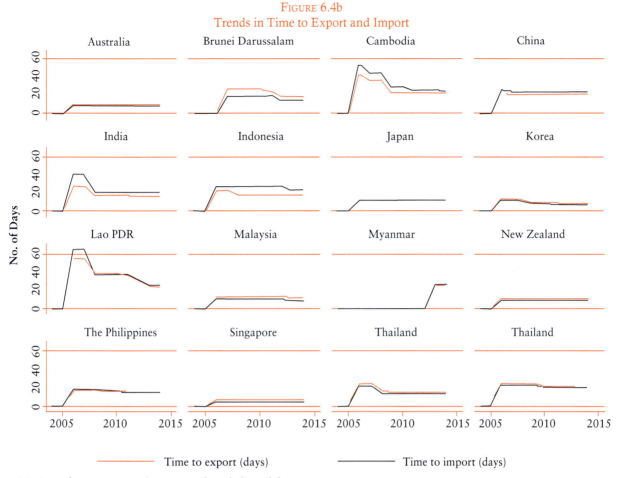

FIGURE 6.4b
Trends in Time to Export and Import

Note: Missing values were treated as zero, to have balanced data.

5. Developing Economic Corridors: Key Policies and the Enabling Environment

Developing economic corridors can help diversify the region's industries and make them competitive globally though technology, logistics and other business support services. An economic corridor network is essential for India and ASEAN countries to get their goods to markets more efficiently, quickly and cheaply. However, an economic corridor alone cannot be successful until and unless other operational priorities such as trade policy, trade facilitation and transit, institutions, energy corridors, telecommunications, etc. are in place. Therefore, a strategic partnership for policy development to setup economic corridor and an action plan to foster regional cooperation and integration have to be in place.

One of the challenges to economic corridors is that their success closely depends on policy reform, capacity development and the strengthening of institutions.[11] This is where regional cooperation assumes importance. The challenges can broadly be divided into two segments. One, the hardware aspects, such as transport facilities (physical infrastructure, logistics networks, maintenance and so on), that are important to ensure the flow of goods and services within and across the ASEAN–India region and beyond. Two, the software aspects, such as trade facilities (customs, time and cost expended at borders, institutions and governance, dispute settlement, safeguards and so on), that are crucial to making the hardware work efficiently. Both will need drastic intervention from governments and policymakers. The task would be to overcome institutional constraints and bottlenecks that are hurting regional competitiveness by making trade expensive.

---

[11] These lessons draw on the experience of GMS economic corridors.

5.1 Multimodal Transport, Transit and Logistics

Transit and trade facilitation are pivotal to the well functioning of economic corridors. The lack of transit is a major reason for the low level of economic exchanges. In general, the task ahead is to revive the transportation networks between ASEAN and India, and establish region-wide multimodal transport and transit to reduce transportation costs. ASEAN and India should have its own regional transit arrangement. To start with, India, Myanmar and Thailand may establish a transit system between the three countries for trilateral highway. Door-to-door logistics approach shall be pursued with no distinction between transnational and domestic connections. At the same time, coordination among key players to achieve efficiency through logistics chain is a must. We also need to know that not all sides will benefit equally from seamless development (for example, India bears cost of Bangladesh road). Highest returns derived from overcoming externalities and bottlenecks in gateways of the region should accede to existing international conventions. Cross-Border Transport Agreement (CBTA), adopted by the GMS or CAREC countries, is an important step towards harmonizing the software related to cross-border transport and transit. ASEAN and India may follow suit while moving into economic corridor development.

5.2 Strengthening and Harmonizing Rules, Regulations and Standards

In order for a transport network to function effectively, the necessary soft infrastructure, such as relevant rules, regulations, and standards, has to be in place. Rules, regulations and standards must meet a common regional benchmark, or more preferably an international one. Trade facilitation initiatives in the area of standards and conformance through reduction of TBT and/or SPS focus on addressing differences between national laws, standards and conformity assessment procedures towards a broader horizontal approach at the regional level. Therefore, India and ASEAN shall harmonize national standards with international standards and develop mutual recognition arrangements (MRAs) among members. Further, to make such an agreement effective, India and ASEAN need to incorporate its provisions into their national laws, regulations and standards. There is the need for higher-level coordination among the stakeholders and agencies concerned, such as transport, customs, immigration, and quarantine authorities. At the same time, the capacity of national institutions has to be enhanced for effective implementation of these agreements. There is also the need for a uniform or compatible standard for developing cross-border transport networks that are beneficial to all stakeholders. The establishment of an efficient management system and capacity building to look after the harmonization of standards would pave the way in developing regional economic corridors. This would ultimately help achieve single-stop and single-window customs offices across ASEAN–India economic corridors.

5.3 Border Policies

Backend integration with regional connectivity projects is essential in order to reap the benefits of growing economic linkages in the region. Countries should focus on borders as connectors and not as walls which separate us (see Saran 2014). Peace dividends become more when borders act as connectors. In India, there has been a perception change while dealing with border barriers. There is a common realization to the fact that a safe and secure border is essential for a faster trade across the borders. Adequate border infrastructure facilitates not only trade but also investment. To deal with border development, the Government of India has recently set up a separate Border Connectivity Division in the Ministry of External Affairs. Among others, this Division deals with projects strengthening connectivity across borders. Besides, development of border infrastructure through Integrated Check-Post (ICP) projects has picked up pace in the country. Border and corridor management will be the key to convert the transport corridor into economic corridor between ASEAN and India. Corridor value chain is thus not beyond reach.

5.4 Financing Cross-border Corridors

Connecting India with ASEAN and vice versa requires large investment. Given the current global economic crisis, this will be difficult to mobilize. This calls for an appropriate financing mechanism to use the region's large savings for infrastructure development. Such a financing scheme should aim to raise resources from the public and private sectors, and multilateral development banks such as ADB on a public-private partnership model.

Bigger economies like Japan, Korea, China and India could have leading roles in filling financing gaps. They could finance and manage missing links, bridges, industrial zones, townships, rural roads, etc.

5.5 Closer Cooperation on Security

India and ASEAN countries have to commit themselves to increasing security for all transport modes, and to promoting policy coherence and coordination among international organizations. New programmes to combat terrorism will involve investment in new technology and infrastructure, possibly raising the costs of trade in the short to medium term. But the prospect of reducing future threats through technology-intensive security and customs inspections should be viewed as an investment in greater efficiency. Automated technology, such as bar codes, wireless communications, radio frequency identity tags, RFID or GPRS-enabled cargo movement, and tamper-proof seals, could improve security and accelerate global trade.[12] Sharing information among security agencies, port and airport authorities, shippers, and customs can expedite the movement of freight through terminals without any new physical investment.

5.6 Completion of Major Cross-Border Corridors

Three major tasks lie ahead for the completion of the Trilateral Highway. We need to complete (a) the construction and improvement of two sections of Trilateral Highway: (i) Kalewa to Monywa via Yargyi, and (ii) replacement of all vintage bridges falling on the highway; (b) Kaladan Multimodal Transit Transport Project and (c) Mekong–India Economic Corridor.

5.7 Accepting Transit and Paperless Trade

ASEAN and India should negotiate and finalize a regional transit transport agreement — first between India, Myanmar and Thailand, and then a back-to-back agreement with the rest of the ASEAN countries and dialogue partners. This agreement, ASEAN–India Transit Transport Agreement (AITTA), has to be ready well before the completion of the Trilateral Highway. Among others, this proposed AITTA will allow vehicles to move seamlessly for regional and international trade transportation purposes. This is the 'software' that is needed in order to operate the 'hardware' — the Trilateral Highway. Through this agreement, we could identify modalities of transportation, introduce operating procedures (OP) for vehicles to ply on the highway, and set up the rule book for public utilities; India, Myanmar and Thailand Motor Vehicle Agreement (IMT MVA) is presently being negotiated. The IMT MVA will allow passenger, personal and cargo vehicles to cross international borders and travel along designated key trade routes between India, Myanmar and Thailand, making cross-border trade more efficient. Third, building a common template for running and maintaining the corridor and signing of mutual recognition agreement (MRA) on logistics and other transportation services between the member countries would be essential for not only removing the barriers to trade but also sharing the benefits and risks. ASEAN and India shall try in achieving common standards in customs, trade documentations, etc. This would facilitate soft aspects of connectivity such as paperless trade and single window.[13]

5.8 Setting up Single Window

We need to assess the trade facilitation conditions between ASEAN and India. Simple, harmonised and standardized trade and customs, processes, procedures and related information flows are expected to reduce transaction costs between ASEAN and India which will enhance trade competitiveness and facilitate the regional integration.

---

[12] These were introduced by the Thanaleng (Lao PDR) and Nonkhai (Thailand) border posts (Author's visit on 10 September 2013).

[13] The ASEAN Single Window is an environment where 10 National Single Windows of individual member countries operate and integrate, being supported by the United States through USAID. National Single Window enables a single submission of data and information, a single and synchronous processing of data and information and single decision-making for customs clearance of cargo, which expedites the customs clearance, reduce transaction time and costs, and thus enhances trade efficiency and competitiveness. India is at a very advanced stage to implement Single Window.

India (and other ASEAN dialogue partners) needs to align customs procedures and trade services with that of ASEAN through interoperability of Customs Single Windows.

5.9 Implementing ASEAN–India Trade Facilitation Programme

Trade facilitation is an area where region-wide a common set of facilitation measures are yet to be undertaken, and compliance to a single standard is yet to happen. The progress has been limited to only individual country initiatives, undertaken mainly as a part of national agenda (for example, e-Customs). Moving to economic corridor warrants a common template of trade transaction in the region. WTO Agreement on Trade Facilitation, signed in December 2013 in Bali, marked the importance of the facilitation agenda for expanding trade across the world. TFA aims to bring paperless trade by reforming trade processes and procedures across the world.

a) **Coordinated border management:** It is based on approaches such as collocation of facilities, close cooperation between agencies, delegation of administrative authority, cross-designation of officials and effective information sharing.
b) **Regional single window:** It is a digital interface that allows traders to submit all import, export, and transit information required by regulatory agencies once via a single electronic gateway instead of submitting essentially the same information numerous times to different government entities.
c) **Regional transit:** Under regional transit, goods and services move freely with compliance to certain rules and regulations in a given region.
d) **One Stop Border Post:** One Stop Border Post (OSBP) allows neighbouring countries to coordinate import, export and transit processes to ensure that traders are not required to duplicate regulatory formalities on both sides of the same border (see Figure 6.6).

ASEAN and India shall implement key trade facilitation projects in the region which will help the countries to streamline border transaction and improve the competitiveness. Table 6.3 presents some key projects that can be implemented suitably in the region.

Customs must operate 24×7. At present, there are differences in working hours between customs. It is recommended that full automation and link-up between customs will reduce transaction time and cost. The trade facilitation measures such as the simplification, harmonization and automation of procedures and documents and streamlining NTMs involve interagency coordination and collaboration. Development organizations like

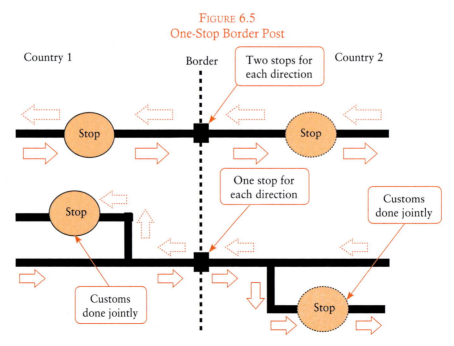

FIGURE 6.5
One-Stop Border Post

Source: Adapted from JICA (2014).

TABLE 6.3
Key Trade Facilitation Priorities

1.	Reduce lengthy customs and cargo handling time at ports of Chittagong, Yangon, Thilawa, Kolkata and Haldia through automation and modernization
2.	Faster opening of L/C account in bank with the help of ICT
3.	Faster cargo insurance with the help of ICT, process reengineering and competition among service providers
4.	Use of ICT to obtain permits and certificates
5.	Simplification and harmonization of trade procedures, more particularly at border
6.	Synchronization of cross-border customs
7.	Acceptance to regional transit, starting with India, Myanmar and Thailand
8.	Development of border infrastructure, particularly between India and Myanmar
9.	Cross-border electronic Customs Transit Document (CTD)
10.	National single window is essential for paperless trade
11.	Fast track lane and priority of goods in transit to cross the border and move towards OSBP
12.	Set up national Single Window (pilot run of authorized economic operator, AEO and mutual recognition agreement) and later linked with ASEAN Single Window
13.	Monitor the performance of corridor and improve the efficiency of border facilities (both side of border improvement in ICP project in parallel)
14.	Enforcement of electronic payment system
15.	Modernization of LCSs in Northeast India and West Bengal
16.	Capacity building and training for CHAs, and other stakeholders
17.	More shipping services between India and ASEAN
18.	ASEAN Airlines to serve some Tier II and Tier III cities in India

the Asian Development Bank, World Bank, UNESCAP, etc. have to play strong facilitating role in developing infrastructure, technical assistance, training and capacity building, etc. in the region.

ASEAN and India have been implementing national level measures of trade facilitation to support and ensure effective implementation of regional and multilateral initiatives. We suggest that ASEAN and India (and also other dialogue partners or the EAS group) have to develop and implement a comprehensive trade facilitation work programme, which aims at simplifying, harmonizing and standardizing trade and customs, processes, procedures and related information flows.

a) Establish a regional trade facilitation cooperation mechanism with dialogue partners;
b) Establish ASEAN+India and/or EAS Trade Facilitation Repository;
c) Develop a comprehensive capacity building programmes to ensure smooth implementation of the work programme.

In light of the acceleration of AEC, the realization of ASEAN Customs Vision 2020 is brought forward to 2015. ASEAN and India shall aim to (a) integrate customs structures; (b) modernize tariff classification, customs valuation and origin determination and establish ASEAN e-Customs; (c) smoothen customs clearance; (d) strengthen human resources development; (e) promote partnership with relevant international organizations; (f) narrow the development gaps in customs; (g) adopt risk management techniques and audit-based control (PCA) for trade facilitation; (h) develop and implement sectoral Mutual Recognition Arrangements (MRAs) on Conformity Assessment for specific sectors identified in the ASEAN Framework Agreement on Mutual Recognition Arrangements; and (i) enhance technical infrastructure and competency in laboratory testing, calibration, inspection, certification and accreditation based on regionally/internationally accepted procedures and guides. Most of these activities have been already undertaken nationally.

5.10 Development of Port Infrastructure and Shipping Networks

Ports and shipping are strong catalysts to economic integration. ASEAN and India are linked by both land and sea and almost 90 per cent of bilateral trade has been carried by sea. Stronger maritime network is essential in order to facilitate production networks, trade and employment. Today, ASEAN and India have long coastline, dotted with many ports. Out of world's top 25 ports, seven ports come from ASEAN and one from India.

TABLE 6.4
UNCTAD's Liner Shipping Connectivity Index

Year	2013	2008	2004
Brunei	4.61	3.68	3.91
Cambodia	5.34	3.47	3.89
Indonesia	27.41	24.85	25.88
Malaysia	98.18	77.60	62.83
Myanmar	6.00	3.63	3.12
The Philippines	18.11	30.26	15.45
Singapore	106.91	94.47	81.87
Thailand	38.32	36.48	31.01
Vietnam	43.26	18.73	12.86
China	157.51	137.38	100.00
India	44.35	42.18	34.14
Japan	65.68	66.63	69.15
Korea	100.42	76.40	68.68

Source: UNCTAD.

Singapore Port with 31.65 million TEUs in 2012 (about 5 per cent global share in container trade) occupied the 2nd position in the world. India's Jawaharlal Nehru Port with 4.26 million TEUs ranked 21 in the world in the same year.

Major container ports in ASEAN are over-utilized. Both Singapore and Port Klang have been running over 100 per cent of capacity. India has also capacity shortfall in ports. At the same time, shipping tonnage in some ASEAN countries are almost nil or way below the regional average. There is high variation in Liner Shipping Connectivity Index (LSCI) across ASEAN (Table 6.4). Singapore, Korea and China are relatively well connected in liner shipping, compared to others. Narrowing the shipping gap is a major challenge for ASEAN countries. Other challenges include few direct calls, high port handling charges, lack of skilled human resources and absence of institutional mechanism.

Cargo produced in India and destined for different locations in Southeast Asia typically moves through the transhipment hub located in Singapore, Tanjung Pelepas or Port Klang. Therefore, the dependency on the Strait of Malacca is high. This sea channel is very important for the world's shipping movement as this connects the growing regions of South Asia and Africa to the economies on the east. At the same time, ASEAN and India have to build new container ports and new shipping lanes. Map 6.3 presents potential container shipping routes between India and ASEAN. Myannar is building a port at Sitwee with assistance of India. Major container ports in ASEAN are adding container handling capacity to manage additional 100 million TEUs by end of the ongoing decade. India is also developing container terminals at New Mangalore, Ennore, Tuticorin, Chennai and Jawaharlal Nehru ports.

Allowing coastal shipping in Bay of Bengal (Short Sea Shipping) would help ASEAN LDCs to increase their market access in India and vice versa. The coastal trade agreement signed by Bangladesh and Myanmar in 2012 may be converted into a regional/agreement with participation of India and Thailand to start with. Institutional links between ports and the shipping community, regional (and bilateral) short sea shipping, and training and capacity building would pave the way for stronger maritime links in the region. Table 6.5 presents a list of projects to strengthen maritime connectivity between ASEAN and India. Countries may think about signing of Mutual Recognition Agreement (MRA) in shipping and logistics services. Regional cooperation initiatives can play an important role to strengthen the maritime network (see AIC 2014).

5.11 *Building a Stronger Coordination Mechanism*

Weak coordination, like high tariffs, hinders trade among countries. Poor coordination between planning, implementing and financing agencies leads to inefficiency in infrastructure development. Coordination among the various agencies or institutions concerned within a country is also required because each one may have different objectives. To implement economic corridors in a timely fashion, effective coordination between countries and other stakeholders is vital. Without this, it is unlikely that an optimal cross-border infrastructure will come into

MAP 6.3
New Shipping Routes between ASEAN and India

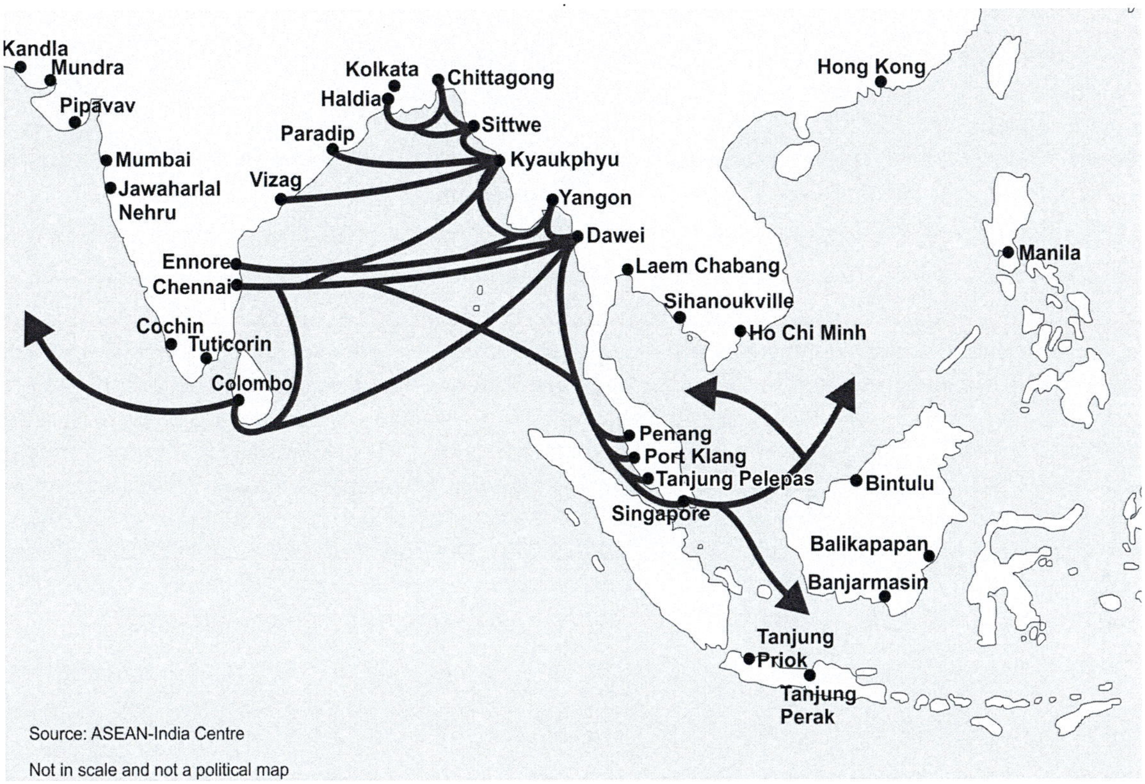

Source: ASEAN-India Centre

Not in scale and not a political map

Source: AIC (2014).
Note: Illustrated by Sachin Singhal.

TABLE 6.5
ASEAN–India Maritime Connectivity Projects

- Connect ports in Myanmar, Thailand and Vietnam with Indian ports with regular shipping services
- Attract more feeder operators to link Indian ports such as Vizag, Kolkata and Haldia with ASEAN countries
- Joining ASEAN Ro-Ro and cruise network, and promoting tourism
- Cooperation for improving efficiency of ports (for example, Singapore)
- Building Chennai and Ennore as gateway ports
- Build ports + SEZ at Dawei on priority
- ASEAN FDI in Indian ports and shipping sectors
- Development assistance to CLMV in maritime sector
- Joint training of human resources
- Connecting to ASEAN Single Shipping Market and signing of MRAs
- Signing ASEAN–India Maritime Transport Agreement
- Strengthen institutions (MoU between APA and IPA, INSA and FASA)

Source: AIC (2014).

existence. An effective coordinating institution will be necessary to generate willingness in countries to partici-pate in projects. It could also resolve conflicting interests between governments and stakeholders.

Regional connectivity has made progresses within different regional frameworks in recent past and ASEAN's dialogue partners are getting increasingly involved and have contributed to their efforts in support of Master Plan of ASEAN Connectivity (MPAC). MPAC projects require US$ 600 billion worth of financing.[14] ASEAN

---

[14] See, for example, the speech of Mr Adnan Jaafar, Dy. Permanent Secretary, Ministry of Foreign Affairs and Trade, Brunei Darussalam, at the workshop on 'Enhancing Connectivity through Multilayered Regional Framework', held at Bangkok on 19 July 2013.

Infrastructure Fund (AIF) is a potential source of financing At this stage, five infrastructure projects, valued at US$ 150 million, have been approved. Additional resources are therefore required to support the connectivity projects, and the ASEAN acknowledges the important role of dialogue partners in achieving greater connectivity in ASEAN. ASEAN Secretariat and ASEAN Connectivity Coordinating Committee (ACCC) hope to achieve concrete outcomes from its engagement with a number of dialogue partners including India. Dialogue partners of ASEAN were requested by ACCC to share their experiences with connectivity projects and also to present their plans and proposals on involvements and contributions in support of MPAC. A stronger coordination between ASEAN and its dialoguer partners would be helpful in building cross-border connectivity.

6. CONCLUSIONS

Efforts to promote regional infrastructure such as economic corridor need to address policy reform in a number of areas. Institutions and investment have an important complementary role in enhancing infrastructure development between ASEAN and India. Regional cooperation also has an important catalytic role to play in this process. By sharing each other's experiences, regional cooperation can make countries efficient by integrating them to the regional market. Economic corridor integrates the markets by fostering trade. Finally, economic corridor can have huge payoffs at a time the region is looking for higher investments in industrial sector, and planning to deepen regional trade through global and regional value chains. Not having economic corridors can stultify regional integration process and also delinks with other regions. Making trade between ASEAN and India seamless would require complementary policy initiatives by countries, regional organizations and multilateral development institutions to strengthen the capacity of countries for development of economic corridors.

7
Removing Non-Tariff Measures

The ASEAN-India FTA (AIFTA) primarily focuses on the coverage of goods and provides safeguards in the event of import causing substantial injury to the domestic producers. The agreement also has strict provisions for Rules of Origin.1 The presence of non-tariff measures (NTMs) under the AIFTA is also an important determinant of the preferential market access. In this chapter we discuss the broad AIFTA-related NTMs such as sanitary and phytosanitary measures (SPS) and technical barriers to trade (TBT), identify the barriers that need to be streamlined, and policy recommendations to strengthen trade relations between ASEAN and India.

1. Non-Tariff Measures and AIFTA Partners

A discussion on the preferential market access scenario under the AIFTA cannot be limited to tariff liberalization alone as it would also include those tariff lines which have been impacted by NTMs, applied by AIFTA partners. Box 7.1 captures how the AIFTA has visualized this possibility. Therefore, trade between ASEAN and India is very much contingent upon how we streamline the NTMs.

In AIFTA, there was no Agreement separately for the NTMs (like SPS and TBT) other than what was provided for under the WTO. Although the Agreement came into effect only in 2010, the NTMs have existed ever since the General Agreement on Tariff and Trade (GATT) period. Since there was no transparency requirement during the GATT regime, it was only in 1995 with the WTO, which mandated the WTO members under the Agreements of Technical Barriers to Trade (TBT)[2] and Sanitary and Phytosanitary Measures (SPS)[3] to notify all their NTMs under the transparency clauses.

1.1 NTM Data

Here, we have taken all the measures notified to the WTO under both SPS and TBT Agreements. Furthermore, the data has been acquired from the Centre for WTO Studies (CWS) at the Indian Institute of Foreign Trade databases on Sanitary and Phytosanitary (SPS) and Technical Barriers to Trade (TBT) measures. This database provides a mapping of the individual notifications to the harmonized tariff lines (HS) at the heading level (4-digit). Once the analysis of NTMs presence at national tariff lines is carried out, we can comment with certainty on the issue of preferential market access scenario under the AIFTA. However, nearly 85 per cent of WTO notifications under TBT and SPS measures made by the members are not linked to national tariff lines or for that to the HS trade classification. Therefore, any assessment of actual market access (the presence of tariff and non-tariff measures on national tariff lines) is made difficult and nearly impossible as the information lacks a vital linkage of HS nomenclature. The database of the CWS helps in linking individual notifications with the

---

[1] The issues laid out in the text are from the basic issues like: Coverage and Application (Article 2); Consultations and Good Offices, Conciliation and Mediation (Articles 4 and 5); Establishment of Arbitral Panels (Article 6); Composition of Arbitral Panel (Article 7); Interim Report (Article 12); Compensation and the Suspension of Concessions or Benefits (Article 16) and Entry into Force (Article 22). Article 10 of the AIFTA agreement covered the provisions on the application of Safeguard Measures.

[2] In the TBT Agreement, Article 2.11 requires that each member shall ensure that all technical regulations which have been adopted are published promptly or otherwise made available in such a manner as to enable interested parties in other members to become acquainted with them.

[3] The SPS Agreement, Article 7, under the transparency clause each member shall notify changes in their Sanitary or Phytosanitary measures and shall provide information on their Sanitary or Phytosanitary measures in accordance with the provisions of Annex B of the SPS Agreement.

Box 7.1
NTM in AIFTA

1. In the case of Non-Tariff Measures of Party:

- The Parties shall not institute or maintain any non-tariff measure on the importation of goods from the other Parties or on the exportation or sale for export of goods destined for the territory of the other Parties, except in accordance with its WTO rights and obligations or other provisions in this Agreement; and to ensure the transparency of its non-tariff measures allowed under subparagraph (a) and their full compliance with its obligations under the WTO Agreement with a view to minimizing possible distortions to trade to the maximum extent possible.

2. The Parties reaffirm their rights and obligations under the Agreement on Technical Barriers to Trade in Annex 1A to the WTO Agreement and the Agreement on the Application of Sanitary and Phytosanitary Measures in Annex 1A to the WTO Agreement, including notification procedures on the preparation of relevant regulations to reduce their negative effect on trade as well as to protect human, animal or plant life or health.
3. Each Party shall designate its contact point for the purpose of responding to queries related to this Article.[5]

Source: AIFTA.[6]

relevant harmonized codes at the tariff heading level, for all countries from January 1995 to as update up to April 2014.[4]

We have used the CWS databases for analyzing the impact of rising NTMs corresponding with tariff liberalization under the AIFTA. While at the macro level, the analysis clearly suggests an increasing trend in cumulative notifications of SPS and TBT measures by all AIFTA parties. On the other hand, tariffs have continued to decrease in accordance with the tariff reduction commitments under the Agreement.

1.2 Applied NTMs

AIFTA parties had a total of 2,094 NTMs, which were notified to the WTO, of which the TBT and SPS accounted for 1,227 and 867 measures, respectively, for the period of January 1995 to December 2013 (see Table 7.1). Since 2010 with the formation of AIFTA, the NTMs have not witnessed any decreasing trend. In fact, both the SPS and TBT measures have accounted for 24 per cent share in the total NTMs.

The analysis of NTMs is radically different from the tariff analysis. In analyzing the NTMs, importance is also given to the previous NTMs, which have been either notified or are presently active, unless they are withdrawn or nullified for various reasons. It can be observed from Table 7.1 that over the years the SPS measures have been gaining significance in the total NTMs by the AIFTA partners. The period of 1995 to 1999 saw the dominance of TBT measures for AIFTA partners accounting for nearly 79 per cent shares of the total NTMs 464 measures/notifications.[7] In subsequent periods, the NTM composition showed an increasing share of SPS measures, almost doubling by registering a share of 46 per cent for later periods. It should be noted that the NTMs notified by the AIFTA partners did not show any declining trend in these periods. Instead, it totalled 1,630 measures/notifications with an average of 544 per period.

In the context of NTMs, there is no distinction between an MFN regime and a preferential regime, unless and until it is built into the FTA Agreement. Figure 7.1 indicates how the application of NTMs by the AIFTA partners has increasingly nullified the benefits of tariff reduction.

---

[4] Updated with a lag of two months.

[5] Refer to Article 8 of 'Agreement on Trade in Goods under the Framework Agreement on Comprehensive Economic Cooperation between the Republic of India and the Association of Southeast Asian Nations', pp. 5–6. Available at http://commerce.gov.in/trade/ASEAN-India%20Trade%20in%20Goods%20Agreement.pdf. (accessed 22 February 2015).

[6] Refer the 'ASEAN–India Free Trade Agreement (AIFTA)'. Available at http://commerce.gov.in/trade/asean-india%20trade%20in%20goods%20agreement.pdf (accessed 22 February 2015).

[7] The Notifications and Measures will be used interchangeably in this chapter as they do mean one thing for the products on which they are applied. For example, if there is a notification with restrictions based on labelling and they are applicable to certain set of products, a measure would also be applicable to certain set of products.

TABLE 7.1
SPS and TBT Measures by AIFTA Parties: 1995 to 2013

NTMs/Phases	1995–99	2000–05	2005–09	2010–13	Total 1995–2013
TBT Measures	366	262	309	290	1227
SPS Measures	98	213	351	205	867
AIFTA Total NTMs	464	475	660	495	2094
Percentage Share (%)					
TBT Measures	79	55	47	59	59
SPS Measures	21	45	53	41	41

Source: Compilation by the author based on the CWS web portal on SPS and TBT measures.

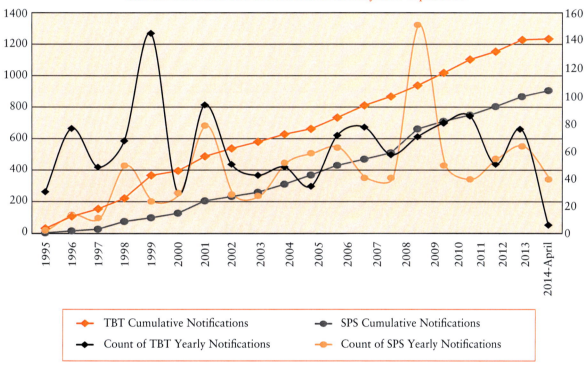

FIGURE 7.1
AIFTA Total TBT and SPS Measures: January 1995–April 2014

Source: Compilation by the author based on the CWS web portal on SPS and TBT measures.

On one hand, the TBT measures have increased from 30 in 1995 to 1,227 by 2013 with a growth rate of 16.2 per cent. The SPS measures, on the other hand, increased with a growth rate of 28.5 per cent from 2 SPS measures in 1995 to 867 SPS measures by 2013, suggesting that there were more notifications under the SPS measures by the AIFTA partners. The yearly notifications can be seen to be fluctuating on a year to year basis, with the highest TBT measures recorded in 1999 with 145 measures/notifications, while in the case of SPS measures, it was in 2009, when these measures touched 151 measures.

1.3 Product Coverage of NTMs under the AIFTA

What makes the assessment of market access challenging under the NTMs notifications/measures is the issue of how to make an assessment on a single notification which has the potential to have product coverage over nearly all the HS tariff lines and at the same time technically restricted to one product. This in itself is very challenging, and compounded to this is how the measure is applied at the border. Sometimes, it may lead to discrimination, due to lack of transparency built-in-to the procedures of application of domestic regulation.

The SPS measures had coverage of 14,865 products during the period of 1995 to 2013,[8] in case of AIFTA partners. It meant that imports of these products were either maximum residual limit (MRL) restrictions or had some other regulations. The product coverage was more than 20 products in the year 1996 (35 products), 2000 (23), 2005 (24), 2006 (37), 2008 (22), and 2011 to 2012 with products 36, 32 and 24, respectively (Figure 7.2). The lowest was in 1998, when 49 measures with average product coverage of 3 per measure/notification. There were two peaks: the first in 2006 having products coverage of 151 products and the second in 2010 with 1,743 products. The average products covered per NTM by the AIFTA partners witnessed considerable variations between 1995 and 2013.

The TBT measures product coverage during 1995 to 2013[9] in case of AIFTA partners were 10,963 products. It meant that imports of these products were either restricted or had some kind of standard/regulations (Figure 7.3). The product coverage was more than 20 products in the years 1996 (23 products), 2000 (20 products) and 2012 (20 products). The lowest was in 1998 with 68 with average product coverage of 4 per measure/notification. There was only one peak, which was in 1996 with product coverage of 1,721 products. The average products covered per NTM measure by the AIFTA partners showed considerable variations during 1995 to 2013.

1.4 AIFTA NTMs and Its Objectives

Both tariff and the non-tariff measures are applied at the border. However, unlike tariff, the non-tariff measures have differential market access impact, based on the quality of the product and the perceived impact from the products entry. What makes a product non-compliable from country X need not be applicable for country Y trading with the country Z. The products which meet the TBT or SPS measures/regulations would be the domestic products and those imported products, which satisfy the regulation. Meeting the regulation can be sometime a challenge for developing and LDCs, which are technologically challenged.

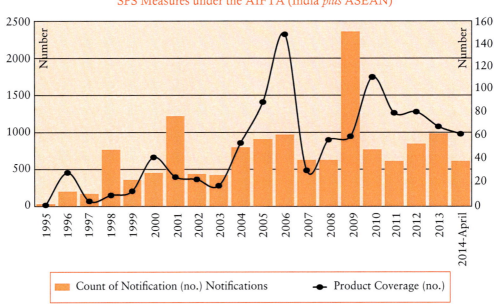

FIGURE 7.2
SPS Measures under the AIFTA (India *plus* ASEAN)

Source: Compilation by the author based on the CWS web portal on SPS and TBT measures.

---

[8] The year 2014 has not been included for analysis as it does represent one whole calendar year.
[9] Ibid.

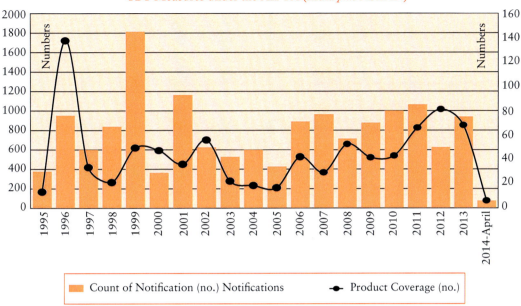

FIGURE 7.3
TBT Measures under the AIFTA (India *plus* ASEAN)

Source: Compilation by the author based on the CWS web portal on SPS and TBT measures.

AIFTA partners regulate the imports under different objectives.[10] The TBT measures are governed by nine broad objectives such as consumer and environmental protection, consumer health, economic stability and security, energy conservation and environment protection, food safety, harmonization with national and international standards, technical standards, cultural and religious reasons and trade facilitation.

The AIFTA partners witnessed a domination of food safety related objective with 62 per cent shares.[11] The regulations on animal health and plant products were second and third in the order of priority with 29 and 9 per cent shares, respectively. The other set of measures which are founded at the national/regional/industry level is called as regional standard.

A majority of AIFTA NTMs are based on international standards. In case of TBT, it was accounted for nearly 62 per cent share of the total measures, and in the case of SPS measures it was 60 per cent. A significant proportion of TBT (38 per cent) and SPS measures (40 per cent) were driven by national standards. Thus, it confirms that the AIFTA partners maintained considerable regulation under the TBT measures, which pose considerable trade barriers, particularly for small exporters.

2. Market Access Barriers Created by NTMs

We analyze the market access barriers, which exist in the form of NTMs on the products bilaterally traded between India and ASEAN countries. We analyze, in detail, India's market access in the ASEAN countries and ASEAN's market access in India.

---

[10] The 18 different minor objective are: Consumer Health; Consumer Health and Protection; Consumer Health and Safety; Consumer Health and Food Safety; Consumer Protection; Consumer Protection and Human Health; Consumer Protection and Safety; Consumer Protection, Human Health and Safety; Consumer Safety Consumer Safety and Human Health; Human and Animal Health; Human Health; Human Health and Protection; Human Health and Harmonization; Human Health and Safety; Human Health and Safety, Consumer and Environmental Protection; Human Safety and Human Safety and Environmental Protection.

[11] Simple changes in the scales of measurement can be called as the use of high-tech method, when there is a shift away from atomic measurements represented in particles per million (PPM) to sub-atomic level (μm) while measuring the level of pesticide contaminations, in the case of food safety objective. Refer to the discussion in Kallummal (2013: 34–42).

For the purpose of consistency, we aggregate the tariff lines with tariff schedule commitments to the heading level (HS 4 digit level) so that it matches with the CWS database on SPS and TBT measures. The harmonized tariff lines at heading levels are for Brunei Darussalam (1,244), Cambodia (1,219), India (1,222), Indonesia (1,221), Lao PDR (1,221), Malaysia (1,222), Myanmar (1,245), the Philippines (1,221), Singapore (1,221), Thailand (1,222) and Vietnam (1,244).

Market access under the tariff alone among the AIFTA partners showed nearly 81 per cent share with 10,878 harmonized tariff lines under the broad category of complete preferential market access, followed by the category of partial preferential market access with 1,688 product groups and under no preferential market access (MFN access) only 936 commodity groups with nearly 7 per cent share. Therefore, there is considerable scope for further liberalization as 81 per cent of the products groups and an additional 12 per cent under partial preferential market access. Figure 7.4 presents the market access barriers under the tariffs.

The market access available for India under the AIFTA, based on tariff alone analysis, shows complete preferential market access of up to 80.62 per cent and an additional partial preferential market access of 12.80 per cent of product groups in the ASEAN Market.[12] While on the other hand, ASEAN partners had preferential market access to the extent of 80.03 per cent of product groups under complete preferential market access and an additional 10 per cent under the partial preferential market access. However, the most important finding is the product groups (HS heading level), which are excluded from the exchange of concessions by the ASEAN (6.58 per cent) and India (10.31 per cent), the difference is close to 3.73 percentage points in favour of India. However, when the presence of NTMs is considered, we get a completely different picture of the preferential market access scenario under the AIFTA.

As noted in Table 7.2, the complete preferential market access provided by AIFTA partners as per the tariff alone was Brunei (1067) with 85.8 per cent shares. Product group-wise analysis of the AIFTA partners and their NTMs coverage under the broad category of complete preferential market access are as follows: Brunei with 19 per cent share, Cambodia with 15.3 per cent share, India with 35.9 per cent share, Indonesia with 48.5 per cent share, Lao PDR with 1.8 per cent share, Malaysia with 41 per cent share, the Philippines with 29.9 per cent share, Singapore with 34.7 per cent share, Thailand with 52.6 per cent share and Vietnam with 51.3 per cent share. It is clear from the broad category of complete preferential market access, which is inclusive of NT-1 and NT-2, that there is considerable presence of NTMs in this category. For India's market access, close to 80 per cent of ASEAN partners markets, which is under complete preferential market access, has witnessed restrictions by the presence of NTMs up to 33 per cent. Similarly, 12.8 per cent of the total product groups falling in the category of partial preferential market access faced NTMs barriers up to 6.6 per cent product group in the ASEAN market. Likewise an analysis of ASEAN market access reveals that 80 per cent of India's market, which is under complete preferential market access, has witnessed restrictions by the presence of NTMs up to 36 per cent. Similarly, 9.6 per cent of the total product groups falling in the category of partial preferential market access may be faced with NTMs barriers up to 4.4 per cent product group in the Indian market.

Let us analyze the NTMs under two separate categories: the TBT measures and SPS measures. In the case of TBT measures, Thailand topped with application on 462 products groups, followed by Malaysia with 394 products, Vietnam with 366 products and India with 312 products (Figure 7.5). However, what is interesting is the presence of Singapore with 161 products groups covered under the TBT measure.

In the case of SPS measures, many of ASEAN partners were seen in the category of complete preferential market access. This means that the benefits of tariff reduction under the AIFTA would be negated by the imposition of SPS measures. Illustrated in Figure 7.6, Singapore topped in terms of SPS measures application with 344 products groups, and closely behind was Vietnam with 315 products. Some of the other ASEAN players which dominated in term of application of SPS measures were Brunei Darussalam (203), Thailand (185), Indonesia (191) and the Philippines (110). India, on the other hand, had relatively less coverage of complete preferential market access products with 130 products ranked sixth in terms of coverage.

---

[12] This is average of products group-wise tariff commitments of 10 members of the ASEAN.

TABLE 7.2
NTMs and Its Significance for Preferential Market Access under AIFTA (Heading Level Analysis)

AIFTA/Market Access	Brunei	Cambodia	India	Indonesia	Lao	Malaysia	Myanmar*	The Philippines	Singapore	Thailand	Vietnam	AIFTA Total
Complete preferential access	1067	1084	978	629	940	978	943	1028	1220	998	1013	10878
No prerential access	94	28	126	85	32	99	149	99	1	109	114	936
Partial Preferential access	83	107	118	507	249	145	153	94		115	117	1688
Heading level (total)	**1244**	**1219**	**1222**	**1221**	**1221**	**1222**	**1245**	**1221**	**1221**	**1222**	**1244**	**13502**
NTMs (SPS and TBT) — count of heading (4 digit HS)												
Complete Preferential access	203	166	351	304	17	401	–	307	423	525	520	3217
No prerential access	5	11	103	76		48	–	81	1	59	47	431
Partial preferential access	1	10	43	213	17	62	–	42		78	71	537
NTMs count (SPS and TBT)	**209**	**187**	**497**	**593**	**34**	**511**	**–**	**430**	**424**	**662**	**638**	**4185**
A. Shares to Total Product Group (heading) Market Access												
A.1 tariff alone market access (%)												
Complete preferential access	85.8	88.9	80.0	51.5	77.0	80.0	75.7	84.2	99.9	81.7	81.4	80.6
No prerential access	7.6	2.3	10.3	7.0	2.6	8.1	12.0	8.1	0.1	8.9	9.2	6.9
Partial preferential access	6.7	8.8	9.7	41.5	20.4	11.9	12.3	7.7	0.0	9.4	9.4	12.5
Tariff coverage (%)	**100.0**	**100.0**	**100.0**	**100.0**	**100.0**	**100.0**	**100.0**	**100.0**	**100.0**	**100.0**	**100.0**	**100.0**
A.2. NTMs alone shares (%)												
Complete preferential access	19.0	15.3	35.9	48.3	1.8	41.0	–	29.9	34.7	52.6	51.3	29.6
No prerential access	0.5	1.0	10.5	12.1	0.0	4.9	–	7.9	0.1	5.9	4.6	4.0
Partial preferential access	0.1	0.9	4.4	33.9	1.8	6.3	–	4.1	0.0	7.8	7.0	4.9
NTMs coverage (%)	**19.6**	**17.3**	**50.8**	**94.3**	**3.6**	**52.2**	**–**	**41.8**	**34.8**	**66.3**	**63.0**	**38.5**

Source: Compilation by the author based databases like, the CWS web portal on SPS and TBT Measures, AIFTA Tariff Schedule and WTO, TAO databases.
Note: *Myanmar has not notified any notification to the WTO.

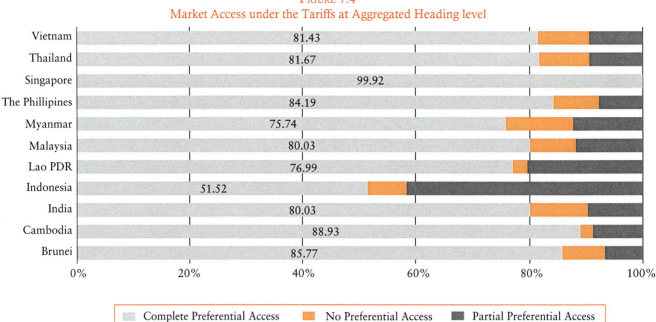

FIGURE 7.4
Market Access under the Tariffs at Aggregated Heading level

Source: Compilation by the author based on the CWS web portal on SPS and TBT measures.

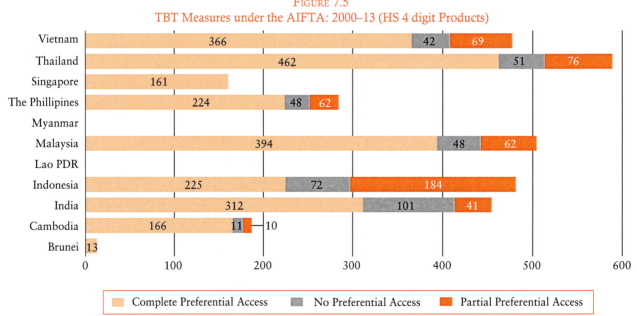

FIGURE 7.5
TBT Measures under the AIFTA: 2000–13 (HS 4 digit Products)

Source: Compilation by the author based on the CWS web portal on SPS and TBT measures.

2.1 How Much of a Market Access Barrier Was the AIFTA NTMs?

Table 7.3 provides a detailed analysis of the composition of all TBT measures under the AIFTA. All the 2088 product groups under the category of complete preferential market access had national measures dominating with nearly 69 per cent share and international measures had only 31 per cent shares. This clearly suggested that all the parties to AIFTA were not operating in the true spirit of providing easy access while committing for zero tariffs.

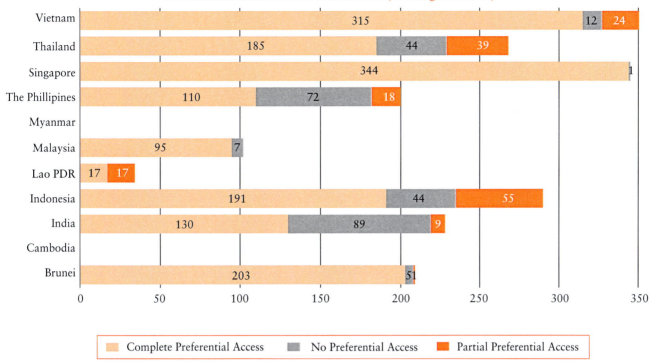

FIGURE 7.6
SPS Measures under the AIFTA: 2000–13 (HS 4 digit Products)

Source: Compilation by the author based on the CWS web portal on SPS and TBT measures.

Also in the category of partial preferential market access the scenario was tilted in favour of national measures with nearly 58 per cent share and international harmonized standard had only 42 per cent shares. Thus, the TBT measure, which is the foundation for industrialization and supply chain creation, the trend suggests that AIFTA parties were moving away from such initiatives. Therefore, the TBT measure under the AIFTA can be concluded as being stringent on our scale. However, since the parties are both at a similar level of technological capabilities and similar stage of development, it should not pose a challenge. Only a deeper study, examining the nature of objectives and the sectors would allow us to conclude firmly.

The total of 1904 products under the SPS measures coverage was distributed across the three broad market access categories like complete preferential market access with 1468 products accounting for 77 per cent share, followed by no preferential market access with 273 products accounting for 14.3 per cent share, and finally, the category of partial preferential market access with 163 products with a share of 8.6 per cent (Table 7.4). We recall that a majority (nearly 62 per cent) of SPS measures objectives was food safety; however, it is important to highlight that out of the 77 per cent coverage, nearly 75 per cent was SPS measures, based on international harmonized standards. This trend is similar across all the categories. Therefore, it can be concluded from the preliminary analysis that in the case of SPS measures, the international standards were dominant.

It was found that there were a significant number of TBT measures, which were based on national standards, when compared with the SPS measures.

3. Conclusions

It is not the tariff liberalization, but the streamlining of NTMs that is important for achieving preferential market access. Only then, any FTA achieve its true goal of promoting trade and investment.

The AIFTA liberalized tariffs across 80 per cent of AIFTA tariff lines. However, there was no clear measure to discipline NTMs. By stating that the parties shall not institute or maintain any NTM on the importation of goods from the other Parties or on the exportation or sale for export of goods destined for the territory of the other Parties, except in accordance with its WTO rights and obligations or other provisions in this Agreement.

TABLE 7.3
Compositions of National and International TBT Measures under AIFTA

Count of Heading (4 Diigit HS)	Brunei	Cambodia	India	Indonesia	Malaysia	The Philippines	Singapore	Thailand	Vietnam	AIFTA TBT Measures
Comp. pref. access	13	166	312	225	394	224	161	462	131	2088
International			51	68	181	28		321		649
National	13	166	261	157	213	196	161	141	131	1439
No pref. access		11	101	72	48	28		51	17	328
International			1	4	26	5		47		83
National		11	100	68	22	23		4	17	245
Partial pref. access		10	41	184	62	32		76	19	424
International			9	41	51	6		72		179
National		10	32	143	11	26		4	19	245
Total TBT measures	13	187	454	481	504	284	161	589	167	2840

Source: Compilation by the author based on the CWS web portal on SPS and TBT measures.
Note: Count of total heading (4 digit HS) which faced TBT measures.

TABLE 7.4
Compositions of National and International SPS Measures under AIFTA

Count of Heading (4 Diigit HS)	Brunei	Cambodia	India	Indonesia	Malaysia	The Philippines	Singapore	Thailand	Vietnam	AIFTA TBT Measures
Comp. pref. access	203	130	191	17	95	110	222	185	315	1468
International	198	120	185	17	41	68	213	155	112	1109
National	5	10	6		54	42	9	30	203	359
No pref. access	5	89	44		7	72		44	12	273
International	5	89	43		3	39		40	9	228
National			1		4	33		4	3	45
Partial pref. access	1	9	55	17		18		39	24	163
International	1	9	50	17		7		34	14	132
National			5			11		5	10	31
Total SPS measures	209	228	290	34	102	200	222	268	351	1904

Source: Compilation by the author based on the CWS web portal on SPS and TBT measures.
Note: Count of total heading (4 digit HS) which faced TBT measures.

The AIFTA lost control over the NTM side of market access. Therefore, the additional preferential market access provided by the tariffs liberalization seems to be nullified by the presence of NTMs.

Some interesting facts about the role of NTMs which have come to light from the analysis is that, although AIFTA has come up with considerable tariff reduction, at the same time it is equally important for such agreements to come to an understanding on the issue of NTMs. This is critical because of the nature of its impact on a product or group of products, whereby these measures have the possibility of totally denying market access. Therefore, there is a growing urgency for negotiations and immediate solution on this issue, by creating and strengthening the discipline around the mutual recognition agreements (MRAs), while dealing with the SPS and TBT measures.

Presently, there is discord in the tariff lines. There is a need to harmonize the tariff schedules of two parties to the agreement. This is important in the context of ASEAN moving towards a common tariff by 2015. However, a majority of ASEAN members have different scheduling under the AIFTA.

This in itself is very challenging and to add to this is how the measure is applied at the border. Sometime, it may lead to discrimination due to lack of transparency built-in to the procedures of application of domestic regulation.

Finally, there is a need to build sectoral MRAs. This is important especially when it is found that a lot of TBT measures are based on national standards. This would help countries to protect the industries within the FTA. India and ASEAN may undertake sectoral MRAs in those areas, which offer higher marginal return from the trade liberalization. Intuitively, MRAs would lead to strengthening production networks across borders.

8
Energy Market Integration and Cooperation

Energy security has long been a major challenge faced by India. Over the last three decades or so, relatively higher economic growth has meant higher demand for energy products and services, which led to even greater energy vulnerability for India. With more than 17 per cent of global population, India accounts for less than one per cent of global oil reserves and global natural gas reserves and about 7 per cent of global coal reserves (BP 2013). Traditional fuels have always played an important part in the energy supplies of India, yet they have become rather stagnant and unable to cope up with the increasing population, which, in turn, also translated into a greater demand for modern commercial fuels. Another aspect of India's energy security challenge is the lack of access to energy for a large section of its population. At 0.60 ton oil equivalent (TOE), India's per capita Total Primary Energy Supplies (TPES) is not only far lower than the global average but also lower than that of Africa (see Table 8.1).

Considering all forms of energy, India's dependence on outside sources is about 28 per cent of its total supplies (see Table 8.2). This is lower than countries like Japan, South Korea, Taiwan, Singapore and many other countries. However, at around US$120 billion in 2013–14, India's net energy import bill was about 2/5th of its total exports, which is higher than many countries that rely largely on imported energy products and services, making India among the most energy vulnerable countries (Government of India 2014). Paucity of domestic oil and gas reserves led India to adopt a coal-centric energy supply strategy as coal was relatively abundant in India (Nanda 2008). Yet, India has emerged as a major coal importer in recent years, along with steady growth in import of natural gas.

In contrast, ASEAN is a relatively (energy) resource-rich region though some countries have higher dependence on imported energy than India. As illustrated in Table 8.2, Singapore (99 per cent), Thailand (46 per cent), the Philippines (45 per cent) and Cambodia (29 per cent) have higher import dependence than India. Yet, ASEAN as a whole is a net energy surplus region. Taking note of this, ASEAN has long considered energy supply to be an important area of cooperation. Except Cambodia, Myanmar and the Philippines, energy supply and

TABLE 8.1
Energy Indicators in India and ASEAN Countries, 2011

Country/Region	Per Capita TPES (toe)	TPES/GDP (toe/thousand 2000 US$)	TPES/GDP (PPP) (toe/thousand 2000 US$)	Per Capita Electricity Consumption (KWh)
World	1.88	0.25	0.19	2933
OECD	4.28	0.14	0.14	8226
Africa	0.67	0.55	0.25	592
India	0.60	0.57	0.19	673
Brunei	9.44	0.38	0.21	8517
Cambodia	0.37	0.57	0.18	168
Indonesia	0.86	0.52	0.21	684
Malaysia	2.63	0.41	0.19	4232
Myanmar	0.29	0.77	0.19	119
The Philippines	0.43	0.30	0.23	648
Singapore	6.45	0.19	0.12	8404
Thailand	1.71	0.57	0.22	2218
Vietnam	0.70	0.78	0.23	1073

Source: International Energy Agency (IEA), Paris.
Notes: TOE = ton oil equivalent; KWh = Kilowatt hour; TPES = Total Primary Energy Supplies; GDP = Gross Domestic Product; PPP = Purchasing Power Parity

TABLE 8.2
Energy Balances in India and ASEAN Countries, 2011

Country/Region	Production (Mtoe)	Imports (Mtoe)	Exports (Mtoe)	TPES (Mtoe)	Net Imports (Mtoe)	Import Dependence (Import/TPES)
India	540.94	277.98	64.52	749.45	213.46	0.28
Brunei	18.69	0.24	14.85	3.83	−14.61	−3.81
Cambodia	3.79	1.57	0.00	5.33	1.57	0.29
Indonesia	394.57	47.30	232.11	209.01	−184.80	−0.88
Malaysia	84.27	43.00	47.04	75.91	−4.05	−0.05
Myanmar	22.39	0.24	8.63	14.06	−8.39	−0.60
The Philippines	23.89	21.36	3.32	40.45	18.04	0.45
Singapore	0.93	135.98	56.98	33.45	79.00	0.99
Thailand	68.74	66.06	11.84	119.15	54.22	0.46
Vietnam	66.60	15.08	21.85	61.21	−6.77	−0.11
ASEAN-1	683.88	330.82	396.62	562.39	−65.79	−0.12

Source: IEA Database, Paris.
Note: Mtoe = million ton oil equivalent.

consumption scenario is far better than that of India (see Table 8.1). India has been importing its energy largely from West Asia and Africa without any long-term systematic cooperation framework.

While ASEAN has been an energy-surplus region for long, its surplus energy has generally moved eastward rather than westward. Table A8.1 provides energy reserves and resources of ASEAN countries and India. In recent years however, India has been importing substantial quantity of coal from Indonesia. The ASEAN region has also made a quiet entry as a supplier of natural gas (LNG) to India. Therefore, it will be interesting to explore if the energy-thirsty India and the resource-rich ASEAN can promote wider cooperation on energy security that can be mutually beneficial to both India and ASEAN countries. An important element in the Plan of Action to Implement the ASEAN–India Partnership for Peace, Progress and Shared Prosperity (2010–15), adopted at the 8th ASEAN–India Summit, held at Hanoi on 30 October 2010, has introduced the cooperation on renewable energy. There has been some progress in this regard since then and the strengths and complementarities in this regard have also been identified.

In the light of this view, we present the approaches of energy cooperation of ASEAN and India, analyze the energy trade between ASEAN and India and discuss the prospects of energy cooperation between ASEAN and India.

1. ASEAN APPROACH TO ENERGY COOPERATION

Region wide energy cooperation in ASEAN started in 1976 when the ASEAN Council for Petroleum (ASCOPE) was established. In the initial phase, the focus was on oil and power grid cooperation. The objective of ASCOPE was to promote active collaboration and mutual assistance in the development of petroleum resources. An important milestone was achieved in the form of ASEAN Petroleum Security Agreement (APSA) in 1986, which was a binding agreement that put obligations on member countries. It established ASEAN Emergency Petroleum Sharing Scheme (AEPSS) to ensure mutual supply of oil by six countries in sudden shortfalls in supplies.

However, power grid cooperation started outside what was then ASEAN. The beginning was made in 1966 when Thailand and Lao PDR concluded a power exchange agreement. This was quite similar to the Bhutan–India cooperation on energy in its objective, scope, modalities and outcomes. Similar agreements were signed between Thailand and Malaysia; and Malaysia and Singapore in 1978. The ASEAN level cooperation started in this regard in 1981 as it established a task force involving the Heads of ASEAN Public Utilities Authorities (HAPUA) with the objective of promoting cooperation on power grid connections. The main focus was on establishing mechanisms to avoid supply disruptions. The mid-1980s saw further deepening of energy cooperation in the ASEAN region.

In another important development, the ASEAN Energy Cooperation Agreement (AECA) was signed in 1986 through which the member countries agreed to cooperate on a wide range of issues to foster efficient development and use of all forms of energy. Cooperation activities included planning, development of resources, conservation, security of supply, capacity building and exchange of information. The 1991 Programme of Action for Enhancement of Cooperation in Energy (PAECE) was followed by 1995 Plan of Action on Energy Cooperation (PAEC 1995–99) and both included oil and gas, coal, new and renewable sources, energy efficiency and conservation with co-ordination bodies for each of the five areas. The resolve to promote deeper energy cooperation in ASEAN got reinforced through the ASEAN Vision 2020 adopted in 1997, which called for ASEAN-wide Interconnection arrangement for electricity, natural gas and water. ASEAN is working towards realizing this vision and have initiated several transmission and gas pipeline projects to eventually develop ASEAN wide power grid and gas pipeline network. Some of the projects are already completed (Sovacool 2009).

The 2004 Plan of Action on Energy Cooperation (PAEC 2004–10) directed actions towards more efficient and sustainable management of energy and an appropriate policy framework and implementation for the same. Hence, clean coal technology as well as energy-environment interface received special attention. The current (2010) Plan of Action on Energy Cooperation (PAEC 2004–10) added a new programme, Civilian Nuclear Energy (CNE) programme to its framework. Consequently, there are now seven areas of energy cooperation that are being pursued in ASEAN (Shi and Malik 2013). The major programmes under this plan are as follows:[1]

a)   ASEAN Power Grid
b)   Trans-ASEAN Gas Pipeline
c)   Coal and Clean Coal Technology Promotion
d)   Energy Efficiency and Conservation Promotion
e)   New and Renewable Energy Development Energy Policy and Environmental Analysis
f)   Civilian Nuclear Energy

2. India's Energy Trade with ASEAN Countries

For a long time, ASEAN countries, such as Malaysia, Indonesia, Thailand and Brunei, have been important sources for India's imports of crude oil. Till recently, India imported substantial quantity of crude oil from these countries. However, in recent years, these countries have reduced their exports of crude oil due to an increase in their own domestic requirements. As of now, India is importing crude oil from the two ASEAN countries, namely, Malaysia and Brunei, in small quantities. In 2013–14, India sourced less than 2 per cent of its crude oil imports from the ASEAN region (Table 8.3), while India imported more than 4 per cent of its crude from the region in 2004–05 (Planning Commission 2006).

In recent years, however, India's trade in energy commodities has undergone some major changes. India has become a major importer of coal and India has also become a major exporter of refined petroleum products. In fact, as of now, petroleum products constitute the largest export item of India. On both these counts, ASEAN is playing an important role. Indonesia is the number one source of coal imports for India, while, another ASEAN country, Singapore, is the number one destination for Indian exports of refined petroleum products.

Table 8.3
Indian Imports of Oil (Crude) from ASEAN Countries

(US$ million)

Country	2012–13	2013–14	Global Rank
Malaysia	1,782.05	1,822.18	14
Brunei	809.86	708.94	18
Total from ASEAN	2,591.91	2,531.12	
Total Indian imports	144,519.72	143,979.96	
ASEAN as per cent of India's import from the World	1.79	1.76	

Source: Export–Import Database, Ministry of Commerce and Industry, Government of India.

---

[1] Available at http://www.aseanenergy.org (accessed 22 February 2015).

Energy Market Integration and Cooperation 101

TABLE 8.4

Indian Imports of Coal from ASEAN Countries

(US$ million)

Country	2012–13	2013–2014	Global Rank
Indonesia	6,061.43	6,943.91	1
Vietnam	17.68	12.54	12
Malaysia		3.68	14
Total from ASEAN	6,079.11	6,960.13	
Total India coal imports	15,951.48	15,446.01	
ASEAN as per cent of India's Import from the World	38.11	45.06	

Source: Export–Import Database, Ministry of Commerce and Industry, Government of India.

In 2013–14, India sourced a whopping 45 per cent of its coal from the ASEAN region (Table 8.4), mainly from Indonesia and its dependence on this region seems to be increasing.

The ASEAN region provides an important outlet for Indian exports of petroleum products and in 2013–14, it absorbed some 15.5 per cent of Indian exports (see Table 8.5). The figure seems to be gradually decreasing over time. India also continues to import some specialized petroleum products. Two ASEAN countries, namely, Singapore and Malaysia are two important sources in this regard. In 2013–14, India sourced about 19 per cent of its refined oil imports from the ASEAN region, which is lower than the same witnessed in 2012–13 (see Table 8.5).

In the year 2013–14, Brunei became one of the suppliers of LNG to India. Though it supplied only US$ 49.62 million worth of LNG in the first year, it became the fifth largest source of LNG for India. With substantial gas reserves, Indonesia becoming one of the suppliers of natural gas to India in the near future is also a distinct possibility.

One important aspect of energy development, transportation and use is that it requires huge volumes of plants, machineries and equipment, and as a result, opens up the possibilities for trade in such goods. Countries engaged in development of coal, oil and gas fields, electricity generation plants, oil refineries, construction of transmission lines, pipelines etc. and a range of goods are required for these activities. As an indicator, one can look at the trade in electric motors and generators between India and ASEAN countries. It is observed that the ASEAN region accounts for only about 5 per cent of Indian exports of electric motors and generators, while it accounts for only about 3.23 per cent of Indian imports of such goods, and the shares are declining (Table 8.6). Hence, there is potential for increasing trade in such goods and greater energy cooperation might facilitate the same.

TABLE 8.5

Indian Oil (Refined) Trade with ASEAN Countries (2710)

(US$ million)

Country	Exports			Imports		
	2012–13	2013–14	Global Rank	2012–13	2013–14	Global Rank
Singapore	7,798.75	7,342.02	1	883.46	518.04	3
Indonesia	1,455.08	1,515.82	12	5.42	3.77	35
Malaysia	711.21	621.10	26	266.84	304.80	6
Thailand	42.63	119.02	37	7.11	28.86	18
The Philippines	7.34	59.62	46	0.46	0.69	45
Vietnam	7.67	8.70	57			
Myanmar	2.96	7.89	58			
Total with ASEAN	10,025.64	9,674.17		1,163.29	856.16	
Total Indian exports/imports	60,346.70	62,420.07		4,851.36	4,420.01	
ASEAN as per cent of India's export/import from the world	16.61	15.50		23.98	19.37	

Source: Export–Import Database, Ministry of Commerce and Industry, Government of India.

TABLE 8.6
Indian Trade in Electric Motors and Generators (8501) with ASEAN Countries

(US$ million)

Country	Exports			Imports		
	2012–13	2013–14	Global Rank	2012–13	2013–14	Global Rank
Vietnam	1.15	6.75	13.0			
Indonesia	6.20	4.36	18.0	11.46	12.00	11.0
Thailand	7.11	4.10	20.0	4.33	7.44	15.0
Singapore	3.15	1.49	37.0	5.71	2.71	23.0
The Philippines	0.98	1.19	43.0	2.47	1.26	25.0
Malaysia				1.19	0.54	33.0
Lao PDR		0.94	51.0			
Myanmar	0.33	0.17	87.0			
Total with ASEAN	18.92	19.00		25.16	23.95	
Total Indian exports/imports	337.88	379.30		715.24	741.63	
ASEAN as per cent of India's export/import from the world	5.60	5.01		3.52	3.23	

Source: Export–Import Database, Ministry of Commerce and Industry, Government of India.

3. ENERGY INVESTMENT AND COOPERATION

India is already active in the ASEAN region through investment in energy sector as well as development of energy infrastructure. While the focus of Indian companies investing in the region are Myanmar, Vietnam, Indonesia and Malaysia, its involvement in energy infrastructure development is by and large limited to CLMV countries through development cooperation and construction of facilities. During April 1996 to March 2013, the cumulative approved Indian FDI outflows (including equity, loan and guarantee issued) to Myanmar stood at US$ 192 million. On the other hand, cumulative inflows into India from Myanmar during April 2000 to March 2013 amounted to US$ 8.9 million. As on December 2012, India occupied 10th rank in terms of foreign investments to Myanmar. Around 98 per cent of Indian investments in Myanmar are in the oil and gas sector with the remaining 2 per cent in manufacturing.[2] Indian energy companies that have operations in Myanmar include ONGC Videsh Limited (OVL), GAIL, Essar Energy and Jubilant Oil and Gas. While some companies have been there since 2000, PSC-1 onshore block in Central Myanmar worth US$ 73 million has been awarded to Jubilant Energy of India on the basis of a global tender in 2011.[3] In 2013, the OVL had successfully bid for two on-shore blocks[4] in Myanmar.

Vietnam continues to be an attractive investment destination for Indian companies and energy sector occupies a prime place in that. India's approved direct investments in Vietnam during April 1996 to March 2013 amounted to US$ 472.9 million. Most Indian investments are in the form of wholly foreign invested projects. OVL and Essar Exploration and Production Ltd are the major Indian investors operating in the energy sector in Vietnam. OVL has signed an Agreement on Cooperation with Petrovietnam. Cumulative FDI inflows into India from Vietnam during April 2000 to March 2013 amounted to US$ 0.24 million.[5] However, energy is not the focus.

A number of Indian companies including Tata Power and Reliance acquired coal assets in Indonesia (Tata Power has recently left), while several others are trying to acquire such assets in the country. To facilitate the process, India and Indonesia have a structured dialogue process in the coal sector having established a

---

[2] Refer, for example, the 'Indian High Commission in Myanmar' website. Available at http://www.indianhighcommission.com.my (accessed 22 February 2015).

[3] For details, refer the Press Release by Ministry of Commerce and Industry, Government of India, 9 June 2013.

[4] These two blocks are: EP3 and PSC B2.

[5] Refer, for example, the 'Embassy of India in Vietnam' website. Available at http://indembassy.com.vn (accessed 22 February 2015).

Joint Working Group (JWG) in 2010. An Energy Forum was created during the visit of President Yudhoyono to India in January 2011. The Forum is co-chaired by the Ministry of Coal from India and Ministry of Energy and Mineral Resources from Indonesia. Furthermore, in the oil and gas sector too pursuant to the signing of the MoU on Cooperation in Oil and Gas in January 2011, a JWG mechanism has been instituted to enhance co-operation in this field.[6]

Malaysian investment in India is estimated at about US$ 7.8 billion, while Indian investment in the country stands at about US$ 3 billion. Power and oil and gas sectors have been the focus of Malaysian investment in India. Malaysia's national oil and gas company, namely, PETRONAS has stake in Cairn India (Indian arm of the UK-based oil and gas company, Cairn Energy Plc). which went up to 14.94 per cent after its acquisition of 2.3 per cent share for US$ 240 million in April, 2011. Ranhill Bhd's US$ 900 million contract for construction of a 2×350 MW thermal power plant in Chhattisgarh, Mudajaya Group Berhad's US$ 150 million E&P power project related contract in Chhatisgarh and Asian Gateways Construction Sdn. Bhd.'s US$ 1.4 billion mega thermal power project (1600 MW) in Andhra Pradesh are some other examples of the involvement of Malaysian companies in India. While Indian investment in Malaysia is relatively more diverse, recently Indian companies have made forays into energy sector as well. Aban Offshore Ltd, Mumbai, has been awarded two contracts worth US$ 55 million in all to drill nine oil wells in Malaysia. Quantum Sigma Sdn Bhd and ES Electronics (India) Pvt Ltd has signed an agreement to establish a manufacturing facility to produce solar panel and energy saving plugs by Quantum Sigma in Bentong, Pahang. The investments by Indian company are on technology transfer and expertise. The proposed project entails an investment of over RM18 million (US$ 5.6 million).[7]

As noted earlier, Indian involvement in development of energy infrastructure through development co-operation and construction activities is mainly in CLMV countries, and Myanmar is the focus in this regard. A line of credit for three power transmission lines and substations to be executed by Power Grid Corporation of India Ltd (PGCIL) was signed in June 2008 along with change in scope of work approved for the project in March 2012. The transmission lines and substations projects are (a) Oakshitpin–Taungup 230 KV transmission line, (b) Taungup–Maei–Ann-Mann 230 KV transmission line and (c) Maei–Kyaukphyu 230 KV transmission line. MoEP and PGCIL signed the contract on March 21, 2012. The scope of the work includes design and engineering, supply of the equipments and supervision of erection of equipments. Renovation of Thanbayakan Petrochemical Complex is another project being financed by another US$ 20 million line of credit signed in 2008–09 (EXIM Bank 2013).

India has been a development partner with Lao PDR for quite some time, where the energy sector has been the focus of such relationship. In June 2004, India provided a line of credit of US$ 10 million for a 115 KV Transmission Line from Ban-Na in Champassak to Attapeu. The project was completed in 2006 (Embassy of India in Lao PDR Website). Similarly, line of credit was extended for supply of equipment for rural electrification worth US$ 4 million, which was completed in September 2009. With Indian assistance, the Paksong–Jiangxai–Bangyo transmission line project worth US$ 18 million was commissioned in September 2010. The Nam Song 7.5 MW hydropower project worth US$ 11 million was also completed with Indian assistance in October/November, 2012. In September 2010, a loan agreement between EXIM Bank and the Ministry of Finance was signed for a US$ 72.55 million loan for the two projects: (a) 230 KV Double Circuit Transmission Line from Nabong to Thabok and substations worth US$ 34.68 million, and (b) 15 MW Nam Boun 2 Hydropower Project worth US$ 37.86 million. The scope of the work includes supply of equipments, goods and services for construction (ibid.)

Indian power equipment manufacturer Bharat Heavy Electricals (BHEL) commissioned the first 100 MW unit at the Nam Chien hydro power project in Vietnam in 2013. The project comprises two Pelton type hydro generating units of 100 MW each. Equipment supplied by the company included hydro turbines, generators, transformers, controls, monitoring, protection system and switchgear. Funded through a line of credit by the

---

[6] For details, see the Ministry of External Affairs, Government of India, India–Indonesia Relations, January 2014. Available at http://www.mea.gov.in/Portal/ForeignRelation/Indonesia_January_2014.pdf (accessed 22 February 2015).

[7] Refer, for example, the 'Indian High Commission in Myanmar' website. Available at http://www.indianhighcommission.com.my (accessed 22 February 2015).

Indian government, the scope of the contract includes design, engineering, manufacture, supply and supervision of installation besides commissioning of the entire electro-mechanical equipment package for the project.[8]

Export–Import Bank of India (EXIM Bank) extended a US$ 35.2 million line of credit to the Government of Cambodia for financing the Stung Tasal Development Project, purchase of the water pumps and for the construction of the electric transmission line between Kratie and Stung Treng Province in Cambodia (EXIM Bank 2013).

4. Prospects for India–ASEAN Energy Cooperation

While ASEAN is going ahead in full force towards comprehensive regional energy cooperation, India's regional cooperation within SAARC is only selective. India has been able to promote cooperation in the electricity sector only at bilateral levels. India's efforts to access natural gas by constructing pipelines through its neighbours, namely, Bangladesh and Pakistan, have not been successful so far. Hence, India would be quite keen to promote its energy cooperation with ASEAN.

India is already engaged in energy infrastructure development in the ASEAN region, particularly in the CLMV countries. India is building hydropower projects, power transmission lines and substations and oil and gas pipelines in these countries. On the other hand, Malaysia is engaged in similar infrastructure development in India. While Malaysia has invested in energy assets in India, Indian companies have also invested in energy assets in ASEAN countries in sectors like coal, oil and gas. When it comes to trade in energy commodities, it is largely limited to Indian imports of coal from Indonesia and Indian exports petroleum products. However, the resource positions of India and ASEAN indicate that India can import much more particularly natural gas and electricity. Energy sector machineries, equipments and other goods can also open up possibilities for substantial trade.

ASEAN is in the process of developing a region-wide grid of natural gas pipelines and electricity transmission lines. India can get connected through these two ASEAN wide grids just by developing transmission line and gas pipeline connections with Myanmar. Indian electricity grid is already connected with Bangladesh electricity grid and Bangladesh is planning to link its electricity grid with that of Myanmar. There has been a significant change in the attitude of Bangladesh with respect to Myanmar–Bangladesh–India natural gas pipeline. The fact that Bangladesh is facing gas shortage now and the discovery of the offshore North-West Myanmar Gas Field has sparked renewed interest in the proposed pipeline and Bangladesh now intends to access natural gas from Myanmar along with India. India and Myanmar have also revived the discussions on the gas pipeline connection between India and Myanmar through Bangladesh. The proposed pipeline would extend from Block A-1, through Bangladesh, to India and various design options are being considered, including a land route via the eastern Indian states of Tripura and Mizoram, an offshore route through the coastal areas of Bangladesh and a deep-sea route. In future, it will be possible for India not only to access electricity and gas from Myanmar but also gas from faraway fields in Indonesia and Brunei and electricity from Lao PDR.

The official discussion on energy cooperation between India and ASEAN has so far focused on renewable energy only. The electricity generation sources indicate that India has developed significant capability in wind energy, Indonesia and Philippines have the same in geothermal energy and Singapore is generating significant electricity from waste. India and Thailand have some experience in solar power as well. India is also the only country to generate nuclear power and use bio-fuel to generate significant quantity of electricity. These countries can help others in developing energy production capabilities in the respective sub-sectors. While India–ASEAN energy cooperation focuses on renewable energy only, India, along with some of its South Asian neighbours and some members of ASEAN are part of BIMSTEC, where energy has been identified as one of the important sectors for comprehensive cooperation including all types of energy. ASEAN-India energy cooperation would depend very much on BIMSTEC energy activities, work as a bridge between SAARC and ASEAN in promoting a comprehensive energy cooperation regime.

---

[8] For details, refer the *Energy Business Review*, 31 January 2013.

TABLE A8.1
Energy Reserves and Resources in India and ASEAN Countries

Resources/ Country	Coal (Million Ton) 2012	Lignite (Million Ton) 2012	Petroleum (Million Ton) 2012	Natural Gas (Billion Cubic Metre) 2012	Technically Feasible Hydropower Potential (GW/Year)	Hydro Generation (GW/Year) 2011	Solar Potential (GW Capacity)	Wind Potential (GW Capacity)
India	56100	4500	800	1074	2638000	130686	657	49
Brunei			100	300				
Cambodia					34400	46.5		
Indonesia	1520	4009	500	2900	401646	12421	62	63
Lao PDR					232500*	3777		
Malaysia			500	1300	123000	7629	13	36
Myanmar				200	348000*	5152		
The Philippines					20334	9699	20	23
Singapore								
Thailand		1239	100	300	16292	8164	33	67
Vietnam	150		600	600	123000	29831	27	44

Sources: BP (2013); IEA Database, Paris; Intpow, Ölz and Beerepoot (2010); Rashid and Islam (2013).

Note: *Gross hydropower potential.

For hydropower, solar and wind power potential, the assessment is for perpetuity and hence no year has been indicated.

9
Strengthening Monetary and Financial Cooperation

The economic performance of ASEAN countries show a wide variation and the economic prospects are mixed. Noted in the *World Economic Outlook* (IMF 2014), Indonesia and Thailand, among the core countries within the bloc (that is, Indonesia, Thailand, Malaysia, Singapore, the Philippines and Vietnam), will grow slower than expected. In particular, political uncertainties in Thailand will drag down public investment, while Indonesia will be impacted by an adverse growth inflation trade-off. Malaysia and Philippines will, however, be on a positive growth path.[1] Notwithstanding the differing growth scenarios, the ASEAN as a whole will continue to be well-positioned to take advantage of the process of global financial market rebalancing. It may be noted that the core ASEAN group counts on around US$ 775 billion in international reserves to counteract any potential stress in emerging market financial asset (IMF 2014). In terms of financial sector's health, most economies in the region have well capitalized banking sectors with satisfactory profitability and high asset quality. This apart, debt sustainability is not an issue of concern as the ASEAN gross public sector debt averages 46 per cent of GDP (ibid.).

We discuss in this chapter the dynamics of financial integration in money and finance in ASEAN as well as between ASEAN and India. A roadmap has been laid out in order to strengthen monetary and financial cooperation between India and ASEAN.

1. Financial Markets in India and the Policies

The money market and the capital market are the organized financial markets in both ASEAN and India. Money market is for trading in government securities, while capital market is for equity securities. In essence, the primary market deals in new issues, the secondary market is meant for trading in outstanding or existing securities. Primary securities are issued by the ultimate borrowers of funds to the ultimate savers, for example, Bank Deposits, Mutual Fund Units, Insurance Policies among others. Financial services include merchant banking, leasing, hire purchase and credit ratings. In India, banks dominate the financial system and the banking system is dominated by commercial banks with the state-owned public sector banks cornering the largest pie. Box 9.1 highlights major banking sector reforms in India since 1991.

1.1 Monetary Policy Stance Differs from Country to Country

The inflation outlook for the major economies in the ASEAN region continues to remain mixed. Consumer price inflation in Indonesia has declined to 4.5 per cent (July 2014) after witnessing a spike with adjustment in fuel prices in the middle of last year. Inflation in Vietnam is high compared with most of its regional peers, whereas inflation has accelerated in the Philippines to around 4 per cent.

Given the fact that the inflation outlook in ASEAN economies remains largely under control, monetary conditions remain mostly accommodative in most of the core ASEAN economies. However, the Indonesian central bank has increased the interest rate several times in 2013 in response to the (then) widening current account deficit and financial market volatility. The Malaysian central bank has in fact raised the benchmark rate in July 2014. Thailand, on the other hand, is likely to maintain loose monetary conditions for an extended period of time in order to restart the economy.

---

[1] ASEAN is a middle-income region having diverse income levels among member countries. Countries such as Singapore and Brunei enjoy a very high GDP per capita at around US$ 49,000 and US$ 39,000, respectively. In contrast, Myanmar and Cambodia have a GDP per capita of just below US$ 900. However, the trend emerging from the growth rates does not indicate any substantial narrowing of the gap that exists between high income and low income ASEAN countries.

Strengthening Monetary and Financial Cooperation

Box 9.1
Major Banking Sector Reforms in India Since 1991

The economic reforms initiated by India in 1991 also embraced the banking system. Following is a short summary of the major reforms aimed at improving efficiency, productivity and profitability of banks.

New banks licensed in private sector to inject competition in the system: 10 in 1993, two in 2003 and recently two in 2014.

FDI+FII up to 74 per cent allowed in private sector banks.

Listing of PSBs on stock exchanges and allowing them to access capital markets for augmenting their equity, subject to maintaining Government shareholding at a minimum of 51 per cent. Private shareholders represented on the Board of PSBs.

Progressive reduction in statutory pre-emption (SLR and CRR) to improve the resource base of banks so as to expand credit available to the private sector. SLR is currently at 22 per cent (38.5 per cent in 1991) and CRR is at 4 per cent (15 per cent in 1991).

Adoption of international best practices in banking regulation. Introduction of prudential norms on capital adequacy, IRAC (income recognition, asset classification, provisioning), exposure norms, progressive adoption of Basel II and most recently Basel II norms to be implemented by January 2019, etc.

Phased liberalization of branch licensing. Banks can now open branches in Tier 2 to Tier 6 cities without prior approval from the Reserve Bank.

Deregulation of a complex structure of deposit and lending interest rates to strengthen competitive impulses, improve allocative efficiency and strengthen the transmission of monetary policy.

Base rate (floor rate for lending) introduced (July 2010). Prescription of an interest rate floor on savings deposit rate withdrawn (October 2011).

Use of information technology to improve the efficiency and productivity, enhance the payment and settlement systems and deepen financial inclusion

Strengthening of Know Your Customer (KYC) and Anti-money Laundering (AML) norms; making banking less prone to financial abuse.

Due to all these reforms, India's financial system is now robust enough and largely unscathed from the vagaries of global financial crisis. However in the last couple of years, India has been facing a growth downturn and higher inflation, which has significantly impacted both deposits and credit growth.

Source: Author.

In September 2013, RBI constituted an Expert Committee under the chairmanship of Dr Urjit Patel to examine the operating framework of RBI's monetary policy. The committee has since submitted its final report. The Committee has recommended CPI inflation as the new nominal anchor for the monetary policy framework. It has also recommended adopting a long-term inflation target of 4 per cent for CPI inflation with a band of (+/–) 2 per cent over a horizon of two years. The panel recommended a 12-month target of 8 per cent and 24-month target of 6 per cent, inflation before migrating to inflation targeting regime.

The arguments for recommending CPI as a nominal anchor and setting a 2–6 per cent CPI target in the medium term is a radical step and can be seen against the backdrop of a stubborn inflation since 2011–12. However, inflation targeting per se in a country like India will face some key operational challenges as it will require close co-ordination with the Government.

1.2 A Region in Need of Investment

During the 1990s, the investment-GDP ratio was 30 to 40 per cent in the core ASEAN countries, except in the Philippines. Investment exceeded domestic savings, as manifested in substantial current-account deficit, funded to a large extent by 'hot money'. This changed abruptly after the 1997 financial crisis. Current-account balances turned to surplus mostly at the expense of domestic investment, which declined to 20–30 per cent of GDP.

Having adjusted its external balances and after becoming an 'excess savings' region, ASEAN now needs to increase domestic investment to get back to its potential rate of growth. Among others, ASEAN countries would benefit from savings being channelled to intra-regional investment. To be sure, this is already happening: intra-ASEAN FDI rose from 14 per cent of total FDI during 2002–09 to 18.5 per cent in 2009–11. Chapter 4 of this Report has detailed discussion on FDI flows between ASEAN and India.

2. Dynamics of Financial Integration in Money and Finance: India and ASEAN+3

It is useful to recognize that, there are several important factors that are relevant for considering greater financial integration in the ASEAN region. First is the wide diversity in the level of economic development across the region. Second is the diverging levels of financial sector development across the region. Third is the limited scope of the existing intra-region resource-pooling mechanism and the lack of institutional frameworks. Fourth is the presence of non-synchronizing business cycles amongst the countries in the region. Such divergences are aptly reflected in the asymmetric transmission of demand and monetary shocks in the region.

There are significant developments that point to emergence of enabling factors for strengthening of economic integration in ASEAN. First, emerging Asia fares quite well in terms of factor mobility and wage and price flexibility. Second, the trade intensity ratios in emerging Asia, particularly the ASEAN region, are quite high and are likely to accelerate. Further, FDI flows within the region are significant. Third, tariffs are being brought down rapidly. Fourth, the free trade agreements are expanding and deepening thus making the prospects of tariff-free and virtual trade integration in Asia sooner than later. Fifth, there are regular and frequent close interactions among Central Bank Governors in Asia which should strengthen the process of cooperation. In the following subsections, we discuss these issues in details.

2.1 Monetary Integration

Since the Asian financial crisis of 1997–98, ASEAN+3 countries have made significant progress in monetary integration. This includes establishing the ASEAN+3 Economic Review and Policy Dialogue (AERPD) under which the Finance Ministers of the 13 member countries meet once a year and their Deputies semi-annually to (*a*) assess global, regional and national conditions and risks, (*b*) review financial sector developments and vulnerabilities and (*c*) exchange views and opinions on areas of mutual interest. Steps have also been taken to monitor short-term capital flows that are volatile in nature as well as to pre-empt currency and banking crises through early warning signals.

Most recently, the ASEAN+3 Macroeconomic Research Office (AMRO) was established in Singapore as the regional surveillance unit of the ASEAN+3. Some of the major activities of AMRO are as follows: (*a*) monitor, assess and report on the macroeconomic situation and financial soundness of the ASEAN+3 countries, (*b*) assess macroeconomic and financial vulnerabilities in any of the ASEAN+3 countries and provide assistance in timely formulation of policy recommendations to mitigate such risks and (*c*) ensure compliance of swap requesting parties with the lending covenants under the Chiang Mai Initiative Multilateralization (CMIM) agreement.

There has also been progress made in establishing regional financing arrangements to address short-term liquidity needs of the countries in the event of a crisis. For example, a US$ 120 billion crisis fund was established in 2010 under the CMIM initiative. The size of the US$ 120 billion crisis fund has since then been doubled. A CMIM Precautionary Line has also been established permitting countries with strong economic fundamentals to borrow large amounts of liquidity for crisis prevention.

A deeper stage of monetary integration is coordination of monetary policy and exchange rates. The current Indian central bank governor has repeatedly emphasized the need for global monetary policy synchronization in the aftermath of the Fed taper. It may be noted that countries like India and Indonesia among others have resorted to interest rate hikes in recent times to control domestic inflation and also possibly as an instrument to avert reverse capital outflows.

As far as exchange rates are concerned, the increasing level of trade integration in ASEAN+3 has now resulted in greater harmonization of output and business cycles in the region. This has resulted in benefits of macroeconomic policy coordination by efforts to introduce a Regional Monetary Unit (RMU), a regional basket of currencies. In principle, the RMU could strengthen the regional surveillance process and could eventually also facilitate exchange rate coordination in the region. Despite the calls made by the ASEAN+3 research group and others for the introduction of RMU, there has been no action as yet.

On 3 May 2012, on the side-lines of the ADB's Annual Meeting in Manila, the ASEAN+3 took a number of significant steps to further deepen monetary integration in the region. The most significant outcome of the meeting was the upgrading of the ASEAN +3 Finance Ministers Meeting (AFMM+3) to the ASEAN+3 Finance

Ministers and Central Bank Governors' Meeting (AFMGM+3). The Central Bank Governors of the 13 member countries (plus Hong Kong) have now been invited to join the deliberations. In the past, the region's firewall for crisis prevention and crisis resolution had been run solely by Finance Ministers responsible for tax and expenditure policies. Officials responsible for monetary and exchange-rate policies were left out. This major gap has now finally been filled. This will also result in close coordination of monetary and fiscal policies across the ASEAN bloc.

The Ministers and Governors have also complimented the ASEAN+3 Macroeconomic Research Office (AMRO) for its success in regional surveillance activities. They have also welcomed Singapore's commitment to provide necessary host country support to the AMRO. Despite its commendable performance under Director Benhua Wei, AMRO faces a number of challenges, of which two needs to be highlighted.

First, AMRO must find out why at the height of the global economic crisis, Korea and Indonesia, who were most affected through the financial channel, decided not to borrow from the CMIM. Korea had decided to borrow from the US Federal Reserve, while Indonesia struck an innovative agreement with a consortium led by the World Bank (Henning and Khan 2011).

Second, modalities must be found so that AMRO can work jointly with the IMF. The G20 Cannes Summit declaration noted that the leaders had 'agreed on common principles for cooperation between the IMF and regional financial arrangements, which will strengthen crisis prevention and resolution efforts' (G20 Secretariat 2011). Lamberte and Morgan (2012) have come up with several recommendations to bring about more effective cooperation between the IMF and regional safety nets. Europe's experience, where the IMF is working closely with the European Union and the ECB as a member of the Troika, could also be useful to those involved in designing such modalities.

As far as next steps regarding AMRO are concerned, it may explore options of introducing the Regional Monetary Unit (RMU), a regional weighted currency basket, as a numeraire currency. The RMU would provide more stable currency values, enable AMRO's surveillance activities, by making sure that countries are avoiding competitive devaluations among each other and make sure that the countries are not engaging in competitive devaluations and are converging their macroeconomic policies for meaningful integration.

Meanwhile, the Task Force constituted by the Government of India, has drawn up a list of 23 countries with which India can trade in local currencies. This is a strategic step towards rupee internationalization. In this context, it may be noted that the Central Bank of China has so far signed 20 such bilateral swap agreements (BSA), where the Yuan is the currency of settlement. Also, with India–ASEAN trade currently at around US\$ 76 billion, this step if taken forward would also help India to reduce the cost of transaction and hedging.

In another development, the BRICS Bank was finally formalized in July 2014. The objective of the BRICS Bank is to increase the flow of funds for infrastructure development projects to the BRICS countries, and act as a lender of last resort in case of currency crises in such economies. Its planned capital base will be comparable to that of the Inter-American Development Bank (IADB), about 60 per cent of the ADB's capital, and somewhat less than half of the World Bank's capital base. The BRICS Bank could also act as a conduit for achieving strategic goals for India, like integrating Indian firms into regional and global production networks such as with ASEAN, and building trust for deeper ties in international trade and investment, both inward and outward. The benefits of strategic integration will be significantly greater.

2.2 Banking and Financial Product Integration

ASEAN economies and India must exploit their mutual common benefit. The region is similarly characterized by complementarities in the demand and supply of other resources such as technology and skilled manpower. Integration through banking could generate significant intraregional demand and reduce the region's vulnerability owing to overdependence on outside regions.

a) **Setting up of regional clearing house:** ASEAN economies and India have ample scope to integrate financially. Tourism remains one of the most potent economic activities, which can create demand for various financial products like travellers' cheque and cards. Vast demand for coastal infrastructure to facilitate trade will need to be supplemented by trade finance. Given the trends in settling trade in local currencies, setting up of regional clearing house for trade purposes can be the next higher level of financial integration.

b) **Expanding Banking Business:** Taking reach of banking sector as proxy one finds that there is considerable scope for India to expand banking network in the region. As on 2013, India had only less than 20 branches in ASEAN countries. In terms of supply of financial banking services the challenges in region are strikingly similar. Banking in the region is still new in harnessing the full technological potential. The use of ATM cards is still low. India has the largest user base among the region and is gradually migrating to its own payment gateway RuPay, which is more cost effective. The region may benefit by migrating to such a framework. The interest rate spread among the banks is very high. Spread between deposits and lending will shrink if banking expansion is taken on agreed mutually beneficial principles. Additionally, Indian banks with their expertise in banking in emerging markets can facilitate transfer of knowledge.

c) **Financial Cooperation:** Monetary and Financial cooperation between ASEAN and India can be accelerated by larger investment. For example, the increase in infrastructure investment in areas such as power, telecommunications, airports, highways and ports all require a corresponding expansion in manufacturing activities. Eventually one can explore the possibility of formation of a larger common market.

d) **Bond Market Developments:** India needs huge investment equivalent to its current GDP to develop the kind of infrastructure required to attain double digit growth on a sustainable basis. The level of investment required is difficult to meet without developing bond markets. Banks, which are major source of finance in the country with around 52 per cent credit-GDP ratio, are constrained on problem of asset-liability mismatches, meeting long-term requirement of infrastructure with short maturity deposits.

Despite number of steps taken in the past to develop bond market, the size of India's corporate bond market, as a proportion of GDP, remained around 2 per cent as compared to the 42 per cent of Malaysia, 75 per cent of Korea, 17 per cent of Japan and 20 per cent of the United States (Table 9.1). So, there is an urgent need to develop Indian bond market with integration to ASEAN+3 countries. Some of the suggestions may include: (*a*) set up specific development banks to meet the financial needs of the member countries (*b*) to allure individuals to invest, the Government should provide tax incentives as in Malaysia and other countries; and (*c*) there is a need to promote guarantee in bond market and for that an organization on lines of deposits insurance be promoted.

In 2003, there was a discussion to develop Asian bond market, with two objectives: (*a*) to develop local-currency denominated bond markets, and (*b*) to develop more accessible and well-functioning regional bond markets both for issuers and investors. We need to actively take forward such an initiative.

i. **Capital Market Integration:** For the development of a bond market, a well-developed capital market is considered necessary. There is a need to build capacity and lay the long-term infrastructure for the development of ASEAN capital markets, with a long-term goal of achieving cross-border collaboration between the various capital markets in ASEAN. The key achievements to date include the adoption of a proposed 'Medium-Term Strategic Framework (MTSF)' to guide the work of the Working Committee on Capital Market Development and to align capital market development to the ASEAN Economic Community (AEC) Blueprint. A Bond Market Development Scorecard is currently being developed to identify market

TABLE 9.1
Size of Bond Market (% of GDP), 2012

Countries	Government (% GDP)	Corporate (% of GDP)	Total
Indonesia	12.99	2.26	15.25
Malaysia	59.10	42.66	101.76
The Philippines	31.68	5.58	37.26
Singapore	50.00	31.14	81.14
Thailand	59.15	16.17	75.32
Vietnam	20.76	0.33	21.09
China	32.86	17.69	50.55
Japan	202.57	17.31	219.88
Korea	46.02	74.59	120.61
India	40.20	2.40	42.60

Source: Asian Development Bank (ADB), Manila.

gaps and to develop a framework for ASEAN to take stock of the progress of its work in relation to the agreed priorities.

The ASEAN Exchange, a collaboration of the seven stock exchanges of ASEAN9, kicked off in September 2012 with the live roll-out of the ASEAN Trading Link, connecting Bursa Malaysia and the Singapore Exchange. The potential for ASEAN capital market collaboration is huge. In 2010, aggregate gross domestic savings of ASEAN nations amounted to US$ 616 billion, with the largest contributions coming from Indonesia, Singapore and Thailand. To facilitate the mobility of savings across national borders, AEC has put in place several initiatives like standardized offering and distribution rules and disclosure requirements, as well as an enhanced withholding tax structure, with an objective to lowering transaction costs and exploiting economies of scale.

ii. **Insurance Market Development:** Insurance penetration is measured as a ratio of premium to Gross Domestic Product (GDP). As per the insurance penetration in the ASEAN countries in 2012, except for Japan and South Korea, for all other member countries the insurance penetration was lower compared to world average (Table 9.2). The other indicator of measuring insurance consumption is insurance density, which is defined as the ratio of premium (in US$) to total population. The numbers again show that except Japan and Korea, all other member countries are below the world average density numbers. So, there is a huge potential to coordinate and improve the insurance markets in the ASEAN region.

In this context, the ASEAN Insurance Regulators Meeting (AIRM) has taken a significant initiative. This includes sharing of insurance statistics among countries with the end goal of achieving a unified form of statistics; exchange of views on regulatory issues and observance of core principles related to insurance markets; consultations with private sector to implement compulsory insurance for motor-vehicles; and conduct of research and capacity building programmes for insurance regulators through the ASEAN Insurance Training and Research Institute (AITRI). However, there is a need for integration between India and ASEAN to penetrate the underdeveloped insurance market in India. This will help the member countries to also help in developing products and policies for developing insurance markets.

iii. **Cooperation on Anti-money Laundering:** In India, there are no official government estimates of black money. There have also been wide variations in the figures reported by different organizations, which further serves to highlight the limitations of the different methods adopted. Ultimately, to deal with the problem of black money, we need tax reforms, particularly introduction of Goods and Services Tax, which would be a major step in integrating the efforts of different agencies dealing with black money. Overall, we need a more holistic approach and sterner regulation to deal with the problem of black money covering all forms of tax evasion including illegitimate activities and corruption. In this context, since 2006 ASEC has entered into a Memorandum of Understanding with the Asia Pacific Group (APG) Secretariat to

TABLE 9.2
Insurance Indicators in ASEAN Countries, 2012

Countries	Insurance Penetration (% GDP)	Insurance Density (USD)
Indonesia	NA	65.3
Malaysia	4.80	514.2
The Philippines	NA	36.0
Singapore	6.03	3362.0
Thailand	5.02	266.2
Vietnam	1.42	22.0
China	2.96	178.9
Japan	11.44	5167.5
Korea	12.12	2785.4
India	3.96	53.2
ASEAN	3.19	134.4
World	6.50	655.7

Source: Swiss Re and Insurance Regulatory and Development Authority of India (IRDA).

coordinate training and capacity building programmes on anti-money laundering and counter financing of terrorism (AML/CFT) for ASEAN countries that are also members of the APG. Both ASEC and the APG Secretariat are in the process of exploring areas where coordination between the two secretariats can be further strengthened in order to identify/develop regional programmes on AML/CFT.

iv. **Capital Flows:** ASEAN countries have witnessed a significant jump in FDI flows since 2010, with Indonesia, Malaysia and Singapore being the key beneficiaries. As far as India is concerned, India witnessed acceleration in net FDI inflows in 2011, but the pace slackened in 2012, but has since then revived. However, the inflows are still lower than the 2008 levels. As far as stable capital flows are concerned (defined as ratio of portfolio equity flows and FDI flows to total foreign exchange reserves), India is fairly well-placed. In the current calendar year 2014, India has received US$ 26.4 billion of portfolio capital flows into India, of which equity flows have been at US$ 12.2 billion (UNCTAD). The region may work for free flow of capital, particularly, stable capital flows in sectors of mutual interest.

3. Concluding Observations and the Way Forward

The economic outlook in ASEAN remains robust over the medium term, anchored by the steady rise in domestic demand. Real GDP growth in emerging Asian economies is projected to be moderating gradually but may remain robust over the 2014–18 period. The changing structure of the global economy with the economic centre of gravity shifting from the developed economies of the United States, the European Union and Japan to China and India would require ASEAN to adjust its own economic structure to enable it to maximize its competitiveness and find complementarities with the high-growth economies in the region. There is a need to reduce export dependence, especially to the developed economies, as a global rebalancing of current accounts is set in motion. The Asian economy and hence ASEAN is now being recognized as the new engine of global economic growth, and it is being increasingly recognized that Asia will be the primary driver of global trade in the coming years. It is in this context that it is extremely vital to enhance regional integration within Asia through stronger regional agreements and institutions.

The ASEAN–India relations have come a long way since their turbulent Cold War phase. ASEAN sees India as an emerging power in Asia and it realizes that India possesses large strategic and economic capabilities. Economically, India, with its burgeoning middle class, can be a significant market for ASEAN manufactures and consequently, an important source of welfare for the region. Some of the recommendations are summarized as follows:

i. The Chiang Mai Initiative (CMI) is a good starting point to build on the various existing initiatives. Although under the present dispensation the CMI is complementary to similar IMF initiatives, it has an important symbolic value in as much as it can signal the markets a regional commitment to supporting any member country's currency that is under speculative pressures. It also recognizes that establishing swap arrangements does not obviate the need to address structural and financial sector weaknesses. It may also be added that while CMI might have contributed to the exchange rate stability in the region, it has also contributed to closer regional economic and financial integration and cooperation. It is useful to explore ways of carrying this process forward.

ii. Banking in the region is still to harness full potential of technology. India is gradually migrating to its own payment gateway RuPay which is more cost effective. The region may benefit by exploring such a framework.

iii. Developing the corporate bond market also needs a special focus. Some of the suggestions include: (*a*) set up specific development banks to meet the financial needs of the member countries; (*b*) to allure individuals to invest, the Government should provide tax incentives like in Malaysia and other countries; and (*c*) there is a need to promote guarantee in bond market and for that an organization on lines of deposits insurance be promoted.

iv. There is a need to build capacity and lay the long-term infrastructure for development of ASEAN capital markets, with a long-term goal of achieving cross-border collaboration between the various capital markets in ASEAN.

v. There is also a need for financial and policy cooperation between the Central Banks. The Asian Clearing Union (ACU), which was established in 1974 at the initiative of the Economic and Social Commission for Asia and Pacific (ESCAP), has eight member central banks. The main objective of the ACU is to provide a facility to settle current international transactions among members on multilateral net settlement basis. The ACU mechanism also provides for a currency swap type mechanism amongst members for trade transactions. ACU aims to promote monetary cooperation amongst the members and has also resulted in closer relations across the banking systems of the member countries. During the last few years trade settled through ACU mechanism has grown at a rate higher than that of total international trade of the member countries. Given the current volatility across financial markets and the fact that the Fed is going to complete the process of withdrawing Quantitative Easing, it is of utmost importance for Central Banks at least in ASEAN region to coordinate on matters relating to monetary policy. This could be a good strategy to ward off contagion in the region.

vi. There is a need for integration between India and ASEAN to penetrate the underdeveloped insurance market in India. This will help the member countries to coordinate themselves, which may help in developing products and policies for a developed insurance market. This is in line with the efforts by the ASEAN Insurance Regulators Meeting (AIRM) that include sharing of insurance statistics among countries with the end goal of achieving a unified form of statistics; exchange of views on regulatory issues and observance of core principles related to insurance markets.

vii. The region may also work for a free flow of capital, particularly stable capital flows in sectors of mutual interest.

viii. The India–Myanmar–Thailand Trilateral Highway is expected to be completed by 2018. This is likely to boost trade, communication and infrastructure in India's northeast region. There is huge potential for tourism that can also be developed between India's Northeast region and Southeast Asia through the creation of this highway. Stable financial arrangements would help promote trade, tourism and technology along this corridor.

10

Science and Technology Cooperation Blueprint

Science and technology (S&T) cooperation has always been one of the main pillars of ASEAN–India partnership. The Plan of Action proposals (2004–10 and 2010–15) most concretely lays down the terms of reference and the agenda for ASEAN–India Partnership for Peace, Progress and Shared Prosperity. The most significant development in the area of S&T cooperation during this period was the setting up of the ASEAN–India S&T Fund (AISTDF) in 2006 by India towards R&D projects and S&T collaborations. S&T capacity building in some of the ASEAN countries have also been receiving support from the earlier ASEAN–India Fund as well. India has extended significant unilateral support for S&T cooperation with ASEAN countries through the ASEAN–India partnership channel as well as through other multilateral/bilateral arrangements that directly benefit ASEAN member states (AMS). The vision statement, emerging out of the ASEAN–India Commemorative Summit in 2012, placed S&T cooperation in the ambit of sociocultural and development cooperation. Although ASEAN–India engagement in S&T has been mature in terms of identifying complementarities and the areas of cooperation; the channels are limited and thin. The potential of appropriate partnership and participation for a robust ASEAN–India S&T Cooperation still remains by and large untapped.

We examine some of these questions in further detail in this Chapter. Here, we discuss the S&T profiles of ASEAN and India, review the broad contour of S&T cooperation between them and present a strategy to strengthen the S&T cooperation between ASEAN and India.

1. S&T Profiles of ASEAN Countries and India

We begin with a short overview of S&T profiles of ASEAN countries and India to understand their relative position in terms of S&T capabilities. We begin with R&D inputs like expenditure and human resources (see Table 10.1). We do not, however, distinguish between private and public expenditures on R&D.

Table 10.1
R&D Inputs

Country	GERD as % of GDP	Latest Year for Which Data Is Available	Researchers[1] per Million People	Latest Year for Which Data Is Available
Brunei	0.04	2004	282	2004
Cambodia	0.05	2002	18	2002
Indonesia	0.08	2009	90	2009
Lao PDR	0.04	2002	16	2002
Malaysia	1.07	2011	1643	2011
Myanmar	0.16	2002	17	2002
The Philippines	0.11	2007	78	2007
Singapore	2.10	2012	6438	2012
Thailand	0.25	2009	332	2009
Vietnam	0.18	2002	113	2002
India	0.81	2011	160	2010

Source: World Development Indicators, The World Bank, Washington DC.

---

[1] Researchers in R&D are professionals engaged in the conception or creation of new knowledge, products, processes, methods or systems and in the management of the projects concerned (definition as per United Nations Educational, Scientific and Cultural Organization (UNESCO) Institute for Statistics as adopted for World Development Indicators). Postgraduate PhD students (ISCED97 level 6) engaged in R&D is included.

The challenge is faced in terms of data availability for recent years (figures for some of the countries are quite dated). The Gross Expenditure on Research and Development (GERD) as a fraction of GDP demonstrates a country's ability to invest in R&D. The ASEAN region poses stark divergences in this regard. The group has among its members, countries like Singapore who spend more than 2 per cent of its GDP on R&D annually as well as those who spend mere fractions (<0.25 per cent) of their GDP in this sector. We find in this group Brunei Darussalam, Cambodia, Indonesia, Lao PDR, Myanmar, Philippines and Vietnam. Malaysia spent little over 1 per cent of GDP in 2011 in R&D. Although, India has robust S&T infrastructure its spending on R&D is still low (<1 per cent) by international standards. The figures on 'researchers per million people' are also widely dispersed. Singapore and Malaysia have high proportion of technical people employed in R&D (6438 in 2012 and 1643 in 2011 respectively). Vietnam stands out among the CLMV group in this regard with a relatively higher proportion of researchers. India with less than 200 researchers per million people apparently lags behind countries like Thailand and Brunei Darrussalam.

To assess the R&D potential of these countries, we look at standard R&D outputs viz. publications and patents. In publications, we take annual count of all scientific journal publications and technical publications for the latest year available, while, for patents, we consider patent applications by residents only in order to capture indigenous innovation capability. We find that India has most scientific publications and maximum patent applications by residents ahead of any other ASEAN country. Among ASEAN countries, Singapore has the highest number of annual scientific publications, followed by Thailand and Malaysia. In terms of innovation capabilities, Singapore, Thailand and Malaysia demonstrate significant strengths with equivalent numbers of patent applications by residents. Among CLMV countries, Vietnam is ahead of the other three both in terms of publications and patents (see Table 10.2).

To mobilize resources for Science & Technology, ASEAN has been liberal to development aids and ideas. ASEAN has been successful in promoting a pool of resources from its dialogue partners in promoting S&T across its diverse member states, in which India stands as one of the foremost partners of ASEAN in S&T.

2. DEEPENING ASEAN–INDIA INTEGRATION AND ROLE OF S&T

After the formalization of ASEAN–India Dialogue Partnership in 1996, an ASEAN–India Joint Cooperation Committee (JCC) was set-up. This was followed by the formation of ASEAN–India Working Groups on Science & Technology and Trade & Investment. Back in 1996, India proposed a 'Technology Vision 2020' by way of future cooperation possibilities, covering a wide range of activities like food processing, health, agriculture, engineering, electronics and communications. Cooperation in S&T between India and ASEAN in its present form was reinvigorated by the Plan of Action (PoA) to implement the ASEAN–India Partnership for Peace, Progress and Shared Prosperity, which was adopted by the Leaders at the Third ASEAN–India Summit in November 2004 in Vientiane. Since, the PoA has been executed through programmes under various existing ASEAN sectoral

TABLE 10.2
R&D Outputs

Country	Scientific Publications	Latest Year for Which the Data Is Available	Patent Applications by Residents	Latest Year for Which the Data Is Available
Brunei	15	2011	–	–
Cambodia	33	2011	1	2012
Indonesia	270	2011	541	2011
Lao PDR	21	2011		
Malaysia	2092	2011	1114	2012
Myanmar	9	2011	–	–
The Philippines	241	2011	162	2012
Singapore	4543	2011	1081	2012
Thailand	2304	2011	1020	2012
Vietnam	432	2011	382	2012
India	22481	2011	9553	2012

Source: World Development Indicators, The World Bank, Washington DC.

work plans, declarations/agreements concluded between ASEAN and India, as well as through participation in ASEAN efforts towards future ASEAN Community (Roadmap for an ASEAN Community 2009–15). The present agenda for ASEAN–India S&T cooperation may be best understood from 2012 ASEAN–India Vision Statement, while the specifics are laid out in the ASEAN–India Plan of Actions. In the Vision document, S&T cooperation has been discussed under socio-cultural and development cooperation, which in a way defines its scope.

2.1 ASEAN Framework for S&T

(i) The Action Plan of Action on Science and Technology

The ASEAN Committee on Science and Technology (COST) was established in 1978. In the following years a series of Plans of Action in Science and Technology have been developed. The most recent plan (The Action Plan of Action on Science and Technology [APAST] [2007–11]) was endorsed by the ASEAN S&T Ministers in February 2007. The Plan was developed taking into account the various directives and initiatives of the ASEAN Leaders (that is, Vientiane Action Programme), and S&T Ministers, Committee on Science and Technology (COST) and the national S&T plans in the ASEAN countries. The Plan, which identifies 6 thrust areas and 24 supporting actions, essentially provides appropriate guidelines for identification and formulation of programmes and projects to achieve better coordination and cooperation to strengthen S&T in ASEAN. The six priority areas under APAST (2007–11) are (a) disaster management, (b) bio-fuels, (c) open source systems, (d) functional food, (e) climate change and (f) health. In view of the six priority areas under APAST, the current S&T co-operation in ASEAN focuses on nine specific programme areas: (a) food science and technology, (b) biotechnology, (c) meteorology and geophysics, (d) marine science and technology, (e) non-conventional energy research, (f) microelectronics and information technology, (g) material science and technology, (h) space technology and applications, and (i) S&T infrastructure and resources development. Area specific sub-committees are responsible for coordinating and implementing activities in each of these areas.

(ii) The Krabi Initiative

The 6th Informal ASEAN Ministerial Meeting on Science and Technology (IAMMST) was held on 17 December 2010 in Krabi, Thailand. The Meeting adopted the report of the STI Retreat and agreed that the outcome of the Retreat shall be called the Krabi Initiative. 'Science, Technology and Innovation (STI) for a Competitive, Sustainable and Inclusive ASEAN' was adopted as the theme for the Krabi Initiative. This initiative was more in the spirit of assessment and sought to harmonize apparently conflicting S&T goals of competitiveness and human development. This process was also meant to reinvent ASEAN scientific community for a meaningful delivery of STI agenda in ASEAN. The thematic areas emerging out of this initiative are (a) ASEAN innovation for global market, (b) digital economy, new media and social network, (c) green technology, (d) food security, (e) energy security, (f) water management, (g) biodiversity for health and wealth and (h) science and innovation for life. The forthcoming ASEAN Plan of Action on Science, Technology and Innovation (APASTI 2015–20) is supposed to align COST programmes with the thematic clusters identified in the Krabi Initiative.

(iii) The Initiative for ASEAN Integration (IAI)

The Initiative for ASEAN Integration (IAI) was launched in 2000 by ASEAN Heads of States to contribute to the objectives of narrowing the development gap (NDG) and accelerating integration of CLMV as the newer members of ASEAN. This is programme has been focused on augmenting the capacity of CLMV to implement regional agreements and participate in the ASEAN regional integration process. This was done with an understanding that ASEAN member states are at varying stages of their economic development. The IAI and NDG are two of ASEAN's frameworks that aim to address these development issues. Both frameworks recognize the value of addressing subregional issues to support ASEAN-wide goals. The current IAI Work Plan is patterned after and supports the key programme areas in the three ASEAN Community Blueprints: ASEAN Political-Security Community Blueprint, ASEAN Economic Community Blueprint and ASEAN Socio-cultural Community Blueprint.

(iv) ASEAN Sociocultural Community (ASCC)

The immediate priorities for ASEAN as per the road map for an ASEAN Community 2009–2015 under ASEAN Sociocultural Community (ASCC) Blueprint are (a) human development, (b) social welfare and protection, (c) social justice and rights, (d) ensuring environmental sustainability, (e) building the ASEAN identity and (f) narrowing the development gap. The goals that crucially draw on S&T capabilities come under (ii) social welfare and protection and ensuring environmental sustainability. Under social welfare and protection, poverty alleviation, food security and safety, health care, control of pandemics and disaster resilience remain key goals that S&T is expected to address. And, under ensuring environmental sustainability, promoting environmentally sound technology would require inputs from S&T.

2.2 ASEAN–India S&T Cooperation: On-going Projects and Programmes

We present a brief account of some of India's important ongoing S&T initiatives in the ASEAN region conceived and implemented by various government departments. These initiatives have been driven by India's well known expertise in information technology (IT), computer engineering, agriculture, biotechnology and space technology among developing countries. Box 10.1 briefly presents India's S&T cooperation with ASEAN.

(i) IT and Computer Engineering

a) The ASEAN–India Science & Technology Digital Library project: The ASEAN–India Science & Technology Digital Library project is being implemented by the Department of Science & Technology (DST), Government of India and the Indian Institute for Information Technology (IIIT), Allahabad. The basic hardware (scanners), developed and tested at IIIT-Allahabad, for Content Digitization Centres have been installed at ASEAN Secretariat Headquarters and sites selected by eight ASEAN member states (except Singapore and Brunei Darussalam). This is meant for complete digitization of printed knowledge resources into an electronic, shareable form in English and translated forms in local languages. The project was funded from the ASEAN-India Fund (AIF) and cost incurred was in the tune of US$ 729,753.

Box 10.1

India's S&T Cooperation with ASEAN

All cooperation projects in S&T are currently funded by the ASEAN–India Fund (AIF) and ASEAN–India S&T Fund (AISTDF). At the 7th ASEAN–India Summit in October, 2009, India announced a contribution of US$ 50 million to the ASEAN–India Cooperation Fund to support ASEAN–India projects across sectors. In addition, India has set up an ASEAN–India Science &Technology Development Fund with an initial corpus fund of US$ 1 million and a US$ 5 million ASEAN–India Green Fund for pilot projects to promote adaptation and mitigation technologies in the field of climate change. The dedicated AISTDF of US$ 1 million was created jointly by the Indian Ministry of External Affairs and the Department of Science and Technology (DST), Government of India with equal contributions. Another US$ 0.5 million has been made available by the DST towards this fund. Other funds, such as the India CLMV Quick Impact Projects Revolving Fund[2] (an annual US$ 1 million), have also been created by the Government of India.

Under the purview of ASEAN–India S&T cooperation several joint projects have been conceived like ASEAN–India projects on surface engineering (completed), S&T digital library, information portals, quality systems in manufacturing etc. Newly launched projects include R&D projects in the areas of marine biotechnology and malaria research. Further, each year children from ASEAN countries are invited for participation in India's National Children Science Congress (NCSC). More than 100 children from ASEAN countries have participated in the NCSC in the last five years. Moreover, in the last couple of years DST has taken initiatives towards several workshop series on areas including functional food, renewable energy, marine biotechnology and the ASEAN food conference within the AISTDF programme. India has been keen on S&T cooperation with ASEAN member states and has often followed benevolent practices with regard to funding and resources. India has also made significant contributions towards the cause of S&T in the CLMV countries.

Source: Various Annual Reports, Ministry of External Affairs and the Department of Science & Technology (DST), Government of India.

---

[2] Short gestation projects under the Mekong–Ganga Cooperation including S&T would be directed towards benefitting local communities with results that are immediate and visible.

b) The ASEAN–India Virtual Institute for Intellectual Property (VIIP) project: The ASEAN–India Virtual Institute for Intellectual Property (VIIP) project, aimed at setting up an ASEAN–India Web Portal on Intellectual Property is being executed by Andhra Pradesh Technology Development & Promotion Centre (APTDPC); Confederation of Indian Industry (CII); Technology Information, Forecasting and Assessment Council (TIFAC), an autonomous organization under DST; and the Government of Andhra Pradesh. The project is funded from the AISTDF with a cost of US$ 120,000.

c) The ASEAN–India Technology Information & Commercialization Portal (TICP): The ASEAN–India Technology Information & Commercialization Portal (TICP) is being developed by CII and Tamil Nadu Technology & Development Promotion Centre (TNTDPC). The portal would act as a dynamic platform for linking existing technology transfer/licensing organizations, R&D institutions, and laboratories in ASEAN and India and facilitating transfer of technologies between ASEAN and India. The project is supported from AISTDF with a cost of US$ 120,000.

d) One Comprehensive Proposal of India to Create a Sustainable IT Infrastructure for Advanced IT Training Using Conventional, Virtual Classroom and e-Learning Technologies: A consolidated project proposal from the Center for Development of Advanced Computing (C-DAC), Noida, entitled 'One Comprehensive Proposal of India to Create a Sustainable IT Infrastructure for Advanced IT Training Using Conventional, Virtual Classroom and e-Learning Technologies' to set up four IT centers in CLMV countries has been approved in 2013.

(ii) Agriculture and Biotechnology

a) The Technology Mission on Functional Food: The Technology Mission on Functional Food would formulate collaborative R&D projects through a joint call for proposals by both India and the ASEAN member states. ASEAN and India have agreed to pursue cooperation on the following themes which could be funded by the AISTDF.

    i. Alternatives for sugar to combat the growing incidence of diabetes and other related consequences (led by the Philippines); and

    ii. Tropical fruit and vegetable processing technology improvement and value added product development (led by Singapore).

(iii) Space Technology

a) Data Reception and Image Processing Facility for ASEAN in Ho Chi Minh City and Biak Telemetry Tracking and Command Station in Indonesia: Indian Space Research Organization (ISRO) convened a meeting of Heads of Space Agencies from ASEAN and India to discuss its proposals for

    i. Establishment of a Data Reception and Image Processing Facility for ASEAN in Ho Chi Minh City and up-gradation of the Existing Biak Telemetry Tracking and Command Station in Indonesia; and

    ii. Provide training to ASEAN Space Scientists at Centre for Space Science and Technology Education in Asia and the Pacific (CSSTEAP), Dehradun, India.

b) India has offered to share satellite imageries from OCEANSAT-2 and RESOURCESAT-2 through the proposed facilities, as also to train space scientists on how to make best use of these satellite imageries for socioeconomic benefits in the region. The proposals have been approved in principle by the ASEAN Committee on Science and Technology (COST) and the Sub-Committee on Space Technology Applications (SCOSA).

We note that the AISTDF was meant to encourage collaborative R&D and technology development to harness knowledge for the creation of wealth. The management of AISTDF is placed with Global Innovation & Technology Alliance — GITA (a PPP company owned by the DST and the Confederation of Indian Industry — CII). The proposed activities under AISTDF include (a) partnership development activities, (b) collaborative R&D, (c) training and short course in S&T and innovation, (d) portals and virtual institutes for information dissemination and services and (e) any other activity as approved by the Governing Council.

3. India and CLMV Countries: Contours of S&T Cooperation

India's sustained engagement with Cambodia, Lao PDR, Myanmar and Vietnam (CLMV) on a multitude of development cooperation arrangements bilaterally and multilaterally is well acknowledged. We note that overwhelming part of India's support for the CLMV countries has been focused on human resource development and capacity building in technical domains. This was recognized in the Vizion Statement of the ASEAN-India Commemorative Summit in 2012. The mechanisms for supporting capacity building and S&T efforts in these countries by India are spread across development cooperation programmes, programmes of South–South collaboration, bilateral arrangements and multilateral routes like the ASEAN, BIMSTEC and Mekong–Ganga Cooperation. India has also been proactively participating in the restoration of historic sites across ASEAN nations. The Angkor Wat conservation project, financed by the Ministry of External Affairs, was the single largest project ever undertaken by India under its ITEC programme in any country.

India has ongoing joint research projects with Vietnam in the areas of smart antennas for 3G/4G mobile communications; power source converter for AC photovoltaic, etc. A Joint India–Myanmar Working Group for Scientific & Technological Cooperation has also been functioning since the formalization of the Indo-Myanmar Agreement on Cooperation in the fields of S&T in 1999. In 2012 India and Vietnam adopted the Programme of Cooperation (POC) in Science and Technology for 2013–14. Under India's support for Initiative for ASEAN Integration (IAI) and through the ASEAN framework itself India has promoted the Lao-India Entrepreneurship Development Centre (in 2004) and Cambodia-India Entrepreneurship Development Centre (in 2006).[3] Myanmar-India Entrepreneurship Development Centre (MIEDC) has also been set up with support from the government of India. The outcomes of such programmes are reportedly very encouraging. Having discussed the primary channels of S&T cooperation between India and the CLMV countries we present a brief account of India's initiatives in the areas of IT, agriculture and space for CLMV countries. As highlighted in the previous section, India is considered sufficiently competent in terms of capabilities in these sectors and has been keen on helping developing countries with such expertise in the spirit of development cooperation.

3.1 IT and Computer Engineering

(i) Cambodia

a) With a view of promoting computer literacy in Cambodia, India has provided 5 Minimally Invasive Education (MIE) IT kiosks to Cambodia that are installed in Siem Reap, Kandal, Takeo and Phnom Penh.
b) Work on establishing India–Cambodia Centre of Excellence & Talent Development (at two locations) for training in ICT is reportedly underway.

(ii) Lao PDR

a) India has established 10 pilot Rural Tele Centres (RTC) in remote areas (along river Mekong) in Lao PDR.

(iii) Myanmar

a) The Myanmar Institute of Information Technology (MIIT) at Mandalay is being set up with the help of the Government of India.
b) India has also supported setting up of India–Myanmar Centre for Enhancement of IT Skills (IMCEITS), Language Laboratories and e-Resource Centre at the Ministry of Foreign Affairs in Yangon and Nay Pyi Taw.

---

[3] India extended support for the Initiative for ASEAN Integration (IAI) and committed to participate in IAI projects, especially in human resource and development during the First ASEAN–India Summit in 2002. In IAI Work Plan 2 (2009–15) India has taken up projects to cultivate entrepreneurship in CLMV countries. During the IAI Work Plan 1 (2002–08) phase India had initiated projects focused on English language training for students and professionals alike in these countries through Centre(s) for English Language Training (CELT).

(iv) Vietnam

a) In Vietnam, India has set up the Vietnam-India Advanced Resource Centre in ICT in Hanoi.
b) A High Performance Computing (HPC) Facility would be set up at Hanoi University of Science and Technology. This grant project is being executed by CDAC (Government of India) and involves installation of a16-node cluster HPC facility.
c) India has extended full support towards IT Training Centre at the National Defence Academy in Hanoi, the Vocational Training Centre in Ho Chi Minh City.

3.2 Agriculture and Biotechnology

(i) Cambodia

a) India-Cambodia Cooperation in the field of agriculture and allied sectors envisages cooperation in a number of areas including integrated pest management, use of pesticides, livestock production and management, disease diagnostics and vaccines, integrated watershed management, aquaculture production management, exchange of information and reports, exchange of germplasm, training and exchange of visits by scientists, agricultural extension services, cooperation in food processing industries and development and improvement of horticulture technology for fruits.

(ii) Lao PDR

a) India is helping Lao PDR in establishing an agriculture college in Champassak province in southern Lao.

(iii) Myanmar

a) India is supporting establishment of Advanced Centre for Agricultural Research and Education (ACARE) in Myanmar and a Rice Bio Park at Yezin Agricultural University, Nay Pyi Taw.

(iv) Vietnam

a) Vietnam defines India as a strategic partner in its international biotechnology research and development cooperation, which is considered crucial for a green industry and sustainable development. India and Vietnam are taking concrete measures to foster biotechnology development in the two countries, especially in agriculture, health, food and the environment.
b) The Programme of Cooperation in Science and Technology for 2013–14 between India and Vietnam is being operationalized. There is also a Programme of Cooperation between the Ministry of Science and Technology of Vietnam and the Department of Biotechnology of India.

3.3 Cooperation in Space

(i) A proposal to set up a Centre for Satellite Tracking and Data Reception and an Imaging facility in Vietnam under ASEAN–India Cooperation mechanism is under consideration. The Centre will be fully funded by India and ISRO will be the implementing agency. It will utilize data provided by Indian remote sensing satellites and harness it for multiple developmental applications.
(ii) India is helping Vietnam in establishing a satellite tracking, data reception and processing centre in Ho Chi Minh City under India–ASEAN Cooperation. India shall also consider launching of Vietnamese satellites using Indian launch vehicles and provide assistance in setting up of earth observation centre in Vietnam.
(iii) The First Myanmar-India Friendship Centre for Remote Sensing and Data Processing (MIFCRSDP) was established in 2001, with the help from the Indian Space Research Organization (ISRO)
(iv) The Decision Support Centre (DSC), India under the aegis of ISRO is a single window information provider on major natural disasters like floods, agricultural drought, and forest fires, cyclones, earthquakes and landslides. The DSC also supports International Charter on Space and Major Disasters and Sentinel Asia. Under this, critical support was extended to Myanmar during Cyclone Nargis (2008), the Indonesian floods (2008) and China earthquake (2008).

4. WAY FORWARD

The Indian External Affairs Minister in her speech at the 12th ASEAN–India Foreign Ministers Meeting in Nay Pyi Taw, Myanmar (9 August 2014) has suggested that dialogue on science and technology cooperation should elevate to senior officials meeting level in 2014 and Ministerial level in 2015 indicating India's willingness to expand the scope of ASEAN–India S&T cooperation. In her statement, she also emphasized the need to strengthen ongoing initiatives in the area of space technology, renewable energy and environment. In the recent past, India has been actively involved in the formalization of the proposed ASEAN–India MoU on Science, Technology and Innovation Cooperation. India has prepared the draft MoU and presented it before the ASEAN Advisory Board for Plan of Action on S&T (ABAPAST) during the recently concluded 67th ASEAN COST Meeting in April 2014. The ABAPAST has also been in agreement with the proposal and has formally responded after consulting ASEAN member states. The MoU envisages engagements at three levels: at the level of S&T Ministers, at the level of very senior officials and at the levels of ASEAN thematic subcommittees. This MoU has provisions that new ASEAN–India Science Technology and Innovation projects would not have to rely solely on AISTDF (maintained unilaterally by India), but, may be supported jointly with equal cost sharing by ASEAN and India.

The enabling role of S&T for economic development has been fully recognized under the ASEAN Framework and a target for the year 2020 has been set to make the ASEAN region technologically competitive through competence in strategic and enabling technologies, with an adequate pool of technologically qualified and trained manpower, and strong networks of scientific and technological institutions and centres of excellence. However, as a group of 10 developing countries with great variance in the level of S&T capability, ASEAN faces considerable difficulties in achieving these goals. The overwhelming concern for India, on the other hand, has been its inability to transform India's S&T potential into outcomes that could measure up in terms of industrial competitiveness and human development. ASEAN–India cooperation in S&T is based on complementarities, where India has generously shared its 'technical knowledge' and 'resources' with ASEAN member states at various levels. The India–ASEAN partnership platform offers the most in terms of opportunities in this regard with maximum consensus on both sides. Over the recent years, India has taken a keen interest in furthering cooperation with the poorer ASEAN members, namely, the CLMV by implementing capacity building programmes in areas, in which India has proven expertise like information technology, agriculture and space. Deepening of such cooperation between CLMV–ASEAN and India is called for, particularly in the area of space science and technology where India can be a lead partner. However, practical bottlenecks like long drawn approvals arising out of multiple stakeholders have slowed the pace of such efforts. There is also a need for greater optimism on both sides about beneficial outcomes of development cooperation between India and ASEAN in the area of S&T.

11

Expanding Food Security and Food Reserves

Food security is one of the foremost challenges faced by the global community, especially by the developing world. Access to food is the most basic human right. Food insecurity can be driven by insufficient availability or insufficient access to food (FAO 2013). In 2010–12 there were about 870 million chronically undernourished people in the world (FAO 2012). Developing countries face a great challenge to provide sufficient food for their ever rising population on sustainable basis. As a result, food security has become a national issue for many countries, particularly in South and Southeast Asia. Attaining food security is also a major concern for India, where more than one-third of its population still suffers from hunger and malnutrition. Adequate food production, stability in domestic food supplies, malnutrition and the physical and economic access to food are the major concerns for India as well as for the Southeast Asian countries. In a sense, food insecurity is a regional problem that could be best tackled through effective regional approach. As ASEAN moves towards to establish an ASEAN Economic Community in 2015, there is an urgent need for each ASEAN country to review its status of food security and cooperate with the spirit of regional perspective.

This chapter presents a broad contour of ASEAN–India cooperation in food security and discusses what further can be done in strengthening the cooperation in food security and food reserves.

1. DIMENSIONS OF FOOD SECURITY

Merely increasing physical availability of food both at the household and community level is not adequate to be self-sufficient in food production, but improving the individual's potential for access to nutritious food is essential. Economic accessibility of food depends entirely on poverty, employment, income security and economic status of the individual households. This insight led to the recognition of multidimensional approaches of food security by FAO (FAO 1996). This definition also suggests that food security can only be achieved if various dimensions like availability, physical access, economic access, utilization and stability are simultaneously met. However, all these multiple dimensions are complementary for achieving overall food security in any region.

The issue of food security is multifaceted and complex, as it is replete with challenges like small land holdings, low productivity, long supply chains, high transaction costs and post-harvest losses. In addition to that, the food security situation is compounded by a number of secondary factors like high incidence of poverty, high population growth, low levels of human development, nutrition, access to drinking water and sanitation, housing, intra-household food distribution etc. Despite the availability of sufficient and balanced diet, food insecurity can arise due to lack of food safety and hygiene. Further, the concept of food security extends beyond production availability and demand for food, since countries with high per capita cereal production are not necessarily food secure.

1.1 Hunger and Malnutrition a Serious Challenge

Poverty, hunger and food security are inseparable (SAARC 2013). Globally poverty can be recognized as the most common cause of food insecurity. Rise in food prices and volatility directly affect poor people, who spend a substantial amount of their income on food items. Further, in the long term, higher food prices also diminish their capacity to move out of poverty. In this context, the global food price crisis of 2007–08 highlighted that food insecurity threatens peace and stability, and is a key cause of conflict and violence (Desker 2013). Regional integration has a very positive role in food security and food reserves.

As ASEAN moves towards an integrated community in 2015 and beyond, food security becomes an integral part of the ASEAN community building agenda. The problem of food insecurity ultimately paves the way for regional cooperation in addressing the issue of food insecurity around the world including the ASEAN region

Expanding Food Security and Food Reserves 123

and India. There are substantial variations in the incidence of extreme poverty at regional, subregional as well as individual country level. Table A11.1 presents the poverty data of the region. The highest incidence of extreme poverty has been recorded in South and Southwest Asia, 28.7 per cent in 2010, as compared to Southeast Asia's, which has recorded the fastest absolute reduction in poverty rates from 45.5 per cent in 1990 to 13.4 per cent in 2011 (UNESCAP 2013). Although, extreme poverty is falling in every country of the ASEAN region and India, hunger and malnutrition remains a serious challenge. The poor households in the region cannot afford even the minimum daily requirement and encounter food insecurity challenges in access and utilization of food. Consequently, physical and economic barriers to food remain the major concerns among the poor households in the ASEAN region and India.

1.2 Prevalence of Undernourishment

A total of 842 million people all over the world are estimated to be in chronic hunger during 2011–13, as compared to 868 million in 2010–12 (FAO 2013). Out of these, around 827 million hungry people live only in developing countries, of which 65 million hungry people live in Southeast Asian countries, down from 80 million reported for the 2008–10 period (UNFAO 2013). Southeast Asia in the last few decades has made substantial progress in reducing hunger which is evident from the reduced number of undernourished people in the region. As per the Global Hunger Index (GHI) for 2013, out of the 78 worst countries, in terms of hunger, India ranks 63 in comparison with other Southeast Asian countries like Malaysia (6), Thailand (9), Vietnam (16), Indonesia (23), the Philippines (28), Cambodia (47) and Lao PDR (54) (IFPRI 2013).

Table 11.1 shows that the ASEAN region has exhibited the biggest decline in terms of number of undernourished people from 140 million in the 1990s to 80.5 million in 2008–10, and more recently to 64.5 million from 2011–13 (FAO 2013). At present, the challenge to feed 64.5 million undernourished people in the region still remains. The prevalence of undernourishment also decreased from 31 per cent of the population to 10.7 per cent over the same period. In contrast, situation in India is not satisfactory, with its large population, has the greatest number of undernourished people. As compared to Southeast Asia's 65 million undernourished people, India has as many as around 214 million undernourished people, which is a matter of concern.

Over the past few decades, despite the increase in food production in the ASEAN region, the incidence and the depth of malnutrition has aggravated the health problems faced by women and children, increasing their susceptibility to diseases. India has the highest number of malnourished people and children under the age five. Over 45 per cent of Indian children are malnourished, followed by Bangladesh and Pakistan during 2000–08. India is among the seven nations (Bangladesh, China, the Democratic Republic of the Congo, Ethiopia, India, Indonesia and Pakistan) where over two-thirds of the worlds undernourished live (FAO 2010). Table 11.2 presents the data on the estimates of the number of undernourished people and their prevalence in the total population of India and the select ASEAN countries. Further, additional figures are presented for the prevalence of food inadequacy, which indicates the risk that individuals will be living on a diet that prevents them from effectively discharging an economic activity requiring physical effort. In India during 2010–12 the prevalence of

TABLE 11.1
Prevalence of Undernourishment in Asia*

Region/Country		1990–92	2000–02	2005–07	2008–10	2011–13*
Eastern Asia	No. of undernourished	278.7	193.5	184.8	169.1	166.6
	prevalence of undernourishment	22.20	14.00	13.00	11.70	11.40
South-eastern Asia	No. of undernourished	140.3	113.6	94.2	80.5	64.5
	prevalence of undernourishment	31.10	21.50	16.80	13.80	10.70
Southern Asia	No. of undernourished	314.3	330.2	316.6	309.9	294.7
	prevalence of undernourishment	25.70	22.20	19.70	18.50	16.80
India	No. of undernourished	227.3	240.7	233.1	228.6	213.8
	prevalence of undernourishment	25.5	22.5	20.1	18.9	17.0

Source: The *State of Food Insecurity in the World*, Food and Agriculture Organization (2013), United Nations, Rome.
Note: *Projections **No. of undernourished in millions and prevalence of undernourishment in per cent.

TABLE 11.2
Inadequate Access to Food

Region/Country	Prevalence of Undernourishment %		Number of Undernourished Million People		Food Expenditure of the Poor %	Depth of the Food Deficit kcal/cap/day		Prevalence of Food Inadequacy %	
	1990–92	2010–12	1990–92	2010–12	2000–10	1990–92	2007–09	1990–92	2010–12
Brunei Darussalam	< 5	< 5				14	6	6.3	< 5
Cambodia	39.9	17.1	4	2	84	250	145	49.7	27.1
Indonesia	19.9	8.6	37	21	22	129	83	30.3	15.8
Lao PDR	44.6	27.8	2	2	84	332	212	52.9	38.3
Malaysia	< 5	< 5	1	1		23	18	902.0	6.9
Myanmar			17	10				57.3	29.5
The Philippines	24.2	17.0	15	16	61	155	97	32.9	23.8
Singapore					31				
Thailand	43.8	7.3	25	5		357	67	54.6	15.5
Vietnam	46.9	9.0	32	8	65	357	96		
Southeast Asia	29.6	10.9	134	65		214	93	40.1	18.1
India	26.9	17.5	240	217	68	176	135	35.4	27.5

Source: The State of Food Insecurity in the World, Food and Agriculture Organization (2013), United Nations, Rome.

undernourishment was estimated as 17.5 per cent as compared to Southeast Asia's 11 per cent. As against this, the prevalence of undernourishment in Brunei and Malaysia was reported to be less than 5 per cent followed by Thailand's 7 per cent in 2010–12. Likewise, Vietnam and Indonesia were able to reduce the figure to below 10 per cent by 2010–2012. Since 1990, Vietnam has achieved significant success in reducing hunger by reducing the proportion of undernourished from 47 per cent to only 9 per cent.

In order to address the problem of food insecurity, India and ASEAN region as a whole have recognized the need to initiate concerted efforts for enhancing the means of making more food available for their citizens, including production enhancement, increased trade and effective stock management. With regard to the severity of the crisis, ASEAN countries and India have initiated series of policy initiatives and programmes at national and regional level to ensure food availability for all.

2. SITUATION OF FOOD SECURITY IN ASEAN

Many Southeast Asian countries face an uphill task to manage the rising demand of food due to changing food consumption patterns. As the ASEAN region becomes more affluent, demand for wheat, fish and animal protein has gone-up heavily (Chng 2013). All the ASEAN member states have recognized the need for enhancing food security and expressed that food security should be an integral part of the ASEAN Economic Community (AEC).

Agriculture is the most dominant sector in the ASEAN region and is the key driver of growth and employment. Except for Singapore and Brunei Darussalam, the rest of the ASEAN countries are agrarian in nature, and are well endowed with natural resources, fertile river basins and favorable climatic conditions, which are suitable for agriculture in the region. It has been observed that most of the ASEAN countries have been facing a rise in inflation in agriculture and food. In the ASEAN region, there are inter-country variations in the incidence of poverty and food insecurity, particularly between ASEAN 6 and Cambodia, Lao PDR, Myanmar and Vietnam (CLMV). Various factors such as the sharp increase in population, global financial crisis, demand for bio-fuel, scarcity of land and water, climate changes have been identified as the challenges to regional food security. Besides, the rise in cost of agricultural production led by fuel and fertilizers, decline of yield and production resulting from irregular climatic patterns among others, have contributed substantially to the rise in food prices in the region (AIFS & SPA-FS, 2009–13).

Smallholder farmers dominate Southeast Asia's agricultural landscape, with about 100 million smallholders operating in the region. Farming on less than two hectares of land, at the mercy of changing weather patterns and commodity prices, with very low access to technology, information and markets, these farmers form the bulk of the poor and are also food-insecure. In an effort to survive, they overuse land and water resources, extend their farms at the expense of forests, use low-quality inputs and technology — all of which have high negative consequences on ensuring food security (Prakash-Mani and Tanvir 2014).

Rice is one of the most important staple foods for the world's poor. In fact, the ASEAN region includes some of the world's largest rice exporters (for example, Thailand and Vietnam) and importers (for example, The Philippines and Indonesia). Normally rice production mainly relies on the ample water supply and thus is more vulnerable to drought stress (Nelson et al. 2012). On one hand, the ASEAN region is highly endowed with natural resources; while, on the other, it is also prone to natural disasters. In 1997–98, drought caused huge crop failures, water shortages and forest fires in different parts of Indonesia, Lao PDR and the Philippines. Since 2009, rainfall has been consistently below the normal average in Southeast Asia, particularly causing drought in Cambodia, Lao PDR, Myanmar, Thailand and Vietnam. According to an estimate, 50 per cent of the world's rice production is affected by drought only (Bouman, et al. 2005). In 2010, the water level of Mekong River, which flows through the heart of many Southeast Asian countries, shrank to its lowest level, affecting livelihood of millions of people in the region. Similarly, in the Philippines, the El-Nino induced drought, affected the irrigation system of the most productive rice areas in Luzon which resulted in huge rice production losses and food scarcity in the country (FAOSTAT 2012).

Therefore, ensuring food security is a common concern to all ASEAN nations. The need for having an explicit and holistic strategy to address the issue of food insecurity in these countries cannot be over emphasized. Each of the country in the region has its own strategy and programme of action to address this crisis. There are also common threads in the policy response, as many of the issues being addressed are similar or identical and the larger sociocultural context is common.

3. India–ASEAN Cooperation in Food Security

India has strengthened its relations with all the Southeast Asian countries in the last two decades. The Vision Statement of the ASEAN–India Commemorative Summit, 2012, recognized the need to ensure long-term food security and energy security in their region, and the use of appropriate technologies for this; they welcomed the efforts to strengthen cooperation in the agriculture sector and cooperation among centers of energy in ASEAN and India. Likewise, the 11th ASEAN–India Summit 2013, stressed on the enhancement and strengthening of cooperation on food security through the widening of food production base and exchange of expertise between ASEAN and India to enhance resilience in food security planning to address price volatility of food commodities.

ASEAN–India cooperation on agriculture and forestry has been progressing well through the implementation of Medium-Term Plan of Action (POA) for ASEAN–India cooperation on Agriculture and Forestry (2011–15). The ASEAN–India farmers exchange programme was organized in India and Malaysia in 2012–13, and provided a good platform for the young, progressive and enterprising farmers of ASEAN member states and India who came across new opportunities and development in agriculture sector, exchanged views and shared best practices and innovations in agriculture. As part of their initiative to enhance the quality of higher agricultural education and research as well as extension through cooperation between agricultural communities, a conference of Heads of Agricultural Universities and research institutions of ASEAN and India was also held in India. Cambodia provides good lessons on mechanism of rice intensification.

In recent years, milk consumption has gone up mainly due to increase in birthrates, improvements in diet, rapid urbanization and an increasingly health conscious citizenry throughout the ASEAN 6 countries, that is, Indonesia, Malaysia, the Philippines, Singapore, Thailand and Vietnam. As a result, India, due to its locational advantage in Asia, can cater to the Southeast Asian market. India has recently lifted the ban on the export of milk powder.

During the 21st ASEAN Summit in Cambodia in 2012, ASEAN leaders declared that 'food security remains a major challenge for ASEAN and the world as a whole, at a time of high commodity prices and economic uncertainty'. In view of these, it is imperative to review the scope and extent of regional strategies in enhancing food security as an integral part of their national initiatives.

Box 11.1

SEWA's Model of Institution Building: Empowering Small-scale Women Farmers

Self Employed Women's Association (SEWA) is an Indian membership based trade union founded in 1972 in the state of Gujarat. Its main goal is to organize women for full employment and self-reliance. Until 1994, its members were predominantly from urban areas because of its base in the city of Ahmedabad. However, in the late 1980s SEWA intensified its activities in rural areas. In 2009, two-third of the membership was from the rural areas out of which 54 per cent of the members were engaged in agriculture. For small-scale women farmers, agriculture is the only source of income. In a patriarchal society, their lack of economic assets, low level of education leads them to be very vulnerable to agro-climatic conditions and economic shocks.

In order to address several socioeconomic constraints faced by marginalized women farmers through an integrated approach, SEWA has been making concerted interventions in capacity building and market linkages. SEWA initiated agri-campaigns to educate and create awareness among women farmers on technical advancement, input requirements and marketing trends through regular meetings at village level. Access to credit and other financial services like insurance and pensions etc. helps in asset building.

Self Help Groups (SHG) have been created to bring collective strength to women farmers, where members share their common problems and solutions. As a result, their bargaining power increases in the market through a collective voice. In order to train grassroot members of SHG in managerial and leadership skill, capacity building programmes have been provided by professional organizations like SEWA Academy and SEWA Manager's School. Tele-agri sessions and tele-training of farmers are being conducted to discuss their problems with experts and scientists. For this SEWA has built partnership with Anand Agriculture University (Gujarat) and Indian Space Research Organization (ISRO) to involve both farmers and researchers via video-conferencing for technology development, advance weather forecasting, control of diseases in order to make agriculture economically viable. Authorized seeds, pesticides and fertilizers distributors provide reasonably priced quality inputs to the women farmers at the beginning of each season.

SEWA's SHG have radically improved women's livelihood, increasing their members' income and food security at household level and generated surplus for the market contributing to local and national food security.

Source: FAO 2012.

As agriculture is a critical sector for the economy of India as well as ASEAN member states, an India–ASEAN Working Group on Agriculture was constituted to facilitate promotion of joint research for development of technologies for increasing production and productivity of crops, livestock, and fisheries and to meet the challenges of food security. ASEAN countries can draw lessons from the SAARC Food Bank with respect to meeting food demands under disaster conditions and other climatic-driven uncertainties. SEWA's model of institution building through empowering small-scale women farmers would be useful for CLMV countries (see Box 11.1).

India and other countries in the ASEAN region share many striking similarities and face common challenges such as poverty and food insecurity and exclusion of the majority from the benefits of social and economic development. They have taken similar paths and are moving towards providing social protection through the policies and programmes for enhancing food and nutritional security and cash transfers schemes through the targeted PDS.

4. NATIONAL INITIATIVES

So far ASEAN countries have a number of food-based social safety net programmes, including supplementary feeding programmes, food-for-work programs and food price subsidies for the vulnerable section of the society. ASEAN countries have also concentrated on the concept of food availability through sustainable primary production and supply of food, including through trade and building of food reserves.

4.1 Indonesia

Among the ASEAN member countries, since 1990s, Indonesia has been vigorously trying to achieve food security, where rice is a symbol of prosperity. *Lumbung*, the traditional rice is extensively used by all ethnic groups' projects as a symbol of guarantee for food security. Moreover, the policy of 'one day, no rice, has also led to the reduction of rice consumption whereby wheat consumption increased by 6.63 per cent per year (Subejo and Padmaningrum 2013). According to the Indonesia's New Food Law, 2012, food security in Indonesia has been based on local specific needs of the population. National Food Logistic Agency (Bulog) is responsible for managing buffer stock operations and price control mechanisms through its monopoly over imports, which helped the Government to ensure food security. Apart from this, Indonesia has been a pioneer in providing conditional and non-conditional cash transfer programmes.

4.2 The Philippines

In the Philippines, given the significance of rice, National Food Authority (NFA) is responsible for ensuring food security in the country by protecting the interests of both rice farmers and consumers through various activities and strategies like procurement of rice from individual farmers and their organizations, organization of buffer stocks and importation of rice during food crisis. The International Rice Research Institute (IRRI), whose motto 'Rice Science for a Better World', could be replicated in other countries of Southeast Asia as a trend setter. In fact, the IRRI has played a very significant role in enhancing the knowledge base of rice farming in Vietnam. Thailand and Vietnam are well known for rice breeding for new rice cultivars and aquaculture research. In the ASEAN region, the active role played by the private sector in developing new improved seeds and innovative production technologies for corn and some vegetables are worth mentioning. In 2010, the Rice Action Plan for ASEAN has been proposed by IRRI through the Global Rice Science Partnership (GRiSP), which brings together hundreds of scientists from across the world to harness the power of science to solve the problem of hunger and poverty.

4.3 Malaysia

Malaysia has initiated a number of programmes to ensure that the population has easy access to food at all times. The National Food Security Policy, 2008–10 (NFSP) focused primarily on ensuring the self-sufficiency in rice. Under this programme, government introduced number of subsidies for rice farmers in an effort to encourage increased production. The NFSP included subsidies linked to fertilizer prices, seed prices, yield rates, overall production rates and the retail cost of rice. The primary goals of the NFSP include turning the agro food industry into a competitive and sustainable industry, boosting income among rural householders and agricultural entrepreneurs and ensuring food supply through the cooperation from the private sector. In 2012, National Farm Mechanization and Automation Plan (NFMAP) was launched by the Ministry of Agriculture and Agro-based Industry (MOA) to implement series of initiatives aimed at addressing innovation and technology use in agriculture.

4.4 Cambodia

Since the formation of the new Royal Government of Cambodia (RGC) in 1993, many new policy frameworks have been developed to alleviate poverty and to improve food security in the country. Improving food security and nutrition is a development priority of the RGC reflected in the Strategic Framework for Food Security and Nutrition (SFFSN) 2008–12 in Cambodia. The SFFSN, a plan document was prepared to design and planning of programmes and projects on the cross cutting issue of food security and nutrition. For food-insecure households, the main objectives of the Plan were to increase food availability from their own agriculture and livestock production, forests and fisheries; enhance accessibility of food by increasing household income and increase the stability of their food supply.

4.5 India

India has made considerable progress in increasing production of food grains, particularly wheat and rice. India's policy regarding food procurement of food grains has the broad objectives of ensuring minimum support prices (MSPs) for farmers and also ensuring availability of food grains for the vulnerable section of the population at affordable prices. In order to maintain the food economy of the country, Buffer Stocking Policy has been planned out, as adequate quantity of buffer stocks. In order to address the issue of food security at household level, Government has implemented Targeted Public Distribution Scheme under which subsidized food grains are provided to the poorest of the poor. Similarly, the National Food Security Bill (NFSB) is India's recent initiative for ensuring food and nutritional security to the people of India (see Box 11.2).

5. REGIONAL STRATEGIES AND ACTIVITIES

Globally, the sharp increase in international food prices in 2007–08 led to food insecurity and exposed the flaws of the world food system. These circumstances paved the way for ASEAN to adopt the ASEAN Integrated Food Security (AIFS) Framework in 2009 to advance cooperation in food security among member states and work towards long-term food security. The AIFS Framework has been supported by the Strategic Plan of Action on Food Security (SPA-FS), a five-year plan (2009–13) whose ultimate goal has been to ensure long-term food security and improve the livelihoods of farmers in the ASEAN region. Following this, all the ASEAN countries have initiated measures in addressing the food security challenges by adopting several national and regional initiatives. The key component of this success has been the regional cooperation amongst the ASEAN countries.

5.1 ASEAN Integrated Food Security (AIFS)

The AIFS framework comprises four inter-related components, supported by some strategic thrusts, supported by action programmes and activities, responsible agencies and work schedules. Firstly, this framework considered

Box 11.2

National Food Security Bill of India

National Food Security Bill (NFSB) gives right to the people to receive adequate quantity of food grains at affordable prices. It has a special focus on the needs of the poorest of the poor, women and children. In the case of non-supply of food grains, now people would recieve Food Security Allowance. Under this scheme up to 75 per cent of the rural population and up to 50 per cent of the urban population will have uniform entitlement of 5 kg food grains per month at highly subsidized prices of ₹3, ₹2 and ₹1 per kg for rice, wheat, coarse grain, respectively. Further, the poorest of the poor households would continue to receive 35 kg food grains per household per month under Antyodaya Anna Yojana at subsidized prices of ₹3, ₹2 and ₹1. There is a special focus on nutritional support to women and children. Pregnant women and lactating mothers, besides being entitled to nutritional meals would also receive maternity benefits of at least of ₹6000. Children in the age group of 6 months to 14 years would be entitled to take home ration or hot cooked food as per prescribed nutritional norms.

Source: Economic Survey 2012–13, Ministry of Finance, Government of India.

food security, emergency and shortage relief as the core components while focusing on strengthening national food security programmes like timely supply of rice as food aid for emergency relief. Secondly, the sustainable food production is an important aspect of securing food security, which could be achieved through improving agricultural infrastructure development, minimizing post-harvest losses, reducing transaction costs and maximizing the potential of agricultural resources. In addition, it identified the establishment of an integrated food security information system through early warning and monitoring and surveillance mechanisms for encouraging sustainable growth in food production. The framework also stressed on the promotion of agricultural innovation to encourage greater investment in food and agro-based industry to enhance food security in the ASEAN region. Rice, maize, soybean, sugar and cassava are initial prioritized commodities for food security for the region. Increasing food production, reducing post-harvest losses, promotion of conducive market and trade for agricultural commodities and inputs, ensuring food stability, promotion of availability and accessibility to agricultural inputs and operationalizing regional food emergency relief arrangement are the objectives of this strategic framework. The SPA has made good progress through strengthened cooperation with dialogue partners, international and civil society organizations by carrying out awareness programmes, research studies and providing technical assistance.

5.2 ASEAN+3 Rice Reserve

Among various measures, the East Asia Emergency Rice Reserve (EAERR) was launched by ASEAN in 2004 on a pilot basis for a period of three years, which was later converted into a permanent mechanism for rice reserves. In support of ensuring food security, within the process of ASEAN community building, the ASEAN and Plus three countries viz. Japan, China and South Korea, in 2012, agreed to the establishment of a permanent mechanism under the ASEAN Plus Three Emergency Rice Reserve (APTERR). Ensuring availability of rice during acute food emergencies and to maintain stability in the price of rice were the main objectives of the APTERR. From national rice reserves, earmarked pledges have been committed by the member countries for allocation to the APTERR. Initially, a total of 787,000 tons of rice were physically committed by the ASEAN plus three countries, against the estimated combined consumption of 542,000 tons of rice per day by both Southeast Asia and East Asia together (Desker, et al. 2013). Bearing this in mind, there is enough scope for these member countries to increase their individual contributions to APTERR, as some of the member countries are among the world's largest rice producers and consumers. Likewise, there is enough scope for some member countries to increase their financial commitment to the APTERR Fund to boost its operational capacity.

Since its establishment, several initiatives of rice distribution programmes to countries like Lao PDR, Indonesia, The Philippines, Cambodia, Myanmar and Thailand under different emergency relief programmes have been implemented from time to time. Recently, APTERR has distributed 800 tons of rice, donated by China to aid the typhoon Haiyan victims in the Philippines.

5.3 Food Safety and Handling

Apart from this, in order to ensure the free movement of safe, healthy and good quality food within the region, ASEAN Good Agricultural Practices (GAP) for Fresh Fruits and Vegetables was adopted in 2006, which aimed at promotion of sustainable agricultural practices with due consideration on environmental hazards and safety and welfare of farmers/consumers in the agricultural sector. GAP has been used as a supplement to adding nutritious value to fruits and vegetables grown in the region for safe consumption. Around 802 harmonized maximum residue limits (MRLs) for 63 pesticides have been established by ASEAN. In a step towards regional networking among ASEAN member efforts, a pesticide database has also been established to improve the marketability of agricultural products. Standardization of vaccines for the livestock industry has been established to control the spread of infectious diseases in animals.

Common standards for some fresh fruits have also been adopted to ensure availability of standard quality of fruits to the consumers. A total of 49 standards for animal vaccines, 13 criteria for the accreditation of livestock establishments and 3 criteria for the livestock products have also been endorsed as harmonized ASEAN standards.

In order to expand intra-ASEAN trade in meat and meat-based products, ASEAN established the 'ASEAN General Guidelines on the preparation and Handling of Halal Food' prepared in consultation with the Association of Religious Ministers of some Southeast Asian countries. A dedicated ASEAN Food Safety Network website has also been developed to provide valuable information on food safety.

Responding to the vulnerabilities of climatic changes, ASEAN has made a timely move towards developing a regional strategic framework covering crops, livestock, forestry and fisheries sector, by developing ASEAN Multi-Sectoral Framework on Climate Change and Food Security (AFCC) in 2009. The broad coverage of AFCC shows that climate change is a cross-sectoral issue, hence, cooperation among different sectors in adaptation and mitigation effort is indispensable.

Owing to the growing concern over food security in Southeast and East Asian countries, ASEAN+3 countries launched an ASEAN Food Security Information System (AFSIS) project in 2002, coordinated by Thailand's Ministry of Agriculture and Co-operatives with financial support from Japan through the ASEAN Trust Funds. The focal point of the project was on human resource development through knowledge sharing and mutual technical cooperation among ASEAN member countries. The main objective of the project was to facilitate the member countries to provide accurate, reliable and timely information required for the construction of regional food security information and the development of the early warning system to strengthen food security policies. However, the AFSIS project revealed overall concerns regarding the reliability of data collection and the extent of technology transfer among member countries.

Given the multidimensional approach of food security in the present scenario, it is imperative for the ASEAN countries to recognize these changing perceptions regarding the food security. Therefore, agricultural R&D plans should be prioritized on new technologies only to influence 'availability' and 'physical access' dimensions of food security. Given their different levels of development, mere availability does not guarantee economic access, as it is a critical component of food security in ASEAN-6 and CLMV countries. In this regard, ASEAN countries at the national level should adopt strategies for food security through concerted action plans and policies by ensuring affordable food prices even for the lower strata of the society. Food utilization is another crucial dimension as it comprises the qualitative and quantitative aspect, hygienic preparation, food storage, feeding practices and general well being of an individual household etc.

As agriculture is a critical sector for the economy of India as well as ASEAN countries, an India–ASEAN Working Group on Agriculture was constituted to facilitate promotion of joint research for development of technologies for increasing production and productivity of crops, livestock, and fisheries and to meet the challenges of food security. Exchange visits and training programmes for farmers have been organized. In order to identify strategy to work out on the modality of cooperation among the agricultural universities and research institutes in ASEAN and India, India organized a conference of Heads of Agricultural Universities and research Institutions of ASEAN countries and Vice Chancellors of Indian Agricultural Universities and Central Universities.

6. Conclusions and the Way Ahead

ASEAN region along with India has been struggling hard in reducing food insecurity, as the fruits of efforts have not been distributed evenly across the region. The challenge of ensuring food security for the growing population cannot be tackled only with the increase in agricultural productivity or food-stocking mechanisms, but greater attention is needed for achieving nutritional security.

Despite the numerous measures like food reserves system and price stabilization of rice for food emergency purposes by almost all the member countries of ASEAN to resolve the challenges of food security issues, there is need for long-term solutions rather than the short one. One suitable option to deal with this is the establishment of regional food bank in collaboration with India. SAARC Food Bank offers several lessons with respect to meeting food demands under disaster conditions and other climate-driven uncertainties. It would maintain food reserves and support national as well as regional food security through collective action among the member countries.

An integrated food security approach may be initiated with ASEAN dialogue partners such as India. It may be emphasized here that the results achieved so far in terms of food availability and reduction in hunger, have been the outcome of the positive initiatives undertaken at the regional level. ASEAN governments with involvement of the NGOs and civil societies have to play very effective role in order to bring significant improvement in enhancing food security through regional cooperation. Both ASEAN and India gain from a deeper cooperation.

TABLE A11.1

Incidence of Poverty in India and ASEAN

Country/Region	Population Living in Poverty (US$ 1.25 per day in 2005 PPP) (% of Population)			Poverty Headcount Ratio at US$ 2 per Day in 2005 PPP (% of Population)			National Poverty Line (% of Population Living below)		
	Earliest	2000	Latest	Earliest	2000	Latest	Earliest	2000	Latest
Cambodia	44.5 (90)		18.6 (09)	75.2 (94)		49.5 (09)			20.5 (11)
Indonesia	54.3 (90)	47.7 (99)	16.2 (11)	84.6 (90)	81.6 (99)	43.3 (11)	17.6 (96)	23.4 (99)	12.0 (12)
Lao PDR	55.7 (92)	49.3 (97)	33.9 (08)	84.8 (92)	79.9 (97)	66.0 (08)	45.0 (92)	38.6 (97)	27.6 (08)
Malaysia	1.6 (92)	0.5 (97)	0.0 (0.9)	11.2 (92)	6.8 (97)	2.3 (09)	12.4 (92)	6.1 (97)	1.7 (12)
The Philippines	30.7 (91)	21.6 (97)	18.4 (09)	55.4 (91)	43.8 (97)	41.5 (09)		24.9 (03)	26.5 (09)
Thailand	11.6 (90)	2.1 (98)	0.4 (10)	37.1 (90)	15.3 (98)	4.1 (10)	58.1 (90)	38.7 (98)	13.2 (11)
Vietnam	63.7 (93)	49.7 (98)	16.9 (08)	85.7 (93)	78.3 (98)	43.4 (08)			20.7 (10)
Southeast Asia	**45.5 (90)**	**33.8 (97)**	**13.4 (11)**	**70.9 (90)**	**60.8 (97)**	**34.5 (11)**	**32.1 (90)**	**25.8 (97)**	**15.3 (12)**
India	49.4 (94)		32.7 (10)	81.7 (94)		68.8 (10)			29.8 (10)

Source: Statistical Yearbook for Asia and the Pacific, United Nation Economic and social Commission for Asia and Pacific (2013), Thailand.

Note: ( ) Figures in brackets indicate year.

12

Towards a Stronger Cultural Link

Regional cooperation and integration is a process through which people from different countries and cultures come closer, transcending political boundaries. The ASEAN–India partnership, therefore, implies enhanced interactions and cooperation not only at the inter-governmental level but also at the level of business, civil society, media and people.

People-to-people connectivity, via media and other forms of communication, can strengthen community groups, academic institutions and institutions of arts and culture. Travel, study, academics, science and technology, work and professional links, cultural activities, sports, religious affinities, etc. are aspects of people-to people connectivity. Regional cooperation and integration can only be substantive and meaningful if ordinary people, not just government leaders, perceive cooperation as beneficial to the development of their potential. While media can play a vital role in shaping perceptions and enhancing communication between India and ASEAN, academic and civil society interactions lay the groundwork for these perceptions to be internalized. Political and economic integration is not sustainable without integration of people and societies. This is where sociocultural issues in ASEAN–India partnership, the policy instrument through which India attempts to promote economic integration and strategic objectives in the region, assume special significance.

In this Chapter, we discuss the scopes and opportunities in strengthening people-to-people connectivity between ASEAN and India.

1. Relevance of India's Soft Power

The promotion of India's strategic objectives could be more effective through the exercise of its 'soft' power in terms of education, culture and democracy. The liberal institutional approach emphasizes soft power aspects along with cultural attraction, ideology and international institutions as valuable resources. Soft power strategies rely more on common political values, peaceful means for conflict management and economic cooperation in order to achieve common solutions. India's ability to play a major role in Asia in fact lies in its human resources, democracy and culture in which it has a distinct advantage over other Asian countries. Knowledge of English, the language of globalization, is India's another advantage.

2. Sharing of India's Democratic Experience

India's democracy has shown a lot of creativity in managing a multicultural society, and in the processes of people's empowerment. It is here that India can make an abiding contribution to the process of democratization and nation-building in the region by helping them with human resource development and capacity building towards enduring democratic institutions. Southeast Asian countries are not only multiracial and multicultural, but some of them are also in the process of democratic transformation. The Western model of democracy may not be of much relevance to these countries, as the societal and historical circumstances are quite different. It is India's experience in nation-building and democracy that grew and evolved out of its own social and cultural base and created its own resilience that could be much more relevant to them. Helping the countries of Southeast Asia in their journey towards democratization of their polity and society can further India's interests in the region. Organizing elections for a potential constituency of more than 700 million voters is an incredible undertaking that India is proud of. Countries like Indonesia, Thailand and even Cambodia, where elections are now taking place periodically, could learn much from the speed and transparency with which votes are tallied and the extensive powers accorded to the Indian Election Commission (EC). Thailand is currently passing through political uncertainty and is now under a military government, which professes to return the country to democracy soon. An offer from India to share its experiences in building an independent and transparent Election Commission in ASEAN should be welcome. Many Indonesians, including the late former President, Abdurrahman Wahid and former President, Susilo Bambang Yudhoyono, have great respect for India's ability to practice democracy despite its many shortcomings. While the central government in Indonesia has already implemented a devolution of power hoping that a fairer distribution of national wealth will reduce separatist sentiments and regional violence, there is still a lack of institutions at the local level to absorb such autonomy. India's federal experiment may be an effective arrangement to manage complex issues and distribution of resources in its Centre-State relations. This is where India can help through its ITEC (Indian technical and economic cooperation) programme, training in local self-government and institution-building at the grassroots level. With little investment, India can reap rich dividends in terms of both promotion of democracy in a vitally important neighbouring country and goodwill from the leadership and the people.

Another country in Southeast Asia that can benefit from India's experience in nation-building, democratic experiments and managing centre-periphery relations is Myanmar, which is facing multidimensional challenges in its transformation from a military-authoritarian state towards a possibly guided democracy and managing inter-ethnic tensions. Myanmar lacks experience and capacity in almost every sphere of its democratic undertaking, and India can and is providing useful support and help to Nay Pyi Taw. India can help Myanmar in this transformation and help in building a stronger and inclusive society.

3. BUILDING HUMAN RESOURCE POTENTIAL AND SYNERGY

Higher education is another area in which India can make an important contribution to the development of human resources from the countries of the region to enable them to reach their fullest potential. Education is critical for promoting sustainable development and improving the capacity of the people to address environmental and developmental issues. Both formal and informal education are indispensable to changing people's attitudes so that they have the capacity to assess and address their sustainable developmental concerns. It is also critical for achieving environmental and ethical awareness, values and attitudes, skills and behaviour consistent with sustainable development and for effective public participation in decision-making. Human resource development holds the key to employment and wealth creation, particularly in this age of globalization.[1] India has extended technical assistance valued at about US$1 billion towards skill development in ASEAN.

While some countries of Southeast Asia attained spectacular economic growth in the 1980s and early 1990s, there was no commensurate growth of higher education, particularly in the technical and scientific field. Singapore was the only exception, which helped it to overcome the economic crisis faster than others by shifting its economy from manufacturing and services to higher value-added economy. As a result, increasingly in recent years, governments and stakeholders in Asia have demonstrated renewed interest in investing in higher education as a means of promoting competitiveness and economic growth. This has spurred higher education leaders to seek ways to effectively utilize the available resources to raise quality and efficiency in higher education. To achieve this goal, there needs to be greater regional cooperation and cross-border collaboration among higher education institutions in the form of student and faculty exchanges, dual and joint degree programmes, twinning between pairs of universities and the formation of university networks. While the process of educational expansion through collaboration was started by the Western universities there is now an increasing interest among the leading universities of advanced Asian countries to open branch campuses in developing countries in the region. The purpose is to build quality and harmonization of education and skills qualifications to support labour mobility and regional economic integration.

India is actively contributing to the development of educational skills and technical training to a large number of people in the region. Undoubtedly, Indonesia has been one of the prominent beneficiaries of Indian technical cooperation programmes meant for fellow developing countries. Around 1,000 Indonesian experts as well as officials received training in India under ITEC, and India offered more than 1,100 scholarships to Indonesian students to study at Indian universities. In May 2006, India opened a Vocational Training Centre in the country and another one in Aceh in 2013. A third VTC in Papua had been announced during the visit of Prime Minister

---

[1] Refer the speech of Indian Prime Minister during his visit to Indonesia in April 2005, commemorating the Bandung Conference.

to Indonesia in October 2013. During the State visit of President Yudhoyono to India in January 2011, an MoU for cooperation in the field of education was signed between the two countries. Pursuant to the MoU, the second meeting of the Joint Working Group took place in Yogyakarta in July 2012. Indonesia is a major recipient of ITEC (90 slots) and TCS of Colombo Plan (15 slots) scholarships. Indian Council for Cultural Relations (ICCR) offers 20 scholarships every year to Indonesian students for pursuing higher studies at the undergraduate, postgraduate, doctoral and postdoctoral levels in 181 participating universities and educational institutions all over India under its General Cultural Scholarship Scheme (GCSS). A delegation from EdCIL comprising of representatives from three universities, namely, Gujarat University, Ahmedabad, Sam Higginbottom Institute of Agriculture Technology and Sciences, Allahabad and SRM University, Chennai participated at the World Education Expo held in Jakarta in February 2013. An IT Lab was set up in Magelang, West Java, and handed over to the Indonesian Military Academy in May 2011. An MoU on IT is also on the anvil with Timor Leste.

However, there are further potentials for India-Indonesia cooperation in education, which will be of benefit to both countries. Everywhere in Asia, there is greater demand among the younger generation to learn English. Myanmar and the two least developed countries of Indochina, Cambodia and Lao PDR, can benefit from India's abundant English language teachers, who could help those countries at much less expense than others.

India has a lead in information technology (IT) and Indian institutions, such as the Indian Institute of Technology (IIT) and Indian Institute of Management (IIM), across different cities, have a very high reputation in those countries. Many Southeast Asians have expressed their interest not only to come and study in these institutions, but also to have these institutions open their campuses in their countries, particularly in Indonesia. There are businessmen of Indian origin who would only be too glad to raise the money for opening these campuses and support the faculty. What they want is the brand name and some experienced backup faculty from India. The dividends that India will get will be rich and unmatched. In this respect, the MoU between TERI University, India and Bandung Institute of Technology (ITB), Indonesia that was signed in Jakarta on 5 May 2014 paving the way for mutually beneficial cooperation between the two institutions in a range of areas, including exchange of faculty, joint research activities and publications, participation in seminars and academic meetings, conducting special short-term academic programmes, short and medium-term research visits for graduate students and postdoctoral fellows, joint supervision for doctoral candidates and joint/dual degrees and master's programme, is a positive development in expanding India's educational reach in Indonesia.

We have already mentioned earlier the support India is providing to Myanmar and Cambodia in their efforts to develop their educational potentials and development. Lao PDR is another country, which has been a beneficiary of India's support for education and human resource development. Under human resource development, the Government of India has been providing over 210 scholarships to Lao nationals through the ITEC programme (150 slots), the TCS Colombo Plan (40 slots), the Mekong-Ganga Cooperation Scholarship Scheme (12 slots) and the General Cultural Scholarship Scheme (eight slots for higher studies). So far, under ITEC, the Government of India has trained about 1,000 Lao nationals. An MoU was signed with the Ministry of Information and Culture in May 2007 for the restoration of the world heritage site at Vat Phu. The work on the project began in June 2009. India is likely to spend US$ 4.1 million on the project over an eight-year period. A Work Plan for Cultural Exchange Programme for the years 2011–13 was signed in 2010. India has set up an IT Centre in Vientiane in November 2004, as well as a National Data Centre in May 2006. Ten Rural Telecommunication Centres were set up, seven in provinces and three in the Ministry of Health, the Prime Minister's Office and the office of the Governor of Vientiane.

While India has been offering support to Myanmar in the sphere of education and human resource development, more needs to be done in that area. The educational system in Myanmar needs improvement. The younger generation in Myanmar today are very keen to learn English in order to avail opportunities that are arising out of globalization. India has opened schools in many ASEAN countries and some of them are a great success stories. Even in highly competitive and quality conscious Singapore, the two Indian schools that are operating there are major attractions not only for Indian expatriates but also for Singaporeans. The Indian government can negotiate with the Myanmar government to open some Indian schools, which would offer not only quality education but also relatively cheaper than the schools opened by the Western countries. There was a time when Indian teachers and professors played an important role in the educational development of Burma. There is no reason why India cannot use its soft power in education to offer a niche in cementing bond with Myanmar. India can also train Myanmar citizens in various technical areas through our ITEC programme. While many technical assistance programmes, including help in education and human resource development exists officially, they must be pursued vigorously and offered in attractive packages so that the Myanmar government feels sufficiently pursued towards accepting them. The MoU that was signed during former Prime Minister Manmohan Singh's visit to Myanmar in 2012 between the University of Calcutta and the Dagon University in Yangon has not progressed much and is still dormant.

4. CULTURE AS A TOOL OF DIPLOMACY

Yet another area that can promote India's soft power in Southeast Asia in general is its culture. Indian culture is an inseparable part of Indonesian customs, and our cultures and values are closely related, bearing in mind the history of civilizational contacts between India and the countries of Southeast Asia, which spans over 2000 years. The ASEAN declaration on cultural heritage defined 'culture' and 'cultural heritage' in this way: 'Culture means the whole complex of distinctive spiritual, intellectual, emotional and material features that characterize a society or social group. It includes the arts and letters as well as human modes of life, value systems, creativity, knowledge systems, traditions, and beliefs.' Cultural heritage means significant cultural values and concepts; structures and artefacts; sites and human habitats; oral or folk heritage, including folkways, folklore, languages and literature, traditional arts and crafts, architecture, the performing arts, games, indigenous knowledge systems and practices, myths, customs and beliefs, rituals and other living traditions; the written heritage and popular cultural heritage. India's own definition of culture, traditions and heritage fits in well with the ASEAN declaration and the commonalities provide a platform for building synergies with the countries of Southeast Asia. If carefully and imaginatively pursued, Indian cultural diplomacy can further cement the bond between the two regions, based on pluralist traditions and the need for maintaining 'unity in diversity'. There is an active cultural exchange between India and Indonesia. The Cultural Exchange Programme (CEP) for the period 2011–14 was signed in January 2011 during the visit of the Indonesian President to India. An MoU has been signed between ICCR and the University Gadjah Mada in February 2012 to set up a Rotational Chair on Indian studies. A chair on Indian studies has also been set up in Mahendradatta University, Bali. People-to-people contact was further strengthened through an active cultural exchange between the two countries, via the focal points at the Indian Cultural Centres in Jakarta and Bali. Several events have been organized in Indonesian provinces to enhance India's visibility in these regions and facilitating business contacts. Slice of India events have been held in universities across Indonesia to showcase Indian culture. A series of events were organized in Yogyakarta, Manado and Bali in October/November 2012 as a part of the India–ASEAN Commemorative event.

To enhance people-to-people contact, the India Cultural Forum was inaugurated on 15 August 2012 bringing together all India focused sociocultural groups in Indonesia on one platform. A Facebook page of the Embassy of India and a Twitter account has been created to connect with the younger generation of Indonesian people who are among the largest users of social media in the world. The Embassy produced two Youtube video's titled 'Old Heritage New Partnerships' and 'India–Indonesia—An Enduring Relationship' and took out various publications on Yoga, Education, Film Festival, India–ASEAN economic engagement, and on India highlighting our strengths. In 2013, 'India Corner' was established in Atmajaya University in Yogyakarta and Udayana University in Bali by donating books on India. A special publication titled 'Studying in India' in Bahasa language was also brought out to facilitate Indonesian students wishing to pursue higher studies in India. A photographic exhibition, release of book and a Seminar on India–Indonesia Relations were held on 30 November 2012 in Yogyakarta to mark the establishment of six decades of diplomatic relations between India and Indonesia. The Embassy organized 'Culinary Connection–India and Indonesia' in March 2013 to explore the links between the culinary traditions of the two countries. A pottery exhibition by Arti Gidwani and AdhyPutrakaIskandar was organized by the Cultural Centre in April 2013. Painting exhibit on 'Women by Women' was held in Affandi Museum in Yogyakarta and in various cities of Indonesia. A Panel Discussion on Women titled 'Women of India and Indonesia: Common Perspectives' was held on 2nd April 2014 at the prestigious the National Gallery in Jakarta. The panel discussion was the focal point of a major exhibition of over 50 exhibits created by Indian women artists on Indian women, which were specifically flown in from India by the Indian Council for Cultural Relations (ICCR).

Notwithstanding, such cultural activities organized by the ICCR Centre in Indonesia that undoubtedly brings Indians and Indonesians closer to each other, there is still scope for more imaginative use of cultural diplomacy in Indonesia. The ICCR runs two cultural centres in Jakarta and Bali that manage to attract local interest. Yoga and Dance classes in particular are popular. Today yoga practitioners not only keep fit but have employability in Gyms and Exercise Parlours! With a little more imagination, say by adding space for regular film shows, a tea room to serve simple Indian snacks, exhibiting (and selling) art works from India, etc. the two Centres could become regular meeting spots for Indonesians young and old who share an interest in Indian culture. It is more than high time that India opened a cultural Centre in the University town of Yogyakarta, the city of Borobudur and Prambanan, a city rich in Indian art and architecture. Several important countries already have cultural centres there (not in Bali, which is essentially a tourist spot) and the Sultan of Yogyakarta had some years ago offered land to the Indian Embassy to build one. Indian cultural centres need to be manned by people, who not only have an extensive knowledge about social, cultural, political and economic issues in the respective country, but must also have a good command, both written and spoken, over the local language, which alone can facilitate access to and build rapport with the people.

Rabindranath Tagore's experiments in education at Santineketan inspired Ki Hadjar Dewantoro, a renowned Indonesian nationalist and educationist to start the Taman Siswa Movement in Indonesia. Conversely, Indonesia's unique batik printing and gamelan orchestra had a profound influence on Tagore in 1927, when he sent his daughter-in-law to learn the art and adapt it to Indian systems of dyeing and printing, while Santideb Ghosh, a renowned exponent of Tagore's songs, synthesized gamelan music into his compositions. India's oldest Cultural Agreement is with Indonesia (1955). Under various Action Plans, both India and Indonesia are expected to undertake translations of classical and modern literature, exchange artistes, cooperate in the field of archives, exchange reproduction of arts, facilitate exchange of shadow puppets, audio-video recording, photographs, slides, recorded music and publications on performing arts, etc. The promises have grown over the years to include archaeology, museology, conservation, restoration and history, exchanges of books and film weeks/ festivals. As a recognition of Tagore's contribution as a cultural bridge-builder and a pioneer in cultural and educational cooperation that he initiated in Santiniketan, his bust was installed at the Borobudur temple in Yogyakarta on 26 November 2012.

Vietnam is another country with which we have very close political and cultural links, and is also a recipient of India's capacity-building support and in sociocultural sphere. It has been a large recipient of training programmes under the ITEC programme. Currently, 150 ITEC slots are being offered to Vietnam every year along with 16 scholarships under the General Cultural Scholarship Scheme (GCSS), 14 scholarships under the Educational Exchange Programme (EEP) and 10 scholarships under the Mekong Ganga Cooperation Scholarship Scheme (MGCSS). A US$ 2 million Advanced Resource Centre in Information and Communications Technology (ARC-ICT) was inaugurated by the External Affairs Minister in Hanoi in September 2011. The Centre has been set up by the Centre for Development of Advanced Computing (CDAC) and trains students and Government officials in various areas such as web designing, network systems, java, GIS applications and e-governance. On 12 November 2013, the High Performance Computing facility at the Hanoi University of Science and Technology was inaugurated by Vice-Minister of Education and Training, Indian Ambassador to Vietnam, and Director General of CDAC. The 16-node cluster with basic visualization laboratory and a 5-node Grid Computing facility has been gifted to Vietnam by India. This is the highest configuration of supercomputer ever gifted by Indian Government till date. The year 2012 marked the 40th anniversary of the establishment of full diplomatic relations between India and Vietnam as well as the 20th anniversary of partnership between India and ASEAN. The two sides celebrated it as the 'Year of Friendship between India and Vietnam' with activities such as commemorative seminars, business events, performances by cultural troupes, organizing film festivals, and culinary week and art exhibitions. A Sail Training ship 'INS Sudarshini' paid a goodwill visit to Danang from 31 December 2012 to 3 January 2013, cultural programmes and a business seminar were also held to coincide with the ship's visit. India has decided to open a Cultural Centre in Hanoi in 2014. The Centre will strengthen India's cultural presence in Vietnam and constitute an important dimension of the friendly partnership between the two countries. In line with the ASEAN declaration of conserving and restoration of cultural heritages, the Archaeological Survey of India will execute a conservation and restoration of Cham monuments project at the UNESCO heritage site of 'My Son in Vietnam'. The project will highlight the old linkages of the Hindu Cham civilization between India and Vietnam. An MoU is under discussion; project duration would be 5 years. One of the major problems India and Vietnam face to further their cooperation in cultural sphere and promotion of tourism is the absence of direct flights between the two countries. A revised Air Services Agreement was signed in November 2013 and a direct flight between the two countries has started operating since 2014. This recent air connectivity is expected to facilitate travel of not only business travelers but also ordinary tourists and Buddhist pilgrims willing to travel to Bodh Gaya and other Buddhist religious sites in India. In the meantime, both India and Vietnam have accorded visa-on-arrival facility for their respective nationals with effect from 1 January 2011.

5. Tourism as Part of Cultural Diplomacy

Promotion of tourism as a means of people-to-people contact can be an important instrument of Indian cultural diplomacy. Promoting the development of tourism in each ASEAN country is an important part of the region's cultural development and also an important topic in ASEAN regional cooperation of recent years. Therefore Cambodia, a country with rich tourism resources and historic and cultural heritage, hosted three ASEAN meetings on transnational tourism. The 14th ASEAN Tourism Conference was held in Phnom Penh on 12–13 July 2001. The conference discussed implementing an ASEAN tourism strategy, establishing an ASEAN tourism website, promoting ASEAN tourism projects, boosting international and intra-ASEAN tourism, encouraging the private sector to organize activities that could promote ASEAN's tourism strategy, etc. On 4–5 November 2002, ASEAN leaders signed the ASEAN Tourism Agreement at the 8th ASEAN Summit; the theme of the agreement was to further boost the development of ASEAN tourism. Even while taking advantage of the ASEAN tourism drive and initiative, India should create its own niche in promoting tourism through culture. Indonesia, for instance, happens to be the largest Muslim country in the world, yet its cultural heritage is essentially Hindu–Buddhist in origin and manifests in the temple architecture of Prambanan and Borobudur in Central Java and innumerable Candis scattered all along the nation. While their origin might have been from India, Indonesians themselves have contributed significantly in improvising and enriching that culture. Indian tourists could be encouraged to travel in larger numbers to those sites to discover the inherent genius of the Indonesian people in preserving such culture and values, and in the process build a common bond between the two countries. Similarly, Islamic cultural heritage and monuments are part of the composite Indian civilization, which need to be presented before the Muslims of Indonesia and Malaysia. The Taj Mahal, Fatehpur Sikri, Ajmer, Delhi, Hyderabad, the abode of Tipu Sultan in Mysore and innumerable Islamic cultural sites and Sufi shrines in India could be a spiritual feast for these tourists.

Cultural ties need to be strengthened between India and Myanmar through tourism. One major hurdle in the way of promotion of tourism is the lack of connectivity between the two countries. There is only one direct flight going to Yangon from India, which is from Kolkata, and that too twice a week. Needless to say, the Buddhist sites in India are undoubtedly a major attraction for the people of Myanmar, where more than 85 per cent of the people practice Buddhism. Even though they practice a different form of Buddhism, they consider India a Mecca of Buddhism and would like to travel to India for pilgrimage. To enable even the poor Burmese to travel to India, our Tourism Ministry in collaboration with private operators must offer economy packages that would include airfare, accommodation and tours in not only Buddhist sites, but also other attractions in India. China does this to the countries of Southeast Asia as part of their cultural diplomacy and it earns huge dividends out of this strategy. India also needs to do more to restore the old links through cultural interactions. For this to materialize, India also needs to improve the infrastructures in our tourist destinations and also to establish more budget hotels/motels for the bag packers. Those moves will automatically increase the number of people from Myanmar willing to travel to India and will help to increase the number of flights going between the two countries. More importantly, connectivity should be increased through development of infrastructures between India's Northeast and Myanmar, and tourism should be encouraged in the border areas. Our interactions with Myanmar are essentially inter-governmental. To build enduring relationship between the two countries, there is an urgent need for developing people-to-people contacts.

Indians traveling to Myanmar are few in numbers. However, there are tremendous potentialities of packaging Myanmar as a major tourist destination for the Indians. For one, Myanmar has cultural sites that are no less rich than any other countries in the world and more importantly are familiar to the Indians — Shwedegon pagoda and Bahadur Shah Zafar Mosque in Yangon, innumerable temples and pagodas in Bagan and in Mandalay. There are many other places in Myanmar, which offer tremendous tourist attractions. And importantly, traveling within Myanmar is affordable as the hotels are quite cheap. The Tourism Ministry needs to encourage some private operators in India to establish links with Myanmar's operators to develop attractive packages for Indians. Once there is an increase in the flow of people from India to Myanmar and larger number of flights ply, connectivity will automatically increase between the two countries. This is urgently needed not only to restore the old ties between the two peoples that are broken after the military came into power in 1962 and practically closed the country to the Indians, but also to build newer ties based on commonalities like pluralism, economic modernization, security and democratization of the polity and society.

India's Buddhist links with countries like Thailand, Myanmar, Vietnam, Lao PDR and Cambodia need to be nurtured and further developed with its cultural diplomacy. Nalanda is one of the oldest universities in the world, whose revival in the coming years with the help of countries like Singapore, Japan, South Korea and China will herald a major transformation in regional cooperation. Bodh Gaya, Sarnath and Nalanda could be developed as places of pilgrimage for Buddhists in Southeast Asia. At its peak, the university attracted scholars and students from Korea, Japan, China, Tibet, Indonesia, Turkey, Greece and Persia. The subjects taught included religion, history, law, linguistics, medicine, public health, architecture, metallurgy, pharmacology, sculpture and astronomy. The university has been opened recently and 15 students have sought admission in various subjects (see Box 12.1).

6. Socio-cultural Cooperation between India and ASEAN

While the above narrative dwells on the sociocultural cooperation between India and ASEAN at bilateral level, cooperation in human resource development, science and technology (S&T), people-to-people contacts, health and pharmaceuticals, transport and infrastructure, small and medium enterprises (SMEs), tourism, information and communication technology (ICT), agriculture, energy, people-to-people exchanges, etc. have been undertaken at the regional level. All cooperation projects are funded by the ASEAN–India Fund (AIF). Cooperation in this area is carried out through the implementation of the Plan of Action (PoA) to implement the ASEAN–India Partnership for Peace, Progress and Shared Prosperity, which was adopted by the Leaders of ASEAN and India at the 3rd ASEAN–India Summit in November 2004 in Vientiane. The above PoA, in turn, is carried out through activities which were prepared by the ASEAN Secretariat in the form of a matrix incorporating the proposed activities under the various existing ASEAN sectoral work plans, Declarations concluded between ASEAN and India as well as priority activities under the Roadmap for an ASEAN Community 2009–2015 that could be implemented with India.

India is also actively contributing to the implementation of the Initiative of ASEAN Integration (IAI) Work Plan with the implementation of some of the IAI projects/activities such as the Entrepreneurship Development Centres (EDC) and the Centres for the English Language Training (CELT) in Cambodia, Lao PDR, Myanmar and Vietnam, as we have already mentioned in the bilateral section. India has also agreed to support the establishment of a CELT in Indonesia. India contributed US$ 50 million to the ASEAN Development Fund (ADF) in 2010. Visa on arrival (VOA) facility has been extended to eight ASEAN countries (Cambodia, Lao PDR, Vietnam, Myanmar, Singapore, Thailand, Indonesia and the Philippines).

Cooperation between India and ASEAN is also being intensified in the cultural, educational and academic fields, through the promotion of people-to-people contacts, and ongoing initiatives such as the Youth Exchange Programmes, Media Exchange Programmes and Special Training Courses for ASEAN Diplomats and Eminent Persons Lecture Series. Delhi Dialogue is a Track 1.5 event held annually in New Delhi, where leaders, opinion

Box 12.1
Nalanda University

Nalanda University (NU) came into being by a special Act of the Indian Parliament — a testimony to the important status that Nalanda University occupies in the Indian intellectual landscape. Nalanda is a standalone international university unlike any other established in the country. It is more than 800 years after the ancient seat of learning, the Nalanda Mahavihara, was reduced to ruins that classes commenced at the 21st century varsity, conceptualized with the same philosophy, from September 1, 2014. Located in the town of Rajgir, in the northern Indian state of Bihar, Nalanda University is mandated to be 'an international institution for the pursuit of intellectual, philosophical, historical and spiritual studies'. This new university contains within it a memory of the ancient Nalanda University and is premised on the shared desire of member States of the East Asia Summit countries to re-discover and re-strengthen educational cooperation. Located just 12 km from the ancient site, a total of seven schools have been planned at NU on about 450 acres of area. Once completed, it will accommodate about 7000 people. The Government of India has sanctioned funds to the tune of ₹27.27 billion over a period of 10 years for the development of this University.

Source: Available at http://www.nalandauniv.edu.in (accessed 1 March 2015).

makers, diplomats, academia and think tanks of India and ASEAN come together to discuss ways to intensify and broaden political, strategic, economic and civil society interaction between the two regions. Two major events were organized in the run-up to the Commemorative Summit. For example, the 2nd ASEAN–India Car Rally and a Shipping Expedition of the sail training ship, INS Sudarshini, to ASEAN countries were intended to bring the two regions closer to each other by highlighting the importance of connectivity. The INS Sudarshini Expedition was flagged off from Kochi on 15 September 2012. The Ship's port of calls included Padang, Bali, Manado, Brunei, Cebu, Manila, Da Nang, Sihanoukville, Bangkok, Singapore, Klang, Phuket and Sittwe, before it returns to India via Port Blair to conclude at Kochi on March 29, 2013. The ASEAN–India Car Rally 2012 was flagged off from Yogjakarta, Indonesia on 26 November 2012. The rally traversed through eight ASEAN countries (Indonesia, Singapore, Malaysia, Thailand, Cambodia, Vietnam, Lao PDR and Myanmar) and reached Guwahati on 16 December 2012, after covering a distance of about 8,000 kms over 21 days. Among other initiatives, the Government of India has set-up the ASEAN-India Centre (AIC) at New Delhi in 2013.

7. Conclusions and Recommendations

Durable and abiding relationships are based not on inter-governmental contacts, but on people-to-people contacts. Culture is the best bond between the people of India and ASEAN. Even though tourism is an important item in Indian dialogue with ASEAN, not much has been done to develop this area to promote people-to-people contacts. So far, tourism has been moving in only one direction — Indians going to Southeast Asia but not the reverse. Imaginative packages need to be evolved and sufficient incentives offered to attract tourists from countries in Southeast Asia, and from Myanmar, Malaysia, Indonesia, Thailand and Vietnam in particular, by promoting cultural and religious tourism. This will not only bring revenues to India but will also cement civil society interactions, an important component of mature and enduring state-to-state relations.

Cooperation in the field of education need to be widened and deepened further by showcasing some of our premier educational institutions and attracting bright students from the countries of ASEAN. Even though the Indian government offers a number of scholarships to students from the countries of ASEAN, it has not been able to attract the brighter ones essentially because of the lack of information about the quality and achievements of our premier educational institutions available to them. Like the Australians and the British, India also must vigorously promote our universities and institutions to the students in the region by emphasizing quality education as well as lower costs compared to the Western universities. After 9/11 and the Global War on Terrorism, students from countries like Indonesia and Malaysia are finding it difficult to travel to the West for higher education. Singapore and China are taking advantage of this and attracting large number of students to study there by offering quality education at relatively cheaper costs. In another 5 to 10 years time, the number of Southeast Asian students studying in China will outnumber the students going to the West. These students will eventually occupy critical positions in each and every sector in their country and the dividends that China will earn will be enormous. India's comparative advantage is in higher education and it must utilize that advantage to reap benefits of its revenue as well as the goodwill that it will generate. India may appoint professional organizations to manage the scholarships and the educational exchange programmes efficiently. Educational and cultural agreements need to be concluded with a view to narrow the knowledge gap that exists between India and Southeast Asian countries. The future educational and cultural interactions should be carried out with a clear-cut view of training a core of experts in each country who would be able to provide better perspective of their country of specialization and give nuanced feedback to their respective policymakers.

Finally, cultural and religious tourism need to be promoted to bring the people from India and Southeast closer to each other. It would be appropriate if both ASEAN and India initiate an innovative political, educational and cultural climate to give more substance to economic engagement process.

References

ASEAN Secretariat (2012a) "ASEAN–India Commemorative Summit 2012: Vision Statement", Jakarta.

ASEAN Secretariat (2012b) *ASEAN Investment Report 2012*, Jakarta.

ASEAN Secretariat (2013) "ASEAN Integrated Food Security (AIFS) Framework and Strategic Plan of Action on Food Security in the ASEAN Region (SPA-FS), 2009–2013", Jakarta.

ASEAN–India Centre (AIC) (2014) *ASEAN–India Maritime Connectivity Report*, ASEAN–India Centre (AIC) at RIS, New Delhi.

Asian Development Bank (ADB) (2007a) *Annual Report*, Manila.

Asian Development Bank (ADB) (2007b) "Is Intra–Asian Trade Growth Driven by Independent Regional Demand?", *Asian Development Outlook 2007*, Manila.

Asian Development Bank (ADB) (2014) *Economic Corridor Development for Inclusive Asian Regional Integration: Modeling Approach to Economic Corridors*, Manila.

Asian Development Bank (ADB) and Asian Development Bank Institute (ADBI) (2009) *Infrastructure for Seamless Asia*, Manila.

Athukorala, Prema-Chandra (2008) "China's Integration into Global Production Networks and Its Implications for Export-led Growth Strategy in Other Countries in the Region", ANU Working Paper on Trade and Development, No. 2008/04, Australian National University (ANU), Canberra.

Athukorala, Prema-Chandra (2010) "Production Networks and Trade Patterns in East Asia: Regionalization or Globalization?", ADB Working Paper No. 56, Asian Development Bank (ADB), Manila.

Athukorala, Prema-Chandra (2013) "Global Production Sharing and Trade Patterns in East Asia", Departmental Working Papers 2013-10, Arndt-Corden Department of Economics, The Australian National University, Sydney.

Backer, Koen De and Sébastien Miroudot (2013) "Mapping Global Value Chains", OECD Trade Policy Paper No. 159, Organisation for Economic Cooperation and Development (OECD), Paris.

Baldwin, R. (2014a) "Impact of Mega Regionals: The Economic Impact", in *Mega Regional Trade Agreements: Game Changers or Costly Distractions for the World Trading System*, World Economic Forum (WEF), Geneva.

Baldwin, R. (2014b) "Multilateralising 21st Century Regionalism", Paper Presented at the *Global Forum on Trade: Reconciling Regionalism and Multilateralism in a Post-Bali World*, OECD, Paris.

Banik, Nilanjan (2014) "India–ASEAN Free Trade Agreement: The Untapped Potential", Mahindra Ecole Centrale, Hyderabad and MPRA Paper 57954, University Library of Munich, Germany.

Basu, Nayanima (2014) "India–ASEAN Services FTA in Limbo over Retail FDI", *Business Standard*, New Delhi.

Bedi, Priyanka and Ekta Kharbanda (2014) "Analysis of Inflows of Foreign Direct Investment in India: Problems and Challenges", *Global Journal of Finance and Management*, Vol. 6, No. 7, pp. 675–684.

Bhattacharyay, B. N., R. Nag and M. Kawai (2012) *Infrastructure for Asian Connectivity*, Edward Elgar, Cheltenham.

Bhattacharyya, R. and A. Mandal (2014) "Estimating the Impact of the India–ASEAN Free Trade Agreement on Indian Industries", *South Asia Economic Journal*, Vol. 15, No. 1, pp. 93–114.

Bouman, B. A. M., S. Peng, A. R. Castaneda and R. M. Visperas (2005) "Yield and Water Use of Irrigated Tropical Aerobic Rice Systems", *Agricultural Water Management*, Vol. 74, pp. 87–105.

British Petroleum (BP) (2013) *BP Statistical Review of World Energy*, British Petroleum, London.

Chng, B. (2013) "Southeast Asia's Food Security Challenge: More than 'Stock' Solution Needed", RSIS Commentaries, No. 185/2013, S. Rajaratnam School of International Studies (RSIS), Singapore.

De, Prabir (2011) "ASEAN-India Connectivity: An Indian Perspective", in Kimura and Umezaki.

De, Prabir (2014) "India's Emerging Connectivity with Southeast Asia and East Asia: Progress and Prospects", ADBI Working Paper No. 507, Asian Development Bank Institute, Tokyo.

De, Prabir and Jayanta Kumar Ray (2013) *India-Myanmar Connectivity: Current Status and Future Prospects*, Institute of Foreign Policy Studies, Calcutta University, Kolkata.

De, Prabir and Kavita Iyengar (eds.) (2014) *Developing Economic Corridors in South Asia*, Asian Development Bank (ADB), Manila.

Deloitte-Federation of Indian Chambers of Commerce and Industry (FICCI) (2012) *Services Trade: India's Advantages*, New Delhi.

Department of Science and Technology (DST) (2006) "Indo-ASEAN Joint Declaration on S & T Cooperation", Government of India, New Delhi.

References

Department of Science and Technology (DST) (2014) *India Attractiveness Survey 2014: Enabling the Prospects*, Ernst and Young (EY), New Delhi.

Department of Science and Technology (DST) (various years) Annual Report, Ministry of Science and Technology, Government of India, New Delhi, available at: www.dst.gov.in.

Desker, B. M. C. Anthony and P. Teng (2013) "ASEAN Food Security: Towards a More Comprehensive Framework", ERIA Discussion Paper 2013–20, Economic Research Institute for ASEAN and East Asia (ERIA), Jakarta.

Economic Research Institute of ASEAN and East Asia (ERIA) (2012) "Developing ASEAN Economic Community (AEC) into a Global Service Hub", ERIA Research Project Report 2011–1, Jakarta.

Edmonds, C. and M. Fujimura (2008) "Impact of Cross-border Road Infrastructure on Trade and Investment in the Greater Mekong Subregion", *Integration and Trade*, Vol. 28, pp. 267–296.

Ernst and Young (2014) *India Attractiveness Survey 2014*, New Delhi.

Export-Import Bank of India (2013) "India's Trade and Investment Relations with Cambodia, Lao PDR, Myanmar, Vietnam (CLMV): Enhancing Economic Cooperation", Occasional Paper No. 161, Mumbai.

Fally, T. (2012) "Production Staging: Measurement and Facts", University of Colorado-Boulder, Colorado.

Food and Agricultural Organisation (FAO) (1996) "Rome Declaration on World Food Security and World Food Summit Plan of Action", World Food Summit, 13–17 November, Rome.

Food and Agriculture Organization (FAO) (2010) "The State of Food Insecurity in the World", FAO, United Nations, Rome.

Food and Agriculture Organization (FAO) (2012) "Good Practices in Building Innovative Rural Institutions to Increase Food Security", Case Study, FAO, United Nations, Rome.

Food and Agriculture Organization (FAO) (2013a) *FAO Statistical Yearbook*, FAO, United Nations, Rome.

Food and Agriculture Organization (FAO) (2013b) *The State of Food Insecurity in the World*, FAO, United Nations, Rome.

Fukunaga, Y. and I. Isono (2013) "Taking ASEAN+1 FTAs Towards the RCEP: A Mapping Study", ERIA Discussion Paper Series No. ERIA-DP-2013-02, Economic Research Institute for ASEAN and East Asia (ERIA), Jakarta.

Government of India (2014) *Economic Survey 2013–14*, Ministry of Finance, New Delhi.

Grainger, A. (2011) "Developing the Case for Trade Facilitation in Practice", *World Customs Journal*, Vol. 5, No. 2, pp. 65–76.

Henning, R. C. and M. S. Khan (2011) "Asia and Global Financial Governance", Peterson Institute of International Economics Working Paper Series No. 11–16, Peterson Institute of International Economics, Washington, D.C.

International Energy Agency (IEA) (2013a) "Key Energy Statistics", International Energy Agency (IEA), Paris.

International Energy Agency (IEA) (2013b) "Key World Energy Statistics", International Energy Agency (IEA), Paris.

International Food Policy Research Institute (IFPRI) (2013) "Global Hunger Index—The Challenge of Hunger: Building Resilience to Achieve Food and Nutrition Security", IFPRI, Washington, D.C.

International Monetary Fund (IMF) (2014a) "Asia and Pacific Sustaining the Momentum: Vigilance and Reforms", *Regional Economic Outlook*, Washington, D.C.

International Monetary Fund (IMF) (2014b) *World Economic Outlook: Recovery Strengthens, Remains Uneven*, Washington, D.C.

International Monetary Fund (IMF) (2014c) *World Economic Outlook*, Washington, D.C.

Kallummal, Murali (2013) "SPS Measures and Market Access Implications for Agricultural Trade: WTO's Systemic Issues and Changing Scale of Technology", Lap Lambert Academic Publishing, Germany.

Kimura, F. and A. Obashi (2011) "Production Networks in East Asia: What We Know So Far", ADB Working Paper, No. 320, Asian Development Bank (ADB), Manila.

Kimura, F. and S. Umezaki (eds.) (2011) *ASEAN–India Connectivity: The Comprehensive Asia Development Plan, Phase II*, ERIA Research Project Report 2010–7, Economic Research Institute of ASEAN and East Asia (ERIA), Jakarta.

Kimura, F. and I. Kobayashi (2009) "Why Is the East Asia Industrial Corridor Needed?", Working Paper, Economic Research Institute of ASEAN and East Asia (ERIA), Jakarta.

Koopman, R., W. Powers, Z. Wang and S. J. Wei (2010) "Give Credit where Credit is Due: Tracing Value Added in Global Production Chains", NBER Working Papers Series 16426, National Bureau of Economic Research (NBER), Cambridge.

Kumar, N., K. Kesavapany and Y. Chaocheng (eds.) (2008) *Asia's New Regionalism and Global Role: Agenda for the East Asia Summit*, RIS and ISEAS, New Delhi and Singapore.

Lamberte, M. and P. J. Morgan (2012) "Regional and Global Monetary Cooperation", Working Paper No. 346, Asian Development Bank Institute (ADBI), New Delhi.

Ministry of Petroleum and Natural Gas (2006) *Report of the Working Group on Petroleum & Natural Gas Sector for the XI Plan (2007–12)*, Government of India, New Delhi.

Mohanty, S. K. and S. Pohit (2007) "Welfare Gains from Regional Economic Integration in Asia: ASEAN+3 or EAS", Discussion Paper, Research and Information System for Developing Countries (RIS), New Delhi.

Nag, B. (2012) "Prospects for Integrating India into Asian Production Network", Paper Written for ADBI/ADB's Study on "Role of Key Emerging Economies—ASEAN, PRC, and India—for a Balanced, Sustainable, and Resilient Asia", Asian Development Bank Institute (ADBI), Tokyo.

Nanda, N. (2008) "Trading in World Energy Market", in Ligia Noronha and Anant Sudarshan (eds.) *India's Energy Security*, Rutledge, London.

Nelson, S., T. Frankenberger, T. Spangler, and M. Langworthy (2012) "Enhancing Resilience to Food Security Shocks in Africa", Discussion Paper, Tango International, USA.

Ölz, S. and M. Beerepoot (2010) "Deploying Renewables in Southeast Asia: Trends and Potentials", Working Paper, International Energy Agency (IEA), Paris.

Organization for Economic Cooperation and Development (OECD) (2013) *Economic Outlook for Southeast Asia, China and India 2014: Beyond the Middle-Income Trap*, Paris.

Organization for Economic Cooperation and Development (OECD) (2014a) *Economic Outlook for South East Asia, China and India*, Paris.

Organization for Economic Cooperation and Development (OECD) (2014b) *Southeast Asia Investment Policy Perspectives*, Paris.

Petri, P. A., M. G. Plummer, and F. Zhai (2010a) "The Economics of the ASEAN Economic Community", Brandeis University, Massachusetts.

Petri, P. A., M. G. Plummer and F. Zhai (2010b) "The ASEAN Economic Community: A General Equilibrium Analysis", Available at: http://ssrn.com/abstract=1682200 orhttp://dx.doi.org/10.2139/ssrn.1682200.

Petri, P. A., M. G. Plummer, and F. Zhai (2011) "The Trans-Pacific Partnership and Asia Pacific Integration: A Quantitative Assessment", East West Centre Working Paper Series, No. 119, East-West Centre, Hawaii.

Planning Commission (2006) "Integrated Energy Policy: Report of the Expert Committee", Government of India, New Delhi.

Prakash-Mani, Kavita and Tania Tanvir (2014) "How Can We Strengthen Food Security in Southeast Asia?", Paper Presented at the World Economic Forum (WEF) on East Asia, Held in the Philippines, 19 May.

Rashid, T. H. M. Sumon and Md. R. Islam (2013) "Prospects of Renewable Energy Resources and Regional Grid Integration for Future Energy Security & Development in SAARC Countries", *International Journal of Research in Engineering and Technology*, Vol. 2, No. 1, pp. 43–51.

Research and Information System for Developing Countries (RIS) (2012), *ASEAN–India Connectivity Report: India Country Study*, New Delhi.

SAARC Secretariat (2013) *Regional Poverty Profile 2009–2010: Food Security Challenges for the Poor and Social Inclusion*, Kathmandu.

Saran, Shyam (2014) "Opening Speech", Delivered at the RIS Conference on Cross-Border Connectivity, Research and Information System for Developing Countries (RIS), New Delhi, 12 May.

Shi, X. and C. Malik (2013) "Assessment of ASEAN Energy Cooperation within the ASEAN Economic Community", ERIA Discussion Paper 2013-37, Economic Research Institute for ASEAN and East Asia (ERIA), Jakarta.

Sikdar, C. and B. Nag (2011) "Impact of India–ASEAN Free Trade Agreement: A Cross-country Analysis Using Applied General Equilibrium Modelling", ARTNeT Working Paper No. 10711, Asia–Pacific Research and Training Network on Trade (ARTNeT), UNESCAP, Bangkok.

Sikdar, C. and B. Nag (2014) "Will India Gain from India–ASEAN FTA? Analysis of Simulated Scenarios based on Phased Implementation", Mimeo, ASEAN–India Centre (AIC), New Delhi.

Sovacool, K. Benjamin (2009) "Energy Policy and Cooperation in Southeast Asia: The History, Challenges, and Implications of the Trans-ASEAN Gas Pipeline (TAGP) Network", *Energy Policy*, Vol. 37, No. 6, pp. 2356–2367.

Subejo and D. Padmaningrum (2013) "Tackling Food Security Problem in Indonesia", *Jakarta Post*, Jakarta.

Uchikawa, S. (2011) "Linkage between Organised and Unorganised Sectors in Indian Machinery Industry", *Economic & Political Weekly*, Vol. 46, No. 1, pp. 45–54.

United Nations (UN) (2013) *World Economic Situation and Prospects*, United Nations, New York.

United Nations Conference on Trade and Development (UNCTAD) (2012a) *World Investment Report 2012*, United Nations, New York and Geneva.

United Nations Conference on Trade and Development (UNCTAD) (2012b) *Development and Globalization: Facts and Figures*, United Nations, New York and Geneva.

United Nations Conference on Trade and Development (UNCTAD) (2012c) Technology and Innovation Report 2012—Innovation, Technology and South-South Collaboration, United Nations, New York and Geneva.

United Nations Conference on Trade and Development (UNCTAD) (2013) *World Investment Prospects Survey 2010–2012*, United Nations, New York and Geneva.

United Nations Conference on Trade and Development (UNCTAD) (2014a) *World Investment Report 2014: Investing in the SDGs: An Action Plan*, United Nations, New York and Geneva.

United Nations Conference on Trade and Development (UNCTAD) (2014b) *Trade and Development Report 2014*, United Nations, New York and Geneva.

United Nations Economic and Social Commission for Asia and the Pacific (UNESCAP) (2012) *Statistical Yearbook for Asia and the Pacific 2011*, Bangkok.

United Nations Economic and Social Commission for Asia and the Pacific (UNESCAP) (2013) *Statistical Yearbook for Asia and the Pacific 2013*, Bangkok.

World Bank (2007) *World Development Indicators*, CD-ROM, Washington, D.C.

World Bank (2009) "Impact of the Global Financial Crisis and Recent Economic Developments in Lao PDR", No. 13, Washington, D.C.

World Bank (2011a) "Air Connectivity Index", World Bank Policy Research Working Paper No. 5722, Washington, D.C.

World Bank (2011b) *World Bank Development Report 2011*, Washington, D.C.

World Bank (2013) *World Development Report 2013*, Washington, D.C.

World Bank (2014a) *World Development Report 2014*, Washington, D.C.

World Bank (2014b) *Doing Business Report*, Washington, D.C.

World Bank–ASEAN Secretariat (2014) *ASEAN Integration Monitoring Report*, Washington, D.C. and Jakarta.

Xing, Y. (2013) "Rethinking the Success of China's high-Tech Exports", in G. Wang and Y. Zheng (eds.) *China: Development and Governance*, World Scientific, Singapore.

Yamashita, N. (2011) "Production Sharing and Trade Flows: A Comparative Analysis of Japan and the US", *Journal of Asian Economics*, Vol. 22, No. 5, pp. 383–397.